AS I KNEW THEM

KENNIKAT PRESS SCHOLARLY REPRINTS

Dr. Ralph Adams Brown, Senior Editor

Series in
AMERICAN HISTORY AND CULTURE
IN THE TWENTIETH CENTURY
Under the General Editorial Supervision of
Dr. Donald R. McCoy
Professor of History, University of Kansas

AS I KNEW THEM

PRESIDENTS AND POLITICS
FROM GRANT TO COOLIDGE

BY

HENRY L. STODDARD

Volume II

*"Great men have been among us; hands that penned
And tongues that uttered wisdom; better none."*
—Wordsworth

KENNIKAT PRESS
Port Washington, N. Y./London

AS I KNEW THEM

Copyright, 1927, by Harper & Brothers
Reissued in 1971 by Kennikat Press by arrangement
with Harper & Row, Publishers, Inc.
Library of Congress Catalog Card No: 77-137980
ISBN 0-8046-1435-0

Manufactured by Taylor Publishing Company   Dallas, Texas

KENNIKAT SERIES ON AMERICAN HISTORY AND
CULTURE IN THE TWENTIETH CENTURY

CHAPTER XXX

McKINLEY'S HANNA OR HANNA'S McKINLEY?

The Campaign Manager Wants A House In Washington But McKinley Says "It Would Never Do, Mark"—He Insists That Hanna Must First Have A Title—John Sherman Goes To State Department And Hanna To The Senate—Hanna's Keenest Disappointment—The Philadelphia Convention of 1900 When Dawes Received The Message That Forced Hanna To Say To Roosevelt, "Teddy, You're It!"

TURN now to 1896—McKinley, President-elect; Mark Hanna, President-maker, and long-time friend. Hanna wanted no Cabinet portfolio; all his life he had been a business executive; he was determined to lessen not to increase responsibilities. He wanted to be the trusted friend and counsellor of a President but not to hold office. Probably he wanted a home in Washington.

His famous corned beef hash breakfasts in Cleveland (made after a recipe he had worked out years before in the iron ore camps of Duluth) had brought many a doubting delegate into line for his candidate. Why not try the same breakfasts in Washington on temperamental Senators and Congressmen? No office, no title, just a citizen friend of the President!

Politicians wondered; newspapers kept guessing the future of this Citizen President-maker. It seemed clear to Hanna; it perplexed McKinley. He knew it could not be as Hanna planned. He had been too long in Washington not to realize that there could be no overlord. Of course, Woodrow Wilson was not then even dreaming of the Presidency, or of making Col. Edward M. House his personal ambassador-extraordi-

245

nary and other self here and in Europe. McKinley, therefore, had no precedent by which to determine Hanna's status except his instinctive feeling that there could be only one President and one White House.

"IT WOULD NEVER DO, MARK"

The two men talked it over.

"It would never do, Mark," said McKinley. "You know everybody would be running to you either before or after seeing me. You owe it to me to come to Washington with a title to office or not at all."

Still, Hanna demurred. He saw no reason why he could not sacrifice time, thought and money for the success of the President he had done so much to elect. Fourteen years later, Wilson turned to Colonel House and made him an ambassador without credentials, to whom those "in the know" would go quietly with their ambitions, and their troubles. McKinley foresaw the inevitable consequences of such a relation.

Together he and Hanna sought a way out. Just one way was possible—persuade John Sherman to resign as Senator and become Secretary of State. Sherman was consulted. It was known that he would like to have held that portfolio under Harrison. Had he the same ambition now? Hanna's future rested on the Senator's reply. Several weeks of uncertainty elapsed—then an unheralded letter of acceptance reached Canton.

Promptly Hanna was appointed to the Senate vacancy by Ohio's Governor. Thus, he went to the national capital in his own right and title, and his famous corned beef hash breakfasts in the old Cameron mansion facing Lafayette Park were accepted as the hospitality of a Senator, not of a President's spokesman.

It was McKinley, not Hanna, who foresaw the unwisdom of the latter rôle.

As I Knew Them

A modest, genial figure in national Republican politics those days was Henry C. Payne, then in control of the Wisconsin State organization—the last of the "Old Guard" to control before La Follette took it over. Hanna's deepest interest in the McKinley Cabinet was to have Payne made Postmaster General. All of Payne's colleagues on the national committee urged the appointment, too. In earlier years Payne had been about the Capitol in the interest of the Northern Pacific Railroad; McKinley was then a Congressman and familiar with Payne's activities. He told Hanna he could not name Payne. Always a good fighter for a friend, Hanna persisted.

"Mark," said McKinley during their final talk in Canton, "you know I want to do anything so close to you as this seems to be but I cannot bring into my Cabinet a man who has been a lobbyist around Congress."

McKinley did not appoint Payne; five years later, Roosevelt did.

Thus, in two matters of consequence before his inauguration McKinley made decisions that showed Hanna a better way than the way he urged. And no one realized McKinley's ability to make such decisions better than did the man who newspapers were then declaring controlled McKinley's mind.

MCKINLEY'S WAY MEANT HANNA'S KEENEST DISAPPOINTMENT

There were to be other occasions when McKinley's way had to prevail over Hanna's counsel, but only once throughout their long friendship was there any keen feeling of disappointment on Hanna's part. That was when he was unable to persuade McKinley to indicate a choice for Vice President to be nominated by the 1900 national convention. He not only refused Hanna but he authorized Charles G. Dawes to say to the delegates that he had no choice. Hanna keenly felt that double blow at his prestige.

That convention, held in Philadelphia, was distinguished by the fact that more men refused to be nominated for Vice President than in any other convention of either party.

Even Roosevelt tried to dodge it.

No one dreamed that it meant the Presidency in fifteen months.

There was nothing but the Vice Presidency for the delegates to quarrel over. McKinley was to be their nominee for President and his record was their platform. They had nothing to do but decide on the man to take the place made vacant by the death of Vice President Garret A. Hobart.

Thomas C. Platt wanted Roosevelt named so as to get him out of the New York Governorship. Matt Quay was interested to force any nomination that would show that Hanna was no longer in control of the national organization. The western delegates were clamoring for a nominee who would be recognized as a "liberal." Platt and Quay used this western sentiment to work up a Roosevelt boom.

The old convention saying that "you cannot beat somebody with nobody" came in here for another demonstration. Hanna found himself without a candidate except John D. Long, of Massachusetts, who had no following. More fatal still was the knowledge among the delegates that he was without support from the President—the man many said he dominated!

Nobody who could be nominated wanted the Vice Presidency!

Fairbanks had dreams of the White House. He preferred to remain in the Senate until the real call came; Allison, of Iowa, was comfortable and contented where he was; Jonathan Dolliver was indifferently willing; Cornelius N. Bliss had refused. Five-foot Timothy L. Woodruff, Lieutenant Governor of New York, had most of the New York delegates, in a complimentary way, and Senator Platt had said "it might taper down to Tim."

DAWES AND PERKINS BEGIN TO FIGURE

I do not know when so much pressure was exerted upon a President to express an opinion as was used to persuade McKinley to indicate a choice. Hanna, realizing that he faced a hard fight without the President's aid, pressed hard for the right to tell convention leaders that he was speaking with authority. McKinley continued to refuse. Here again McKinley avoided a pitfall—one into which Roosevelt eight years later plunged with disastrous results—the mistake of a President naming a candidate for a convention.

Of course refusal meant humiliation for Hanna—better that, than White House domination of candidates.

Two men destined afterward to be prominent in politics were active figures behind the scenes at Philadelphia. Charles G. Dawes—then Comptroller of the Currency, and now Vice President—and George W. Perkins. Dawes indorsed McKinley's attitude; Perkins stood with Hanna. Perkins even went to the extreme of hiring a special train to take him from Philadelphia to Washington to urge McKinley. Fairbanks and Allison also urged.

Under such pressure it seemed probable that McKinley would yield. Hanna believed that he would and so kept steadily making his fight more and more an administration matter. Dawes warned Hanna against his course, protesting that he would be defeated and a nomination made that would be proclaimed as a defiance of White House wishes. Hanna, however, persisted. Dawes then, by telephone, repeated the same warning to the President. McKinley, through George Cortelyou, promptly authorized Dawes to state: "the President's close friends must not undertake to commit the Administration to any candidate; it has no candidate. The Administration wants the choice of the convention."

As I Knew Them

No desire to humiliate Hanna actuated Dawes; he simply wanted to protect McKinley. The message he received was seen by Hanna only. There was no need to show it to others. At once, Hanna knew he was beaten. He accepted defeat good-naturedly, for everything was part of the day's work with Hanna. If he could not get what he wanted he made the best of what he could get. He promptly sent for Roosevelt and said, "Teddy, you're it!"

Thus, a great chapter in American politics was begun, with not one of the figures having the dimmest vision of what it all was shortly to mean.

What different history would have been made had McKinley given Hanna the authority he wanted!

CHAPTER XXXI

HAWAII AND THE WAR WITH SPAIN

Both "Manifest Destiny"—McKinley Delayed War Until Our Army And Navy Could Prepare—He Believed That If The Parliaments Of Both Nations Would Adjourn, Cuba Would Be Free Without War— Foresaw The Problems That Would Follow War—Tells Shafter To Hold San Juan's "Thin Line"—Seeking A Right Basis For Peace— McKinley Ways And Wilson Ways—The Philippines And Cuba "Our Opportunity And Our Burden."

ANNEXING the Hawaiian Islands by treaty was one of the important steps taken by McKinley. His remark to Cortelyou that it was "manifest destiny" was made before there was any thought of the Philippines or Porto Rico. He found a responsible government in Hawaii, functioning as well as an independent government there could function. But it faced local uprisings and possible acquisition by England or Germany. Both considerations settled McKinley's mind. He urged the Senate to ratify the treaty offered by the Hawaiians. Not until after Dewey had taken Manila, nor until Hawaiians had violated neutrality by coaling and harboring our warships, did the Senate ratify the treaty. Thus McKinley closed the chapter Harrison could not, and Cleveland would not, finish.

Perhaps our war with Spain was "manifest destiny," too. Congress evidently thought so,—even to the extent of seeking to speed up destiny by declaring war before our Army or Navy was prepared even for a single battle. McKinley was firm against haste. He made no angry protests against Congress; he won delay by calmly talking over the situation day by day with those who were rampant for war as well as those opposed.

It was true, too true, that we were not ready, but it was

251

equally true that McKinley hoped that, given time, Spain would relieve the tension by freeing Cuba unconditionally. A week or so before the war declaration he told me in the White House that if the Parliaments of both countries would adjourn, he and Sagasta, then Spain's Prime Minister, could free Cuba and peaceably settle all differences. He said also:

"I am not anxious about the result of war. There can be but one result and it will not be long delayed. What I have in mind is what will come after war—the problems we do not see now but that are sure to come in some way. And they will not be easy problems. Other nations have had that experience, and we shall not escape it."

War came; so did the after-war problems. Some of those problems are still unsolved.

MCKINLEY DIRECTED ARMY AND NAVY

History will never credit McKinley with having directed every move on land and sea—but he did. Night and day he followed closely every battleship, every regiment and every plan. In Cuba not a move was made without approval from Washington.

Take one incident as typical, yet an incident that really led to the quick ending of the struggle.

On the night of July 1, 1898, after the day's battle driving the Spaniards over the slope of San Juan Hill, the American troops, exhausted by the tropic heat, were a thin, tired line on the hill-top. I was on the hill that night, and I know the "all in" condition of officers and men. Shafter feared a counter-attack, and did not believe we could withstand one. He cabled Washington that he might retire to a less exposed position. McKinley replied that he must, of course, use his own judgment inasmuch as he was on the ground, but he urged him to hold the hill. The people at home would not understand a retreat. That cable decided Shafter. The hill was held.

As I Knew Them

Holding that hill as well as El Caney made Santiago Bay impossible for the Spanish fleet bottled up there. It was at the mercy of attack by land guns. It had no alternative but to sail out hoping that some of the ships would escape the waiting American battleships.

Such is the caprice of fortune that Roosevelt's name is much more frequently associated with the war than is McKinley's. Just as when you speak of Waterloo the one remembered Britisher is Wellington so when you speak of San Juan the one remembered American is Roosevelt.

In both instances this is unfair to others who contributed as much if not more to the achievement, but it is the way of the world, otherwise known as fate. History is full of it. At times it seems like a conspiracy against the facts. The regular army won the battle of San Juan and the war in Cuba.

SEEKING A RIGHT BASIS FOR PEACE

In all the years I knew McKinley I cannot recall ever having seen him more concerned than when, with the armistice signed, he faced the problems of peace with Spain. He had none of the superior, confident air of a conqueror when, just returned from Santiago, I called at the White House. The war spirit still possessing me, I expected to find him in the same jubilant mood. My first glance, however, told me another story. The power to exact terms of his own liking seemed to rest uneasily on him. Here indeed was a man who had no flare to be absolute. Were we to keep the Philippines and Porto Rico? Were we to interpret the "Platt Amendment" literally as to Cuba, leaving it a free country, or interpret it in the newer light of conquest and take Cuba over, too?

These questions and others only less important were on our nation's doorsteps like unwanted children. If turned away where were they to go? If taken in, what would the consequence be? There was no answer that was not followed by responsibility as closely as one's shadow.

As I Knew Them

Never were the methods and personality of a man more clearly reflected than in the manner in which McKinley entered into peace negotiations; never were one President's ways in sharper contrast with those of another President than were McKinley's with those of Woodrow Wilson twenty years later, when the latter faced the same problems.

Wilson formulated his own conception of the peace he was to impose upon the world; he consulted few, if any. He did not even seek to learn the opinion of the country. When it came to him in the election of a Republican Congress, he rejected it. His course is stated more in detail in the chapter on Wilson.

McKinley sought counsel everywhere. He brought Elihu Root into his Cabinet as Secretary of War "because I want a lawyer to handle the problems of the new islands and you are the lawyer I want." He brought Admiral Dewey from Manila so that he might have by his side during the treaty negotiations the "man on the spot" who knew whereof he spoke. He persuaded Senators Cushman Davis, Frye and George Gray to become members of the peace commission, with Secretary of State Day and Whitelaw Reid.

Furthermore, McKinley took pride in the ability of his Commissioners. He sent them to their task with his confidence *and his respect*. "Be magnanimous" were his instructions—"the true glory and enduring interests of our country would best be served by an example of moderation, restraint and reason."

But McKinley did not stop there. He went west and made speeches, talked with representative men, wrote letters of inquiry. He made a systematic effort to get the reaction of the people to every feature of the peace negotiations, particularly the Philippines, and Cuba.

Step by step he moved to stronger ground—always keeping

ahead of public opinion but not too far ahead to be beyond its influence. He knew the peril any man, particularly a President, invites by attempting to do the thinking for a nation, and he avoided it. In this way McKinley secured a peace that Congress and the country would approve.

MCKINLEY ASKED FOR GUIDANCE

Charles S. Olcott, in his "Life of McKinley," tells how McKinley spoke in November 1898 to a committee of Methodist ministers who had called to pay their respects. As they were leaving the President called them back and said:

"Hold a minute longer. I would like to say a word about the Philippines.

"When I realized that the Philippines had dropped into our laps I confess I did not know what to do with them. I sought counsel from all sides—Democrats as well as Republicans—but got little help. I thought first we would take only Manila; then other islands, perhaps, also. I walked the floor of the White House night after night until midnight; and I am not ashamed to tell you, gentlemen, that I went down on my knees and prayed Almighty God for light and guidance more than one night. And one night late it came to me this way—I don't know how it was, but it came: (1) That we could not give them back to Spain—that would be cowardly and dishonorable; (2) that we could not turn them over to France or Germany—our commercial rivals in the Orient—that would be bad business and discreditable; (3) that we could not leave them to themselves—they were unfit for self-government—and they would soon have anarchy and misrule over there worse than Spain's was; and (4) that there was nothing left for us to do but to take them all, and to educate the Filipinos, and uplift and civilize and Christianize them, and by God's grace do the very best we could by them, as our fellow-men for whom Christ also died. And then I went to bed, and went to sleep, and slept soundly, and the next morning I sent for the chief engineer of the War Department (our map-maker), and I told him to put the Philippines

255

on the map of the United States (pointing to a large map on the wall of his office), and there they are, and there they will stay while I am President!"

"OUR OPPORTUNITY AND OUR BURDEN"

No one who was present at the Ohio Society banquet in the winter of 1900 will ever forget the scene when McKinley there met the challenge of imperialism. McKinley was never more impressive, more earnest, more persuasive and never held an audience more silent and attentive than while he was uttering these words:

> "There can be no imperialism. Those who fear it are against it. Those who have faith in the Republic are against it. So that there is universal abhorrence for it, and unanimous opposition to it. Our only difference is that those who do not agree with us have no confidence in the virtue or capacity or high purpose or good faith of this free people as a civilizing agency, while we believe that the century of free government which the American people have enjoyed, has not rendered them irresolute and faithless but has fitted them for the great task of lifting up and assisting to better conditions and larger liberty those distant peoples who through the issue of battle have become our wards. A self-governed people will never permit despotism in any government they foster and defend. The burden is our opportunity; the opportunity is greater than the burden."

COMPROMISED RATHER THAN "RIDE A WHITE HORSE"

There was still another incident in the McKinley policy toward our new island possessions that brought his methods into contrast with those of both Cleveland and Wilson. Cleveland, it will be remembered, speaking of his free wool message had said, "If every other man in the country abandons this issue, I shall stick to it!" Wilson took the same rigid attitude on measures that he included among his policies.

From Sacramento "Bee"

THE CARES OF A GROWING FAMILY SEEN THROUGH "THE BEE'S" PROPHESCOPIC SCOOPOGRAPH

As I Knew Them

McKinley, strongly believing in a prompt effort to make the people of Porto Rico feel at home with us, declared immediately after annexation in favor of repealing all tariffs against that island's products. "It is our plain duty," he insisted to Congress. But the protectionist Republican majority did not agree with him; he found himself in conflict with them as much as was Taft in 1910 when he urged his Canadian reciprocity bill. Taft passed the bill over the protests of his party in Congress with the aid of Democratic votes. McKinley refused to do this.

"I could ride a white horse in this situation and pass the original bill," McKinley said to me in the White House the afternoon a compromise for Porto Rico was agreed upon. "All the Democratic members are ready to vote to repeal the duties. There is more at stake in this country just now, however, than immediate free trade with Porto Rico. The vital thing is to keep as many votes as possible in Congress back of the whole programme of the Administration. We have insured that. Also, Porto Rico gets free trade in two years, the revenues collected in the meantime go back to the island, and the legislation has a practically unanimous vote. I am content with that result."

"THE FOREIGNER THE BETTER," SAID PLATT

Another example of McKinley's way of handling Congress was his approach to Senator Platt, of New York, when he wanted to send Joseph H. Choate as Ambassador to Great Britain and Horace Porter as Ambassador to France. Both had been fighting Platt in New York politics for years. McKinley wanted no contest in the Senate over confirmation, so he followed his policy of testing a situation before getting into it. He asked Platt to the White House.

"Platt," he said, "two men in New York whom you do not like politically and who do not like you are candidates for important foreign posts. I would like to have your consent to their nomination."

"Who are they?" inquired Platt.

"Choate and Porter," McKinley responded.

"Mr. President," answered Platt instantly, "nominate them quick and the 'foreigner' you send them the better!"

CHAPTER XXXII

"WE'LL STAND PAT!" SAID HANNA

McKinley Had Made Good—Prosperity Reigned Throughout The Land—"Bet-You-A-Million" John W. Gates Typified The Spirit Of The Day—Big Effort, Big Capital And Big Results—So McKinley Got A Mandate From The People "In The Interest Of Business Expansion," As Hanna Explained It.

"WE'LL stand pat!" replied Hanna when asked by a reporter to state the issue of the 1900 campaign to re-elect McKinley.

And "stand pat" the McKinley supporters did with much reason for their confidence.

Following Cleveland's four years of conflict with Congress, the first four years of McKinley were a period of calm that the country prized and during which it prospered greatly.

Prospered? Yes—beyond all expectation. McKinley had made good as "The Advance Agent of Prosperity." Through most of his term prosperity had reached farmer, merchant, mechanic and capitalist with some degree of fair division. "Dollar Wheat," high wages, industrial profits, had infused the people with a jubilant, confident, aggressive spirit. Crossing the line into a new century, our "captains of industry" seemed to feel that they had entered a new land of promise, and that "no pent-up Utica" would hereafter contract their powers or limit their possibilities.

"Bet-you-a-Million" John W. Gates was typical of scores of men to whom new wealth was only an incentive to greater wealth. "Big business" knew no caution. It became a gamble—a gamble with fate. Every capitalist, real or fancied,

259

looking into the future, visioned only big effort, big capital, big results. Today was merely a way station on the great highway to tomorrow. No one thought in terms of the present, splendid as they were; no one was content with what had been and what was. The future was capitalized as confidently as though it were a tale that is told. Men of experience, men of stability, men of hard-earned fortune looked upon every industry as a new Eldorado, whose treasures were to pour into the laps of those who planned on giant scale. The United States Steel Corporation is one of the dreams inspired by McKinley prosperity.

HANNA AND BRYAN SAW DIFFERENT ISSUES

It was while that spirit prevailed that McKinley defeated Bryan a second time; even Bryan's west returned generous majorities for McKinley. It was a campaign without a moment of doubt. Bryan thought the issue was "imperialism," and devoted his speech-making to that issue, but on election night Hanna gave a different interpretation to the verdict. "The Republicans," he said, "have received a clear mandate to govern the country in the interest of business expansion."

Back of that "mandate" too, was the earlier Supreme Court decision giving legality to the Sugar Trust's purchase of two Philadelphia refineries, making absolute its control of the industry. The decision seemingly stripped the government of power over corporate wealth, and such wealth promptly made the most of its opportunity. It assumed that it had received a license from the court; it assumed also that the election gave it in addition, as Hanna expressed it, "a mandate" from the people. What more could be asked?

Apparently nothing. So combination after combination was made. In every industry the "big fellows" united for control. Finally the railroads, too, saw possibilities in combination, and the Northern Securities Company resulted.

As I Knew Them

McKinley watched these developments with doubting mind. He wanted prosperity, but not too much of it; he wanted business to expand, but not too rapidly. He left nothing on the record to reflect his reaction to the get-rich-quick tide surging all about him, particularly after his reelection, but it is known that he often expressed regret that the Sherman anti-trust law had not been better sustained by the Courts. Seven months of his second term had barely passed when an assassin closed his career and the duty of carrying out the "mandate for business expansion" devolved upon the Vice President, Theodore Roosevelt.

CHAPTER XXXIII

MARK HANNA—BUSINESS IN POLITICS

*It Was Clean Business, However, For He Was Not A Speculator—A
Man of Many Kindly Qualities And A Loyal Friend—Sensitive To
Cartoons—A "Big Boss" But A Popular One—Adrift After McKin-
ley's Death—"Of Course Since You Want It, I Will Support It" He
Telegraphed Roosevelt About His Nomination—Dead Before The Con-
vention Of 1904 Met—Hanna And Bryan As Balances.*

IN the picture gallery of the men of politics, the portraits
have no soft tones. Both tint and lines are strong and
emphatic, accentuating good or bad, as the artist sees the
character of his subject. The politician, not the man, is on
the canvas. Thus Mark Hanna is portrayed in the political
history of his time. There he personifies the coarse, ruthless
business man in politics—the kind of business man we see in
theatrical characters or in novels—the kind that delights mer-
cilessly to crush opponents or sacrifice family, honor and
friends for gain.

It is grossly unjust to put Hanna in that class, for he was
not of that type at all. True, he had the decisive ways of
the man at the head of big affairs, but he also had qualities of
friendship and kindness. He was candid, genial and straight-
forward. No pretences, no intrigues, to gain his ends. He
was openly for you or against you. He was a business man
in politics, and naturally had a business man's judgment of the
policies best to pursue.

HANNA SENSITIVE TO CARTOONS

I first met Hanna at the Republican national convention of
1892 in Minneapolis. Later I knew him well. Month by
month as he marshalled the McKinley forces of the country,

he gathered men about him who gave him a loyalty that lasted until his death.

The one trait, suppose we call it weakness, that Hanna never overcame was his hurt feeling when cartooned or wrongly condemned in newspaper editorials. Homer Davenport drew the most offensive cartoon of Hanna—that with the dollar signs all over him,—and Davenport lived to seek Hanna and apologize. Most men in public life become hardened to criticism, but Hanna never did. Frequently he would say that he loved a fair fight but did not like below-the-belt blows.

To McKinley's proposal that he take John Sherman's place in the Senate, his instant response was that he "couldn't talk on his feet." When appointed two months later, he determined to make good in his new job and to secure election by the Ohio Legislature on his own account. He realized his handicaps—he was a "big boss" in politics, a "big boss" in business, a millionaire. It was not a record on which to expect popular support.

Nevertheless, Hanna went after that support. He was no platform speaker; he set apart an hour of each day to make himself one. He was not acquainted with the smaller county leaders of his State—soon he knew them all. Finally, he undertook a stumping tour of Ohio. In his speeches he tried no flights of oratory; he kept to the levels with which he was familiar. His audiences liked his blunt, homely phrases; he spoke their language and had their ways.

When the time came for the Legislature to elect a Senator, Hanna's name, like "Abou Ben Adhem's," led all the rest. He was then established in politics with his own ambitions and his own following. Later Roosevelt, among others, was to realize it.

HANNA ADRIFT WITHOUT MCKINLEY

With McKinley gone, Hanna was adrift for the three remaining years of his life. He frankly told Roosevelt that he could not be with him in certain contemplated policies, but he kept his word to stand by him to the end of his term. Undoubtedly he would have been glad to see a candidate developed against Roosevelt in 1904, but Roosevelt held the stage too completely, and Hanna died while reluctantly watching the tide flow by. There was talk that Hanna would seek the nomination for himself. The newspapers constantly were publishing such stories. He certainly had made himself popular; but he understood public opinion too well to believe that he could run for the Presidency with any hope of success.

Yet many prophesied that he would become a candidate. Hanna enjoyed the talk, but he kept his own counsel. His silence so baffled Roosevelt that the latter authorized Gov. Durbin, of Indiana, to announce that the President thought it time for Hanna to "fish or cut bait."

THE "FOR-ME" OR "AGAINST-ME" TELEGRAMS

About the same time in the Spring of 1903, Senator Foraker decided to challenge Hanna's control of the approaching Republican State convention in Ohio. He used the Roosevelt candidacy as his issue, declaring for his nomination and insisting that the State convention should commit Ohio to him. Foraker cared little for Roosevelt, but he sought an opportunity to show that Hanna no longer spoke for Ohio Republicans. He got from Hanna just what he expected—opposition to the proposed indorsement. Hanna rightly insisted that a year in advance was too soon to pledge a State delegation. He then telegraphed Roosevelt, who was on a tour in the Northwest, that he would have to oppose the issue raised by Foraker, but he was not doing so in any spirit of antagonism to his nomination. He added that he felt sure Roosevelt when apprised of all the facts would approve his course. But the President took a contrary view. He wired that inasmuch as the issue had been raised those who favor his nomination would support it and those who do not would oppose.

That settled Hanna's attitude.

"In view of the sentiments in your telegram," he wired back, "I shall not oppose the resolutions."

The sentiments settled more than the Ohio indorsement. They settled the nomination a year in advance of the 1904 convention. Hanna had died before the convention met.

Next to Roosevelt Hanna did more than any other man to make the Panama Canal a reality. He led the battle in Congress for it.

HANNA AND BRYAN AS NECESSARY TYPES

Hanna, of course, did not have a broad conception of public policies, but his views were honestly held. He looked over the nation as a banker looks over a balance sheet, hunting for "tangibles." He was not without appreciation of those intangible things that go so far toward making the character of men and nations, but their value as collateral was no greater in his eyes than in the eyes of the average banker unless backed by a definite objective. The smoke from a factory chimney had more meaning to him than the dream of the man in the office below.

He wanted results, not dreams, and in politics if results were not forthcoming from one set of men he quickly switched to another group. Power not politics, held his mind, and, like all who seek power, he believed that his use of it would be wise and best.

Such men have a place in the life of every nation, particularly in our own. They are a balance, a check, to extremists on the other side. One type would be as unsafe in complete control of a nation as the other; but one is as essential as the other in fixing the level on which millions of people can stand together contentedly under one government. Hanna had his contrast in Bryan. The year 1896 produced both men as national figures. The two types fought it out stubbornly in two national elections—Bryan getting the hurrahs of the multitude; Hanna getting their votes for McKinley.

CHAPTER XXXIV

DEPEW—MAN OF YEARS AND OF FRIENDS

Everybody Knows Chauncey M. Depew—Why He Abandoned Saloon Campaigning—Seven Decades Before The Public—Chauncey "De Peach"—Supported For President And Twice Elected Senator—Always Sought As A Campaigner.

WHO does not know Chauncey Depew? Who has not heard him tell a story or make a speech? Who has not found his philosophy—laugh and the world laughs with you —the stirring elixir of life when life seemed drab and empty? My recollection of him goes back many years and runs through many events and situations that were dark and confusing until his cheery disposition and clear mind found the way to light and new effort. Depew is not of a type; he is a type by himself.

Depew was two years later than Mark Hanna in entering the Senate at Washington. It was the spirit of the McKinley days not to be fearful of men who had won their way in the business world, but from the presidency of one of the largest railroad corporations directly to the United States Senate was a step never possible before or since Depew's election in 1889 by the Legislature of New York. Not content with giving him one term the Republicans reelected him in 1905. Election for a third term came in 1910 when the break in the Republican party lost Depew his seat to a Democrat because of the anti-Taft tidal wave.

Back somewhere in the eighteen-nineties I heard Depew in a speech before the New York Legislature say that when he was campaigning for election in 1861 and 1862 as Member of Assembly from Peekskill, candidates rivalled each other as to who could visit the most saloons in the district, who could call the most loungers therein to the brass-rail and the mahogany bar, and hand out the largest greenback to the saloon-keeper, with a nonchalant "never mind the change."

Depew followed this practice in his two campaigns but became so disgusted with it and with himself that he resolved never again to seek public office if he had to pay that price. He put the resolution into effect next year (1863) when nominated for Secretary of State of New York. He canvassed different parts of the State, and spoke at many more meetings than he could have addressed had he continued touring saloons. His election by a substantial majority satisfied him that no votes were lost by his different campaign method. He never again entered a saloon for electioneering or any other purpose.

SEVENTY YEARS OF PUBLIC LIFE

In that change of campaign headquarters from saloon to platform, Depew laid the basis for his career as railroad president, as United States Senator, and as orator. Though he has had seventy years of public speaking in Europe and America, he is still sought and honored at every banquet he cares to attend.

I doubt that any other man has had contact with the extremes of life such as Depew has enjoyed.

In New York city they know Depew on the Bowery and east side as "the Peach"; among New Yorkers of average station he is "Our Chauncey"; and among the exclusives he is Senator, or "Mr. President" of the New York Central Railroad. It is an achievement for any man to be accepted in three stations so widely separated. I once asked Depew how he managed it. He said he didn't manage it, he just went along with the day's work, and let nature take its course. Then he added, "with this exception, that I never made a pessimistic speech in my life; I have always looked upon the brighter side; I've always had faith in my country and our people; that strikes home more often than public speakers realize."

The title of "Peach" came to Depew in an interesting way. During the Presidential campaign of 1892 he addressed a Republican meeting on the Bowery for Harrison and Reid. In order to show the opportunity for everyone in America, he said:

"I started in life with these two hands and this head."

Someone in the audience called out: "That head is a peach, Chaunce."

The newspapers took up the phrase and from that time on Depew has been known as "de Peach."

It is not my purpose to use Depew's saloon story as an argument against liquor, but I do want to use it to demonstrate the unwisdom of those who assume that they must descend to low levels in order to be "popular" in politics or in other callings.

Real popularity—the popularity that counts—is not attained that way; rather is it soon lost. I could name a score of able, brilliant men in Congress and in the New York Legislature in the last thirty years who wasted so much time seeking that kind of popularity that they sacrificed their real opportunities. Men of rare ability have gone down like ten-pins, one after another, as I have watched them through their careers, cut short by their inability to realize, as Depew fortunately realized, that respect and confidence are not to be won with your feet on a brass-rail or your hand slapping somebody's, anybody's, everybody's—back.

SLOAT FASSETT'S GREAT MISTAKE

For obvious reasons I cannot use names, but any reader acquainted with the habits of men in public life—in fact with the habits of men in any walk of life—will easily recall many who have frittered away their talent and their chance by their will-o'-the-wisp search for "popularity" based on an appeal to the poorer rather than the better instincts of people. My observation is that those who respect themselves are most respected. Depew did not become a "Peach" to the Bowery-ites by pretending to be one of them; he remained the same Depew on the Bowery as on Fifth Avenue and he achieved popularity in both sections because he was just Depew in both.

A contrasting incident of interest was the experience on the same Bowery of J. Sloat Fassett, when he was a candidate for Governor. He was addressing a house crowded with east side voters. The night was oppressively hot, and many of his audience began taking off their coats. Fassett evidently thought he would win favor by doing the same thing. He threw off his coat and then turned to resume his speech.

Hisses greeted Fassett instead of the applause he had anticipated for getting down to the level of his audience. Though his hearers were shirt-sleeved themselves they did not care to listen to a Governor in shirt-sleeves. Fassett continued his speech until he could find a place to stop; he then gave up and amidst boohs and hisses put on his coat and left the platform.

Next day's newspapers carried the story of Fassett's bad night on the Bowery—wholly due to the fact that, unlike Depew, he did not stick to his own ways on the East Side as he would have done on Fifth Avenue.

ALWAYS SOUGHT AS A CAMPAIGNER

In the years while Depew was the active head of the New York Central Railroad, he was in constant demand as a campaign speaker—particularly in the up-state rural counties. No man has made so many speeches in so many counties. The railroad extends into most of those counties, and has the traditional antagonisms of a railroad in all of them; yet each year when local political leaders would send their list of desired speakers, the name of Chauncey Depew, president of the New York Central, was always there.

As I Knew Them

In 1888 the destinies of the Republican party in New York State were entrusted to the "Big Four"—Platt, Depew, Miller and Hiscock;—the party leaders were not afraid to name Depew as one of the four, despite his railroad interests. Nor were the New York delegates to the national convention of that year fearful of criticism from the folks back home because they supported Depew for President. He received 99 votes, ranking next to John Sherman and Judge Gresham on the first ballot.

BRIGHTENS H. G. WELLS' GLOOM

Depew's philosophy of life was aptly illustrated at a dinner given by Ralph Pulitzer to H. G. Wells, when the celebrated Englishman came over here to report the Washington naval limitations conference for the New York World. Pulitzer called on Wells as the first speaker of the evening. I never listened to a gloomier, more hopeless picture of the future than Wells gave us in his speech.

The banqueters were certainly a depressed crowd when Depew was called upon. I shall not pretend to quote his exact words but in substance he said that with all that Wells had published in his book "The Outline of History" down to Julius Caesar he agreed because he knew little about it.

"But I am a contemporary of Caesar," he added, "and I know history from Caesar to the present, and I do not agree with a word our friend has written about those centuries. Nor do I agree with what he has said here tonight about the present plight of the world and the still darker future ahead of us. We have light, not darkness ahead of us; we have a better understanding among nations, not a poorer understanding ahead of us; we have a realization of the horror and burdens of war to guide us away from war in the future. No, friend Wells, this is not the time for sorrowing, nor the time for despair. This is the time for hope—the time for straightening out for one great big effort to make up for all the

tragedies of the past eight years. This world has never turned
from bad to worse; it gets its jolts, and I admit we have had
a hard one, but it is always getting better and it is not going
to stop now."

When Depew sat down, the clouds had lifted from the
dinner table, and we showed our relief by applause that must
have convinced Wells that he was in the wrong company for
the doctrine he preached.

THE QUALITY OF LEADERSHIP

This is no place to detail Depew's career. Personally, I
believe that had he, as a young man, continued in public life
he might have been President of the nation instead of President of a railroad. He has the outstanding quality of leadership—the ability to sense the purpose of the average man and
to move along with him. He has another great quality in his
determination never to look hopelessly on the dark side of
any situation.

Taft was elected President on his smile, but Depew's laugh
in the midst of a gloomy conference whether of business or of
politics has taken the furrows out of many a brow. And his
reward is in the full life he is still enjoying as I write—full
of friendships, full of honors, full of health and full of years.

CHAPTER XXXV

BRYAN—A CAREER OF PROTEST

Two Pictures of the "Peerless One," Thirty Years Apart—Making and Discarding Issues—Urging a Peace Treaty In Order To Have a Campaign Cry—What Was His Motive In 1912?—A Tragedy in the State Department—His Last Appeal To His Party, and the "Boos" That Greeted Him.

IN 1896 I sat in the press section not fifty feet from William Jennings Bryan when he made his "cross of gold" speech in the Democratic national convention at Chicago; there I watched the tumult that startled a nation and almost won him a Presidency; in 1924 I sat in the press section in Madison Square Garden in New York City, again not fifty feet away, when he made his plea not to denounce the Ku Klux Klan by name; there I heard the "boos" that greeted his last appeal to his party—"boos" so loud and persistent that Chairman Walsh threatened to recess the convention.

Those nearly thirty years!

At first, a man in the full energy of ambitious life—flashing, gleaming eye, broad-shouldered, straight as an arrow, the physique of a gladiator, the spirit of a crusader; voice clear and vibrant; 15,000 spectators emotionally following every word, every gesture. Then the other picture twenty-eight years later—a worn man, eyes dimmed, shoulders stooped, the old spirit glowing faintly like the thin flame from a burnt-out log, voice no longer resonant, many of the delegates and spectators hostile to his pleading, scarcely tolerant of the leader they had followed so many years.

What a career between the day of hurrahs and the day of "boos"! It had led him into all the highways and byways of politics except the one he most desired to travel—the highway to the White House. Its triumphs were of the platform; the only office he ever held by election was that of Congressman—two terms from 1891 to 1895. In those years an anti-Republican tide engulfed the country, making the election of a Democrat possible from Lincoln, Nebraska, normally Republican.

Bryan was a product of his restless day. Such types come in the life of every nation reflecting its passing temper but not its character. They have their "exits and their entrances," and while on the stage seem destined next moment to make a tremendous hit. That moment never comes. Looking back upon their activities, one wonders, as he sees great waves of discontent rising at times perilously high, why such men hold their leadership so long without being swept into the place of power they seek. With that wonder comes a firmer faith in the wisdom of the ballot-box.

THREE MEN WHO HELD THE PEOPLE

I am far from classing Bryan with either Roosevelt or Wilson, but we must not forget that from 1896 to 1919 those three men held the political attention of the country more completely, indeed more exclusively, than any other three men ever held it. Bryan became of national significance before Roosevelt or Wilson, though he was two years younger than Roosevelt and four years younger than Wilson. "The Commoner," as he delighted to hear himself called, was only 37 when first nominated for the Presidency—a fact that led to his being referred to, sarcastically, as "the Boy Orator of the Platte." Roosevelt was 42 when he succeeded McKinley and was the youngest President to enter the White House. Wilson was 56.

The death of Roosevelt in 1919 left Wilson and Bryan the most conspicuous figures in the public mind, though Senator Bob La Follette was steadily emerging. In 1924 as a presidential candidate of his own party, the Wisconsin Senator

polled 4,800,000 votes. Wilson's death in 1924 followed by
La Follette's, left Bryan alone on the national stage for a year
longer—just as he had held it alone for two years before
Roosevelt achieved national prominence, and ten years before
Wilson dreamt of a career outside his college environment.

THE TWO BRYANS MY MIND HAS SEEN

There have always been two Bryans in my mind—the Bryan
in private life with religious convictions to which he clung
with firm, sincere though spectacular faith; the Bryan in public life with so many convictions that he seemed to believe that
he was ordained to discover and redress all the wrongs of
the oppressed, because no other human could do the job so
well. He had a passion for "issues." This habit brought
him under suspicion of constantly shopping in the market
places for something to "sell" the people. Like an omnibus
he carried a great variety of issues so as to be sure he had
gathered up all there were, and could accommodate everybody.

Let me illustrate with the "16 to 1" issue—the foundation
stone of Bryan's career. Cleverly he dramatized that issue
in a single speech that almost as it was uttered changed him
from an unimportant advocate to an historic figure in the fight
for silver. Yet Richard P. Bland of Missouri—"Silver Dollar Dick"—had been the leader of the silver forces in Congress for more than twenty years. The only triumph scored
for the metal was the Bland law of 1878 compelling the free
coinage of silver dollars—the Bland "cart-wheel" dollars.

It was that law, modified by the Sherman law of 1890,
that Cleveland forced Congress to repeal. The issue thus
created seemed to point to the Missourian as the man to lead
in the 1896 battle for silver's restoration. Surely if the
servant were worthy of his hire—and Bland was—Bland
should have been chosen. But Bryan pounced upon the issue
as an eagle does his prey. He knew the moment to act in the
convention. He asked permission to speak last—just before

the balloting for nominee. He was staking all on one opportunity to impress the delegates; he wanted his voice to ring in their ears unchallenged by subsequent speakers.

LEAVING THE TRIED SERVANT FOR A NEW STAR

The political orator, as he reads the "cross of gold" speech can visualize the whole thing as an actor does when he reads a play. He can see every high spot, every chance for effectiveness, every place where the audience will break into applause. And Bryan utilized such opportunities. It was this example of dramatic force and careful political play-writing which led to the gossip in those days that in his youth Bryan had been an actor. His dynamic climaxes moved the delegates to turn hysterically from the man who had served to one who suddenly appeared like a new star in the firmament.

But the new star was not to be as constant as the star grown dim in many battles. The new star was determined always to be of the first magnitude and, if one issue seemed likely to tarnish its brightness, another must be brought forward.

Writing of the 1896 campaign, Bryan called it "The First Battle." When he wrote he knew it was the last battle for silver; he knew he would never use it again as an issue. Promptly he went "shopping" for something else that would arouse the people and keep him "the Peerless Leader." He found it in anti-imperialism. All the passion with which he had appealed to voters in 1896 against the God of Gold was now transferred to the newer issue as readily as you change one coat for another.

The God of Gold had not ruined the country as four years before he had predicted; there was no crown of thorns pressing down upon the brow of labor. Instead the people had prospered mightily and so had Bryan. But Bryan could insist that another God—the God of Imperialism—was being worshipped by the opposing party and was certain to transform our Republic into an autocracy. And all because we had taken over the Philippines! When the votes were counted, and he again found himself denied the Presidency, there was nothing for Bryan to do but go shopping once more for an issue. For the twenty-five remaining years of his life he kept shopping and shopping but never again found another issue that interested the people in a national sense.

ISSUES WERE BRYAN'S STOCK IN TRADE

Some call this just politics; some call it insincerity; some call it opportunism. Call it all or any of these, for the difference is not great, the truth is that Bryan had an unexcelled talent for keeping himself before the public, and in the exercise of that talent he used "issues" as a storekeeper uses his stock. He tried to keep on hand what the people wanted; and if he was out of stock he undertook to sell them something "just as good."

As a grocer Bryan would not have put sand in the sugar or his thumb on the scales, but he would make a sale, as he sold Florida real estate, based on things hoped for rather than on things done. No man with sincerity of purpose would jump grasshopper-like from issue to issue as Bryan did, or could so easily convince himself as Bryan could that he had finished his job before each jump.

Bryan always insisted, for example, that his "16 to 1" issue would have remained an issue until it had won but for the increasing production of gold! Thus he reconciled his yesterdays with his todays,—content with his own dismissal of it and his own reasoning. When he made this statement as to "16 to 1" he confirmed Tom Reed's prophecy in Congress in 1892:

"He (Bryan) finds now that even the Democratic party has got to obey the everlasting laws of common-sense; they have got to act according to the eternal verities, and that is going to be a great shock to him on every occasion."

As I Knew Them

It is amazing that a man of whom that could be said with truth could travel the country over so many times and for so many years and hold so many voters through it all—over 6,000,000 votes were polled for Bryan at each of three elections. What was it Bryan possessed that made it possible for him to do that which no other man in our politics was ever able to do? He had no record of achievement on which to ask public favor; his was a career of protest. Not once was he able to say "I did thus and so," contrasting his own official acts and policies with those of men who had responsibility. Excepting his "cross of gold" speech, Bryan never uttered a sentence that survived longer than its day, or that political historians can use to illustrate his philosophy. Words? Yes—words by the million, but not one thought that revealed a purposeful mind. Nevertheless, Bryan must be credited with something that appealed strongly. No two men ever agreed as to what that something was. Some said a Presence and a Voice. The Voice was magical; few could use it better. And the Presence filled the eye.

His power over the political opinion of the country was a tribute not so much to his convictions as to his adroitness. Perhaps that is the appropriate word for Bryan's statesmanship—adroitness, to the point of suspicion of his sincerity even in policies, such as prohibition, for which he would have made any sacrifice.

RATIFIED A TREATY TO CREATE AN ISSUE

As far back as 1898—only two years after his first campaign for the Presidency—Bryan demonstrated his skill in shifting issues.

In the Senate in February, 1899, the struggle over ratification of the peace treaty with Spain had much the same inten-

MICAWBER-LIKE, BRYAN WAS ALWAYS LOOKING
FOR SOMETHING TO TURN UP

sity as the struggle twenty years later over the Versailles treaty. The proposed purchase of the Philippines from Spain for $25,000,000 split party lines. Senators Hoar, of Massachusetts, and Eugene Hale, of Maine, denounced the treaty as an imperialistic document. They did not believe in the transfer of the sovereignty of any people by bargain and sale, without consent.

Many Democratic Senators, politically disposed to make trouble for McKinley, joined in this view, and began to unite in opposition to ratification. Bryan, who had been Colonel of a Nebraska regiment of volunteers, had resigned his commission, and was again footloose, a candidate for the 1900 nomination. He turned up in Washington with the surprising request to Democratic Senators to vote to ratify. He insisted that no political party could take responsibility for keeping the country even technically at war. His view was reluctantly accepted by enough Democrats to put the treaty through. Bryan's entrance into that situation was timed to be dramatic and pivotal. When the roll-call on ratification showed only one majority in favor, the country did not have to be told that Bryan had saved the treaty. Bryan had seen to that.

HE WANTED THE LIMELIGHT ALONE

Here again, as in 1896, he set the stage with himself in the centre, and the limelight on him alone. He had made himself the decisive factor in confirming the purchase of the Philippines. He would now make himself, or seek to make himself, the decisive factor in setting them free. He demanded our immediate release to the Filipinos of the sovereignty we had acquired from Spain.

Bryan had stood on broad ground while favoring the treaty and had won commendation for his course, but his new turn threw a new light on his motive. The response came quickly from the country that in urging ratification he had been shrewdly building a platform for himself in the presidential struggle just ahead. It was his one chance for a nation-wide issue—the one chance to escape from another "16 to 1" battle. If the treaty were to fail, he could not evoke "Imperialism," for we would be out of the Philippines, but if the treaty were ratified, and the Philippines should come under our flag, then he could demand that we set them free, and pocket our loss of $25,000,000 for temporary sovereignty.

Only a mind with a peculiar bent for creating a situation would have resorted to such strategy, but it made the best issue he could find. "McKinley prosperity" had buried all other issues; the distant Philippines offered the only one available. In that 1900 election he made the poorest showing, proportionately, of any of his three struggles; at its close, anti-imperialism, no longer serviceable, promptly went into the discard along with "16 to 1."

TOOK NO CHANCES WITH T. R., BUT FOUGHT TAFT

No persuasion could lure Bryan into a candidacy against Roosevelt in 1904; he was aware of its certain end. But four years later, he knew that he could not keep his hold on his party without becoming its candidate. Besides he had some hope that he could defeat Taft. All that he did in that campaign, however—indeed the most definite thing of his career —was to make a speech against "Big business" that brought Charles E. Hughes into national attention as a masterful orator and thinker.

At Youngstown, Ohio, Hughes replied. The Hughes speech caught the country; thereafter the election, though six weeks distant, was only a matter of totalling the vote against Bryan. Bryan replied to Taft's speeches, replied to President Roosevelt's 'statements'—but he attempted no reply to Hughes.

I saw Bryan frequently during the Republican national convention of 1912. He was there as a reporter for a newspaper syndicate; he seemed to enjoy talking with Roosevelt and other Republican leaders. I did not attend the Democratic convention at Baltimore a week or so later, but when I read of Bryan standing on the centre of that stage denouncing Belmont and Ryan as unfit delegates, and challenging the election of Alton B. Parker as chairman, my mind turned to the picture of him seated in the press section, a few days before, the calm interpreter of an intense Republican conflict. It was a spectacular transition—few men could have made it. But Bryan did it well. And it was just the thing he liked to do— to come upon a scene as though shot through a trap door, astonishing all by his presence and his purpose.

BRYAN'S GREAT BATTLE AT BALTIMORE

Was he, too, really seeking his own nomination in Baltimore?

Had the spectacle of a divided Republican convention, insuring Democratic victory, stirred his thrice-thwarted ambition anew?

He had been elected to the Baltimore convention under instructions to vote for Champ Clark; the Nebraska delegation was a unit for the Missouri candidate.

When the "break" came in Chicago, however, Bryan frankly lost interest in newspaper writing; the opportunity to elect a Democratic President had his entire mind. In my presence he declared that he was going to Baltimore to fight the Democratic reactionaries to the death. Others in Chicago quoted him as saying that if, after Taft's nomination, Baltimore should nominate a conservative, he would feel that both parties had become reactionary; the only course then left for him would be to support an independent ticket—even Roosevelt. When Bryan's plan was mentioned to Roosevelt, his reply was "I'm not the same kind of cattle." By a "conservative" it was assumed that Bryan meant Underwood, Harmon or the man he was under instructions to favor— Clark.

Though the instructions he had accepted meant the nomi-

nation of Clark there can be no doubt that Bryan had a
different nomination in mind, and his purpose to desert Clark
was revealed the instant he arrived in Baltimore. He gathered his forces to defeat Alton B. Parker for Chairman—and
polled 508 votes for himself against 578 for Parker! That
near-triumph led him to a still bolder effort. In effect the
second effort succeeded too, for in a fiery speech, he secured
a four to one vote for the following resolution, after agreeing
to omit the second paragraph:

> Resolved, that in this crisis in our party's career and in our
> country's history this convention sends greeting to the people of the
> United States, and assures them that the party of Jefferson and
> Jackson is still the champion of popular government and equality
> before the law. As proof of our fidelity to the people we hereby
> declare ourselves opposed to the nomination of any candidate for
> President who is the representative of or under obligation to J.
> Pierpont Morgan, Thomas F. Ryan, August Belmont, or any
> other of the privilege-hunting and favor-seeking class.
>
> Be it further resolved, that we demand the withdrawal from this
> convention of any delegates constituting or representing the above-
> named interests.

WAS HE FOR WILSON OR FOR HIMSELF?

Thus two emotional incidents built a solid foundation under
Bryan's manœuvring to name the candidate. He was now
the pivot of the convention—the man of demonstrated
strength. The Murphys, Taggarts and Brennans had the
numerical force of their delegations, but Bryan had the spirit
of the convention. There was no limit to its possibilities. How
would he use his power? When would his real purpose be
revealed? Would he kill off every candidate but himself?
He was watched closely, suspiciously. The Clark managers
asserted that Bryan would remain true to the instructions
from Nebraska; Colonel House and other Wilson advocates
rested on his assurance that he had forgotten Wilson's plea

that he should be "knocked into a cocked hat" and they believed he was friendly to the Jersey Governor; Roger Sullivan and Tom Taggart asserted that he was out for himself and they acted accordingly.

BRYAN DEFEATS CLARK AND CLARK MAKES RESPONSE

Bryan voted for Clark for nine ballots. He knew that Clark could not be nominated until Tammany swung into line for him. On the tenth ballot Tammany did so. That move gave Clark a majority of the convention; nomination by a two-thirds vote would probably follow on the next roll-call. Bryan's great moment had arrived. Standing on the platform he declared that he could not vote for a candidate whose nomination, if made, would be secured by the votes of Murphy, Belmont and Ryan. He switched to Woodrow Wilson. The Clark column was shattered.

Through thirty-five more ballots Clark struggled vainly; so far as his candidacy was concerned, the end had come. All the time, the one question was, when would Bryan desert Wilson for himself? The Sullivans and the Taggarts, unable to name Clark, were nevertheless powerful to stand in Bryan's way. Rather than take the chance of another candidacy by "The Peerless One," they preferred to defeat him with his own candidate Wilson.

Was Bryan a traitor to Clark? Was the use of Tammany, as a reason for switching, merely a subterfuge? Speaker Clark in his "Memories" said:

> "I never said, 'Great is Tammany and Croker its Prophet.' Bryan did.
>
> "I never welcomed Mr. Murphy at a railroad station and had my picture taken clasping hands with him. Bryan did.
>
> "I never sent a trusted friend half-way across the continent to beg Mr. Murphy not to defeat my nomination under the two-thirds rule by refusing to give him the New York delegation after I received a majority. Bryan did."

As I Knew Them

Most men in political life fail to see any humor in jokes about themselves or in cartoons. Bryan enjoyed them. So did Wilson. So did Roosevelt. The latter was delighted with Finley Peter Dunne's book "Alone in Cuba" and was eager to meet Dunne and laugh over it. Wilson often told stories at his own expense. Bryan got the originals of many cartoons and hung them on the walls of his almost-bookless library. He liked to tell the story of the drunk, who, thrown down the stairs of a dance-hall for the third time, picked himself up and said: "Those fellows can't fool me. They don't want me in there, and they think I don't know it." He applied the story to his own three defeats for the Presidency.

BRYAN IN THE STATE DEPARTMENT

It is a mercy to Bryan to say little of his career as Secretary of State.

That Wilson tolerated him so long is the best tribute I know to Wilson's self-control and patience. Of course, Bryan in the Cabinet was politics; but even politics has its limits. There must have been many embarrassing moments in the Wilson Cabinet sessions. The public could not know of them, but it did know that the serene and dignified office in which the Secretary of State is to be found was a distressing place while Bryan occupied it. Shirt-sleeved (literally) with handkerchief tucked in his collar and a big palm-leaf fan in hand, he sat in the Secretary's high-backed chair like a Hottentot chief on his tropical throne. Bryan's callers were chiefly the cheap grade of politicians who grub a living out of public office or public favor. Men of consequence frequently had to wait while Bryan tried to hunt jobs for the daily procession of "deserving Democrats." He would telephone from one department to another seeking places for the "faithful," as he called them, explaining to his fellow cabinet officers that he had to take care of 6,000,000 voters who had supported his three candidacies for President.

As I Knew Them

"A PECULIAR PRODUCT OF OUR COUNTRY"

Next to hunting offices for his followers, he busied himself with lecturing on tour. Condemnation made no impression on him so long as the receipts held up. He talked of a speaking tour of Europe. President Wilson was told in advance of the Chautauqua tours and consented. But he must have headed off the foreign trip, though the report had reached London that Bryan had arranged to go there. On February 13, 1914, Ambassador Page wrote to Colonel House:

> "It was announced in one of the London papers that Bryan would deliver a lecture here and possibly in each of the principal European Capitals on Peace. Now, God restrain me from saying, much more from doing anything rash, but if I have got to go home at all, I'd rather go before he comes. It'll take years for American Ambassadors to recover what they'll lose if he carries out his plan. They now laugh at him over here. . . . Mr. Asquith . . . met Bryan once and he told me with a smile that he regarded him as a 'peculiar product of your country.' "

In Washington, diplomats were at first amazed, then disgusted; they kept their distance from the State Department except when it was necessary to call on official business.

BRYAN'S LAST CONVENTION

The picture of Bryan pleading for his cause amidst the "boos" of the Madison Square Garden convention in 1924 is something that no witness can recall with pleasure. There were many incidents throughout that unhappy convention that were sad to look upon or to recall in later days. Not in all the history of conventions has there ever been one so pitiful as Bryan on the platform frequently halting his speech until his voice could be heard above the yells of derision. Here was the thrice-named leader of his party, here was the man to

285

whose daring the party owed eight years of Wilson as President, with all that goes with partisan control of government. Yet he could not command even the respect of attention.

Bryan's battle in that convention was not so much over the nominee as over the platform. He seemed to centre on the party platform. He wanted prohibition upheld by a law enforcement plank, and he was against any denunciation of the Ku-Klux-Klan by name. Florida named him as its member of the platform committee.

THOUGH HISSED, BRYAN WINS FOR THE KLAN

A national platform is a delicate thing to write, an exhausting task for the members of the Committee. It was doubly exhausting in seething New York—a citadel of "wet" sentiment and religious antagonisms. The Ku-Klux question moved both sides profoundly; perhaps never before were they so evenly balanced. All day and all night the committee debated. When at last calm came, Bryan suggested closing with prayer, so at six o'clock in the morning Judge McCunn, of Pennsylvania, a Catholic, recited the Lord's Prayer, and Bryan himself prayed fervently in his own words.

Two reports go to the convention for its choice—a majority report that does not name the Klan, and a minority report naming and denouncing it. Bryan urges the majority report. He tries to be conciliatory. But every delegate of Catholic faith has been made to feel that a plank inferentially against the Klan without naming it is directed against his religion.

The heavy, tired speaker seeks to touch some note of common purpose. There is none of the "We will defy them" spirit with which in his early years he had constantly assailed the "money power." He seeks to touch a note of common purpose. But he cannot bring harmony out of such discord. He is greeted with howls from the galleries; despite the howls, he persists. When all is over, the tabulation shows only a single vote margin for the "no name" plank. It is the barest victory possible, but it is a victory. He has his way.

THE STRUGGLE FOR A CANDIDATE

The cost of that victory Bryan is soon to learn. The same elements that were at odds on the platform are at odds on the nomination. Thirty-eight ballots are taken. A deadlock has come. It must be broken. Who shall give counsel? The three-times candidate, the father in Israel of the present Democracy, tries to lead the way to a choice, as he led at Baltimore twelve years before.

But his victory for the Klan still rankles. He rises on a stereotyped excuse—to explain his vote. His reception is hostile. Not even the formal narrative of the official proceedings can conceal it. He is greeted with "cheers and applause mingled with hisses and boos." He tells his hearers that every state has at least one man to whom the convention could safely turn—he will name some. He begins at home. "We have a man in Florida. He is president of our State University (Laughter). His name is Dr. O. O. Murphree (Voices) "We want Smith! We want Smith! (Laughter, applause and cheers). He is a scholarly Democrat." (Voice: "Never heard of one.")

The speaker goes on. Soon he says that this is probably his last convention. His enemies join in a round of applause. Quickly he responds: "Don't applaud, I may change my mind." (Laughter, applause and cheers). He refers to his three nominations and the words "never again" greet him. He speaks of likely timber and at last reveals his real purpose with a good word for McAdoo.

The minutes record "applause, and boos, considerable disorder on the floor and in the gallery." A delegate from New Jersey interrupts to ask about "Doheny and McAdoo and Oil." There are "continuous cries of 'Oil,' 'Oil,' and the Chairman orders the galleries cleared. Bryan asks the man who has heckled him what state he comes from. 'New Jersey,' responds the delegate. 'I voted for you every time you ran. I am sorry.' "

And so it goes. The record is full of such interruptions as "Who's paying you for this?" "Come off, come off," "Great disorder, shouting, boos, cat-calls and cries of out of order." At last Bryan finishes his speech while the Chairman's gavel is pounding for order and Mr. O'Brien, a New Jersey delegate, exclaims "The same old 'Dollar Bill,' the same old 'Dollar Bill.' "

Bryan resumes his seat. His speech has been a failure. Not till sixty-five more—one hundred and three in all—ballots are taken can a nomination be reached, and the nominee is John W. Davis, whose candidacy he had denounced as too close to Wall Street.

In 1912 Bryan had fought and defeated a "Wall Street" candidate. This time he surrendered. The cynical said that he got his price—his brother in second place on the ticket. It was the last use of his influence in a national convention and, like other incidents, it brought his sincerity into question even among his own party associates.

ALWAYS IN A RACE FOR WEALTH

At odds with Bryan's professions, was his greed for wealth. The Bryan one finds denouncing Wall Street's worship of the God of gold is a Bryan in swift and persistent pursuit of the same God. Even while holding the dignified post of Secretary of State the desire for dollars led him to go lecturing through the country like a barn-storming actor. Later, when Florida needed an orator for its land speculation, he joined in the land craze and became its spokesman. It, too, meant gold.

Of course, Bryan was in a numerous company in his desire for wealth, but why should he have regarded himself as the only member of the company with honorable intent? His followers in politics often hoped that he would step out of the ranks of money-seekers, but he became more devoted to money-making as his Florida acres sold higher. He lived to find himself a millionaire and to speak of it with satisfaction. The great fortune he accumulated is the strongest indictment of his sincerity—not because it represented wealth, but because of his constant preaching that the man with a dollar is to be feared as a selfish creature, while the man without a dollar must be accepted as unselfish.

Of course, there is good, a great deal of good, in every man, and more of it in most of our public men than they get credit for. There was good in Bryan. I am reminded of the reply made by a friend when I asked him why he did not seek the gold known to be on some land he owned in New Mexico. "It costs too much to get it out," he said. The gold in Bryan cost too much to get out.

ALWAYS SEEKING, NEVER GAINING, OFFICE

Our people estimated Bryan properly when they kept him always seeking but never attaining power. Half a century is a long penance period but many people believe it would have required almost that time for the country to recover from a Bryan Administration. He had no mind for the practical; none for organization, none for sound reasoning. Not many men with his contacts and experiences would have remained as Bryan remained from beginning to end of his career at the same intellectual level. He was not a student, not even a reader of enlightening literature. Newspapers with their daily offering of something new had his attention. He cared little for books. His collection would not have overtaxed a five-foot shelf. One book, however, he knew thoroughly—the Bible.

In 1907 he toured the world, visiting many of the leading capitals and meeting many leading men. After such opportunity for broadening experiences he was as unchanged as if he had spent his time on a Mississippi river flat-boat. The influence of years, of observation and of travel counted for little. Adroitness in speech, adroitness in manipulating conventions, adroitness in advancing his own opportunity for political power and for wealth remained his dominant characteristic. Against that record must be placed his religious convictions whose fundamental bases he never changed.

He preached against millionaires and died one; he preached against militarists and asked to be buried among them.

CHAPTER XXXVI

J. R.

His Real Interests Were Family, Country And Friends—His Last Ten Years Were Regarded By Many As His Greatest—Always Something Doing In The White House, But In One Direction Only—"Don't Move, We've Got It!" Exclaimed John Singer Sargent—Where Roosevelt Should Be Honored With A Monument—How He Found Money For The Battle-Fleet Cruise—His Loyalty To Friendship—"Teddy" The Whole World Round—The Wide Circle Of His Acquaintances.

TO have known Theodore Roosevelt well and to have enjoyed his confidence is a proud privilege for an American to claim. That privilege is mine—and I rank it among the richest of my life.

I knew him in his days of early ambition; I knew him on the battle-line at Santiago; I knew him in his days of power; I knew him in his days of storm and trial; best of all, I knew him in those later days when he realized that the world was behind him, that his work was done and that all that remained for him was to counsel his fellow citizens as best he could out of his own vast experience.

It would be hard to say definitely in which period of his remarkable career Roosevelt's qualities stood out in most commanding way; but it will always seem to me that he was greatest after titles had become mere symbols of the past and the man, not the office or the power, spoke.

It is not my purpose to write as an historian. Certainly I shall not attempt that rôle with Roosevelt. Joseph Bucklin Bishop, Lawrence Abbott and Roosevelt's own "Autobiography" cover that field thoroughly. What I place on record about that splendid type of vigorous, patriotic and fine-purposed American manhood must swing back and forth

"HE'S GOOD ENOUGH FOR ME"

through the years, as events and conversations range themselves in my memory—at times far apart in date. I prefer to write in a more personal way based on the impressions I gathered on different occasions.

The first statement I desire to make is one that has long been on my mind, but one that I realized could not be made while Roosevelt lived without being regarded as a partisan effort to defend him. I want to put it on record here, as I have said in an earlier chapter, that of all the men in public life I have known and met during nearly half a century of active newspaper work, I can recall none more ready to listen to the views of others, more willing when convinced to put aside his own ideas, more ready to accept group judgment in preference to his own, than Theodore Roosevelt.

Following his return from Africa in 1910, I sat in numerous conferences called to determine the course he was to pursue—including his candidacy for the Republican nomination in 1912—and I was always amazed at the patience with which he discussed the various points of view urged and his own. Once you had his confidence you had an open sesame to his mind.

There were times, of course, when Roosevelt felt deeply on certain matters and stuck to his colors. Nor did he ever fail to state his views with vigor, and one had to be well equipped with facts and reasoning to gain the verdict over him in conference. When his own interests were solely at stake the Colonel felt that his own judgment should prevail.

HIS LAST TEN YEARS

I have said above that I consider the last ten years of Roosevelt's life—the out-of-power years—as his greatest. Perhaps I should qualify that statement by saying that to his friends they are the greatest. Those of us who were privileged to listen to him during those years felt like one thrilled by the warm radiance of a setting sun; how splendidly its strength and beauty shone out in the glow of its fading moments.

Roosevelt was no man to reminisce. He lived in today and tomorrow. His yesterdays served only the purpose of building up his tomorrows.

After his retirement from the Presidency in 1909, and particularly after 1912, he would often preface his talk by saying, "Now I am free to express my own opinions because I shall not be endangering anyone but myself." It was then that his friends heard Roosevelt at his best, and got the true measure of the man.

EVERYONE INTERESTED IN ROOSEVELT

Those seven years in the White House ending in 1909 had a fascination for the people that no other President was ever able to excite. I recall a popular cartoon of the period portraying the head of a household putting aside his breakfast table newspaper and calmly resuming his morning meal.

"My dear," says the astonished wife across the table, "the paper must be dull today."

"It is. Not a thing doing in the White House."

Everybody was keenly interested to know from day to day in what new direction their versatile President would turn his vigorous endeavors. Some had good reason anxiously to seek early information, but people generally indorsed and applauded each day's budget of news because they knew that the activities at the White House, whatever they might be, were directed toward one end.

There was one comment, however, frequently heard, that always angered Roosevelt—the talk that he was a militarist who would delight in forcing America into conflict with another nation. He resented that charge. His militarism was his belief that the way to avoid war is to be prepared and have others know you are prepared. In Chicago in 1903, he summed it up in the phrase "Speak softly, but carry a big stick, and you will go far." He repeatedly cited our peaceful relations with other countries during his Administration as proof that his policy was sound.

Probably no man assailed Roosevelt as a militarist more frequently than did Bryan. Now that both men have passed away, we find one lying, at his own request, in the modest burial ground of his home village, while the other, also at his own request, lies in a conspicuous sepulchre in Arlington Cemetery, Washington, among the brave men whose calling he had always condemned.

The Great Moment plumbs our deepest instincts. When you tapped those wells in Roosevelt you found home, family, his country and his friends. He rests beside them in death, and no martial glory intrudes.

"DON'T MOVE! WE'VE GOT IT"

Perhaps at this point is as good a place as any to tell the story of the John Singer Sargent painting of Roosevelt, now in the White House. The photograph of that painting is probably more familiar than any other of Roosevelt. It shows Roosevelt at the foot of a White House staircase with his elbow resting on the newel post, one hand toying with his watch chain, standing in contemplative mood as though about to state a conclusion that had for some moments baffled him. Such, in fact, is exactly what did happen; the masterful brush of Sargent caught the pose and put it on canvas from a true situation.

For two afternoons President and artist had vainly invaded every nook and corner of the White House for an appropriate place to serve as background. Pose after pose was tried in place after place, without satisfying either man. Roosevelt was not deeply concerned about it, but Sargent was. He wanted the real Roosevelt and he knew that the real Roosevelt could be revealed to him only in the right surroundings.

Roosevelt tired of the search, Sargent was eager to continue it; the painter's keen ambition, the President's thoughts of pressing duties, grated on the nerves of both men. Finally, as they descended the staircase shown in the painting Roosevelt stopped at the bottom, rested his elbow on the newel, and turning to his companion said hopelessly:

"Well, Sargent, we had better give it up. We're after the impossible."

"Don't move, Mr. President!" exclaimed Sargent quickly. "Don't move! We've got it!"

And they had.

DUG THE CANAL—THEN DEBATED ABOUT IT

Roosevelt believed in ideals, but he had no faith in ideals so vague as to be impossible ever to get beyond words and phrases,—impossible of practical application. He wanted results,—deeds not talk.

Take the Panama Canal, as an example. For years Congress had been debating how, when and where to dig a canal across the Isthmus. Even Mark Hanna with all his power and aggressiveness could not force action. The President wanted no more debate. He acted, and let Congress catch up with him.

So it was when he challenged the legality of the Northern Securities Company. There was much uplifting of hands that Roosevelt was leading the country into chaos, but the Supreme Court upheld him even against its own precedents. So, too, with the canal. The debaters in Congress first criticized, then wondered, then applauded and gladly paid the bills.

The Panama Canal is Roosevelt's big historic physical achievement. That is his own judgment of it. In view of his deep interest in it, I cannot understand why the Roosevelt Memorial committee has neglected to appropriate a portion of its funds for a memorial in the canal zone.

Somewhere on the highest mountain top, on each side of the Isthmus, there should be a tower of light to recall to voyagers in the Atlantic and the Pacific the man who made that great waterway a reality. The pending splendid plan for a monument to be located in Washington is not likely soon to become more substantial than a controversy with Congress. Of course, in time, Congress will act, but meanwhile there would be instant, cordial approval of a monument in the

THE NEWS REACHES BOGOTA—From the *Herald* (New York)

canal zone. Like the canal itself it would be built while the Washington enterprise is still being debated.

SENDING OUR BATTLESHIPS AROUND THE WORLD

The enterprise that won Roosevelt's heart was the triumphant voyage of our battleships around the world. He fairly thrilled over every incident as the cables brought the day to day news. It never ceased to interest him. Nothing delighted him more than to tell the story of his manœuvres to get funds for the trip. Nelson Aldrich, chairman of the Senate Finance committee, would not agree to an appropriation. For a time Aldrich was confident he had thwarted the President's plan.

"Loeb and I got to work on the job of digging up funds out of unexpended balances in different departments," Roosevelt once said to me. "We finally found enough money to take the fleet around South America to Japan and China—possibly a little further. It would then be half way around the world. I made up my mind to send the ships that far and then let Aldrich take responsibility for leaving them there at anchor or appropriate the funds to bring them back. I felt sure the country would not stand for ordering the ships back across the Pacific; Aldrich would have no option; he would have to bring them home by way of the Atlantic, which was exactly what I wanted.

"I had the same experience in other matters as in that affair. Once I acted instead of sitting around talking and pleading, I found all the support I needed. Aldrich and his committee of Senators, convinced that I was going ahead with the battleships, surrendered handsomely and the fleet sailed around the world, to be greeted everywhere in friendly spirit."

THE HOSTILE CORPORATION INFLUENCE

"More spying on the corporations" was the outcry when Roosevelt urged Congress to stop talking about establishing a Department of Commerce and Labor, and establish one. The need for such a Department had been obvious for a long time. Its creation was another Roosevelt achievement, gained over powerful opposition. Corporations could not understand why a President was not content with merely recommending; or why he wanted a Department with more than swivel-chair power. What sinister motive prompted him?

The usual "underground" opposition was exerted against the measure by corporation lobbyists at Washington, but they had to give way, finally, and on roll-call it had generous support from both political parties.

As I Knew Them

As I write of this incident, I am led to say that nine-tenths of the legislation to which banking interests and corporations object, and often spend large sums of money to defeat, prove of benefit to them. The Federal Reserve system is perhaps the most conspicuous example of a helpful measure that met the vigorous protests of New York bankers—yet the men who most strenuously opposed it are today its most ardent supporters.

The same story could be told of nearly every law affecting banks and corporations. The banker and the corporation head seem to distrust nothing so much as change; today they know, but tomorrow is a stranger to them; no matter how long the night may be, no matter how hopelessly they grope in darkness, they dread the dawn of a new day with new conditions.

CORTELYOU AND LOEB

The Department of Commerce and Labor, besides serving its purpose, brought two young men to the front who influenced the Executive Department of our national government far more than is generally known—George Bruce Cortelyou and William Loeb, Jr. The President made Cortelyou the first head of the new department. Loeb was made Secretary to the President, and, as in the case of Cortelyou, the title meant confidant and counsellor. Cortelyou had also been secretary to Cleveland and McKinley. Three Presidents, far apart in temperament and policies, depended upon him with equal confidence. Cabinet honors then came to him—first as head of the Department of Commerce and Labor, then as Secretary of the Treasury. Here was a reward for loyalty, industry and modest wisdom. It reflected no "pull,"—just a tribute to one who had served ably and well.

Loeb's experience in the White House did not cover as many years, but it was more intimate. He had been with Roosevelt while he was Governor of New York. No one ever knew every thought, purpose and mood of a President as Loeb knew Roosevelt's. He was in truth the President's other self;—he was the one man who could act for Roosevelt in full confidence that he was doing as the President would have him to do. There is not much in the Roosevelt administration that does not, in some way, bear the impress of Loeb's judgment. To his last years Roosevelt turned confidently to Loeb, though Loeb had gone out of public life and was well established in business. A career of helpful, energetic loyalty to his chief is now crowned with his own success.

ROOSEVELT'S GREATEST TRAIT

I have read many estimates of Roosevelt. I have read of his wonderful vitality, his tireless energy, his courage, his restless eagerness, the amazing extent of his knowledge of and interest in so many subjects—and, of course, it is all true. Indeed, the half has not been told.

The trait that most appealed to me was his loyalty to friendships. Commodore Stephen Decatur's famous toast to his country might well have been paraphrased by Roosevelt to read "My friends! May they always be in the right; but my friends right or wrong!"

More than once I was with Roosevelt in moments of keen personal disappointment, but never did he show the same deep regret over any happening to his fortunes as over evidence that one whom he called friend had turned on him.

And there were some who did.

Those wounds sank deep, though they left no vengeful scar. Where there was a separation it was the friend not Roosevelt who took the diverging path. It was not necessary to agree with him to hold his friendship. "My dear fellow," he would say, "it's bully of you—just bully—to come here and fight it out with me. You're a trump and a fine fellow but on this we don't see it the same way. We'll talk of something else."

Then would come a temptation to abandon your opinion

and accept his—a fatal mistake for one desiring to keep the
Colonel's confidence. He never wanted anyone to surrender
to him because he was President. He lost interest in those who
sought his favor by not battling for an opinion of their own.

TEDDY THE WHOLE WORLD ROUND

I claim neither right nor ability to reveal more clearly than
others have revealed the Roosevelt whose personality held
the attention and admiration of the world through seven years
in the White House. Wherever America was known in those
years, Roosevelt was known; and what America meant in the
minds of peoples, whether the people of Greenland's icy
mountains or those of India's coral strand, there Roosevelt
meant to them the same thing.

No other American was ever accepted so completely during
his own time by the average man everywhere as a sympathetic,
understanding leader as Roosevelt was accepted. He was
Teddy the whole world round and the intimacy of that term in
no degree lessened the universal faith in his endeavor to get a
"square deal," so far as government could secure it, for the
man who found it difficult to get one for himself.

THE WIDE CIRCLE OF HIS FRIENDSHIPS

I like to think of that wonderful friendship with Henry
Cabot Lodge, lasting from young manhood, unchanging
through all the vicissitudes of nearly forty years of political
strife. It revealed the quality that seems to me the foundation of Roosevelt's greatness.

I like to read his favorite hymn, read at his funeral in that
little village church from which he was buried. "How Firm
a Foundation, Ye Saints of the Lord, is laid for your faith in
His excellent word." In its inspiring lines I see the Roosevelt
I knew and followed—firm in his faith in the Lord, firm in
his faith in you, his friend.

As I Knew Them

Both Roosevelt and Lodge were big enough to tolerate differences of opinion that would have separated most men. Lodge kept out of the 1912 controversy, but he voted for Taft for President, and not for his friend Roosevelt. That was a vote of principle and Roosevelt respected it.

But Lodge was only one friendship. There were many, many others. There was Jacob Riis, a police news reporter for the New York Sun, who won Roosevelt's friendship in the early police department days, and kept it to the last; there was "Joe" Murray, a Republican district leader, who gave Roosevelt his start in politics and sent him to the New York Legislature; there was Father Curran, of Wilkesbarre, Penna.; there was Bill Sewall, the Maine guide; and "Bucky" O'Neill, from Arizona,—he of the Rough Riders who, near San Juan Hill, had boasted just a moment before he was killed that "no Spanish bullet was ever moulded to hit me."

Then there were the men who had ranched with him in the Dakotas; and Matthew Hale, of Boston, who had tutored his children before getting into politics; Dr. W. T. Hornaday of the Bronx Zoological Gardens, and John Burroughs, Charles F. McKim, Raymond Robbins, Booker T. Washington, Jane Addams and Sir Edward Grey, now Viscount Grey of Fallodon. Even the fierceness of the 1912 campaign did not lead Roosevelt into one word of dispraise of Senator Murray Crane, although the Senator was a relentless opponent.

High and low in politics, in the professions and in business were within that circle of friendships of infinite variety, and to each he gave something out of his incomparable personality that none could find elsewhere.

AN ARCHBISHOP, AN EX-PRESIDENT AND AN EX-PRIZE FIGHTER

There is one incident of a score that could be told illustrating Roosevelt's contact with men in every walk of life.

One day in the summer of 1916 Roosevelt was lunching at

the Harvard Club. A friend had brought Archbishop Ireland there, confident that the Colonel would forget the clash he had had, while President, with the Archbishop.

Roosevelt saw the two men as they entered the club, and relieved Ireland's doubts as to his welcome; he rushed up to him, exclaiming "My dear Archbishop, I am delighted to see you again."

They sat down for a chat while awaiting lunch.

Soon a tall broadshouldered, bulletheaded figure approached.

Roosevelt had left word at the door to have him shown in when he called. The Archbishop was surprised to see him smile at the Colonel and offer to shake hands.

"Archbishop," said Roosevelt, "meet another good Irishman."

"John," turning to the visitor, "meet the Archbishop."

"Archbishop," continued the Colonel; "this is John L. Sullivan. He has fought many battles that I admire and an Archbishop cannot; but he has fought one battle that an Archbishop can admire—the battle with himself."

"If it had not been for you, Colonel, I never could have stopped drinking," interrupted Sullivan. "I used to think of you busy in the White House taking time to send word to me to keep up the fight, and seeing me there when I called. I couldn't drink with all that on my mind."

"I'm glad to shake hands with you on your last fight," said the Archbishop.

And an Ex-President, an Archbishop and a prize fighter sat there together!

THE ROOSEVELT I KNEW

There may be those who knew, or thought they knew, a different Roosevelt than the Roosevelt I knew; I have no quarrel with them. The Roosevelt I knew is the Roosevelt I am endeavoring to outline. I can speak only from my own experience. I ought to have a fair knowledge of the man, for I knew him as Police Commissioner; I stood with him when the battle of San Juan Hill opened that torrid July morning of 1898; I knew him as Governor and as President;—greatest of all, I knew him as citizen those last ten years of his life —the most potent, most purposeful voice in the country.

I never sought and he never offered me a favor except the favor of his friendship. My newspaper did not always approve his course; we held to our own opinions, but we never questioned the sincerity of his purpose. On some matters on which we differed I realized later that it is possible for editors to be wrong. The one request Roosevelt ever made of me was to support Taft for nomination in 1908. That I could not do. My paper was supporting Hughes. After Taft's nomination I gladly supported him.

CHAPTER XXXVII

TWO MEMORIES OF ROOSEVELT

Opening The San Juan Battle, And A Midnight Conference That Ended At Dawn With Decision For New Party—Munsey Pledges His Newspapers And His Fortune—Only One Inevitable End At Chicago— Never Made Decisions For Expediency's Sake—An Early Dream Of The White House—Harrison Introduces Him As "Impatient For Righteousness"—An Epoch In Himself—The One Title That In His Last Years He Desired.

MANY interesting memories live, of course, in the minds of all who had relations with Roosevelt. Two hold their place firmly with me. One was a midnight-to-dawn session in his bedroom, in the Auditorium Annex in Chicago, when George W. Perkins, Frank Munsey and I discussed with him the possibilities of the step that led to organizing the Progressive party.

What a night that had been! I never saw the Colonel so fagged; for hours his fighting blood had been at fever heat. It was not the crowd that tired him, for he could always handle a crowd, but a score of important party leaders one after another had discussed with him all phases of the serious situation.

The last one (I have forgotten his name) had dragged the Colonel into the bath-room and closed the door against intruders. He was another self-appointed emissary with a plan of compromise but with no authority except his own. Soon we heard a loud voice that all recognized; the door opened and the Colonel stepped out with a hurried, vigorous step that matched the wrath in his countenance.

The crowd had left the Colonel's apartment; their loud cheers and louder oratory still filled the corridors and lobby.

As I Knew Them

Four tired men sat on the bedside planning the strategy of the morrow. The Colonel leaned heavily and wearily against the headpiece, Perkins next to him and then Munsey. I sat at the foot.

While seated on that bedside, Perkins and Munsey urged the Colonel to go on with the third party fight. They pledged their fortunes—Munsey declaring with characteristic intensity: "My fortune, my magazines and my newspapers are with you." Even before that meeting Roosevelt had strayed far off the party reservation; yet the peril of going further, the doubt as to how the country would react to a bolt, loomed larger and larger. For more than an hour discussion went on; we saw the streaks of dawn as we separated with the Progressive party started on its earnest way.

ONLY ONE INEVITABLE END

Of course, there was no one moment, no one conference, when the one big decision was made. All that week every moment had been a moment of decision as to some phase of the exciting struggle, and all decisions pointed to one end.

Roosevelt members of the convention committees were abandoning the scheduled meetings; delegates and spectators in the convention were in constant riotous revolt, Hiram Johnson, the two Pinchots, Medill McCormick, Raymond Robbins, Bainbridge Colby, William Hamlin Childs, Chauncey Hamlin, William M. Chadbourne, "Bill" Flynn and all the Republicans of the corn-belt States were in hourly clashes with the Taft forces, and were straining at the leash with which the Colonel was holding them in line.

Against those influences, an influence more intimate and more potent than politics, was counselling the Colonel not to bolt. Until that midnight-to-dawn conference, it was still possible for him to turn back, and he would have welcomed a compromise eliminating both Taft and himself. No such terms were offered from the Taft side. The midnight discussion therefore settled the course to pursue. The one problem to which all minds were thereafter directed was how and when the new organization was to be brought into being.

After breakfast next morning William L. Ward, who had decided to remain "regular," made a last effort to persuade the Colonel to acquiesce in the Taft nomination. Not so much what he said as what his eyes and snapping jaws indicated made Ward quickly realize that something decisive had happened over night.

NEVER MADE DECISIONS FOR EXPEDIENCY'S SAKE

Many who condemned Roosevelt for his attitude in that campaign were astonished that an astute politician could have believed he could smash through his party organization and elect himself President. Such critics did not know Roosevelt. He never made decisions on the basis of expediency. He always searched for the right or wrong of a proposition, and decided accordingly. Nothing else influenced him in Chicago. The politics of the situation did not interest him; the unrighteousness of it did.

Roosevelt had no illusions about his candidacy. He never thought he would be elected. During one of my visits to Oyster Bay before the Progressive convention in August, he said: "Taft cannot win whether we go in or not; we cannot win. What we can possibly do is to poll more votes in States like New York than the Taft ticket and thus be recognized legally as the second party. With the Democrats we would then be entitled to a party column on the ballot. Thousands of Taft Republicans would flock to us. Let us keep this in mind as our objective, but don't let us ever again say to one another, or even think, that we are not going to win. You cannot fight hard unless you think you are fighting to win, and we must fight hard."

As I Knew Them

The other memory of Roosevelt still vivid takes me back to Cuba, in July 1898—on the knoll called Grimes' Hill, facing San Juan Hill and just in front of the cross-roads called El Pozo. It was called Grimes' Hill because the battery commanded by Captain Grimes had been placed there the night before, with Roosevelt's Rough Riders in support. Col. Samuel Sumner was in command.

I call them Rough Riders because that was the name the regiment had acquired before sailing for Cuba. History knows them only as Rough Riders. They were not Rough Riders at all in Cuba, for their horses were never brought over. Down there we called them Wood's Weary Walkers. Leonard Wood was the Colonel in command and Roosevelt was Lieutenant Colonel—hence the alliterative change. They were a wild lot, those Rough Riders. They did not know what discipline meant, though they knew how to fight.

It was not the intention to take San Juan Hill that day. The only orders from Shafter were to keep the Spaniards there busy by intermittent firing so that they would not send men to reinforce El Caney, a village several miles away, which Lawton and Chaffee had assured Shafter they could capture in an hour or two of fighting.

El Caney is a suburb to the north of Santiago while El Pozo is to the east.

But Lawton and Chaffee found they had a hard and bloody day's work ahead of them. Grimes' battery also found that the Spaniards on the hill could keep us busy, too.

Thus San Juan Hill and El Caney developed rapidly into a stiff battle for possession of both places.

That night our tropic-wearied troops had gained both objectives. They had had twelve hours of fighting, however, instead of one or two as Chaffee and Lawton had anticipated.

Roosevelt stood with Sumner and Grimes when the Battery

As I Knew Them

opened fire. I can see him now, looking thro' his field glasses and then pointing excitedly to different locations on San Juan. He was trying to detect how each shell landed in the Spanish trenches.

Not a shot came in reply from San Juan nor was there a visible sign of life, for 10 or 15 minutes after our first shells went whizzing over. Then a shell must have landed where it hurt, for bang! came a swift one in reply from a Spanish battery well concealed.

So long as our firing got no response, I was interested with Roosevelt and others in trying to locate just where each shell had landed, but when the Spaniards, having our range, began landing shrapnel "in our midst" I lost interest in the skill of our own gunners. With Colonel John Jacob Astor I accepted Sumner's hurried advice to "get out of this hell spot."

Astor and I found ourselves out of the shrapnel zone but in the rifle fire zone.

Finally we reached the narrow valley road already crowded like a sardine box with soldiers waiting delayed orders to move. They were under shell and rifle fire—and yet expected to stand still in an exposed road! It was at that point that Roosevelt made his memorable dash through the almost solid ranks, crossed the road and went up the opposite hill into the dense undergrowth behind which the Spaniards were entrenched. He had been ordered into action. That was my last view of him for the day. The heavy firing told me, however, that there was something doing where he had disappeared.

AN EPOCH IN HIMSELF

"T. R." was an epoch in himself—as much its dominant figure as were Washington and Lincoln in their day. He was all there was to his period, which began when he entered the White House as President and closed seven years later as he rode down Pennsylvania Avenue with Taft to install him as his successor!

I do not mean that the influence of Roosevelt ended then, for it still persists; it is to be found in many laws of recent years and conspicuously in the present desire of great wealth to seek the protecting power of government instead of defying it. The driving force of intense purpose behind his policies ceased, however, when he ceased to be President. As he said himself we may slip back a little now and then, but never to the old levels. The standards have been raised; those who thought their safety was in keeping them low now realize that a square deal for all is the best deal for all.

So it is that many of the things Roosevelt left undone are only now in the way of being done—much too slowly, it is true, yet inevitably. The mills of progress like the mills of the gods grind slowly—but they grind. Roosevelt lives in this slow, eventual development. And as public opinion drives government toward those ideals for which he stood,—his name will remain its symbol and its inspiration for great achievement.

Who is to interpret him? Not anyone of this day. His words and acts are his only interpreters and history must appraise them by the acid test of years.

LIKED THE CENTRE OF THE STAGE

No one could have associated with him without acquiring never-fading memories of a friendship that made you feel its helpful influence. There was a candor, earnestness and vigor about T. R., possessed to the same degree by no man I have ever met, and they were not withheld because of race or color or condition.

Yes—it is true that T. R. liked the centre of the stage— loved it in fact; but when he sought it he always had something to say or to do that made the centre of the stage the appropriate place for him. He preferred to talk to the galleries and against the narrower ideas usually held by those occupying orchestra seats.

There were strenuous, often boisterous times in the White House with T. R. But Roosevelt knew the powerful influences in and out of his party that had to be overcome, if his policies were to prevail, and he realized the futility of soft-stepping and whispered persuasion. He had no faith in "gum-shoe" methods. His faults were not those of secrecy and intrigue; Roosevelt worked in the open, with startlingly frank avowals of his purpose.

His first effort always was to reach the people. He believed that if he got the people he was certain to get the politicians. He worked on the theory that led Charles G. Dawes to punctuate his testimony before a Congress Committee, five years ago, with "Hell and Maria."

Dawes knew that what he said would be printed on the front pages of newspapers if peppered with "Hell and Maria," and on the back pages if merely a dry recital of facts, however important the facts might be. He had a message to get to the country; he deliberately chose the one way certain to get it before it. That was Roosevelt policy, too.

ALWAYS WORKED FAR AHEAD

Of course, I have heard a great deal about Roosevelt's "impulsiveness." On immaterial matters it is true that he was quick and sharp with his "yes" or "no," but he never made a decision of consequence without thoughtful consideration. He acted quickly when he acted; but he always had the matter well in hand before uttering a word or taking a step.

Take his speeches, for illustration. He made many speeches that aroused intense discussion; they were at times denounced as utterances of the moment, the outbursts of impatience. Yet no public man ever prepared his speeches so long in advance of delivery as Roosevelt; none ever gave them more careful revision. Those "impulsive" phrases which his opponents by their denunciation made popular, were the most deliberately thought out phrases of all, and usually got the reaction he anticipated.

Roosevelt's day was always well organized for work. He had no idle moments. At Oyster Bay "on vacation," he was either pulling an oar out on the Sound, laying an ax to a tree, or riding horseback. Then he had hours for reading, for writing and for visitors. He wrote laboriously, and revised so freely that it amounted almost to re-writing. This was especially true when he attempted to dictate. He disliked it and did it poorly.

His reading was almost wholly confined to books; he would go for days without looking at a newspaper. I doubt if all his newspaper reading for twenty years averaged over ten minutes a day. His home reflected his characteristics. You found there none of the ostentation of wealth. Books and trophies of his adventures were the outstanding features. The furnishings were of the kind you would expect in the average country home; there were no gilded sofas and chairs; no grand pianos with elaborate carvings, no rare tapestries and no liveried servants. When you crossed the threshold at Sagamore Hill you stepped into the warm, cordial atmosphere of a real home—the home of an American in spirit, in purpose and in ways. Hayes, Harrison, McKinley and Coolidge went from just such homes into the White House at Washington, and took with them the dignity of modest living and simple ways.

Roosevelt had no time for "leisure" as some persons call it. Idleness was the thing he most detested—unless it was the wealthy idler. He simply could not tolerate the man who could be of use to the world and yet refused to do his part. His persistent denunciation of the idle rich was often charged to "playing politics," but that was not true.

His motive was to drive them to work. To him life had a purpose; it ceased when purpose ceased. To live and to do nothing meant to be dead. The Colonel's leisure was not found in wasting time but in changing his occupation. Every hour counted—and yet I never heard him say he was tired.

AMAZED AT THE DEMANDS OF WEALTH

Roosevelt's long struggle against the power of the group he characterized as "malefactors of great wealth," his determination to have government in the open instead of govern-

THEIR ONLY TEAM WORK

ment by invisible power, were prompted by evidences that came to him in part while Governor of New York State but in full in the White House. They revealed the methods, the purposes and the arrogant attitude of corporate wealth.

The thing that amazed him most was the presumption by influential men that as President he would accept their idea that great wealth, corporate and individual, was to be cared for and protected as something more sacred than government

313

itself. Roosevelt felt that the Presidency was a big enough office to deny that theory, and he determined to give it battle.

He fought to establish the supremacy of the government over every other influence, to put the interest of the people as a whole in advance of all other interests. To him conservation meant not merely conservation of the nation's forests, waterways and other natural resources, but conservation of the government's power to command obedience to its statutes.

Wealth was blind to this theory of government; its big lawyers had taught it how to be "law honest" and yet do as it pleased; it regarded as heresy the Roosevelt theory that there must be teeth in the law so that "law honesty" would be "dishonesty."

We have not yet reached the millennium in "big business" ethics; we still have lawyers whose chief practice is in counselling restless wealth how to do what it wants to do and yet not find itself "out of bounds"; but we have made a good start in the right direction. Whatever advance has been scored had its beginning in the Roosevelt stand for a "square deal," and in the Roosevelt insistence that the best protection for wealth is its fair attitude toward others.

WHAT ROOSEVELT HAD IN MIND

No man who ever sat in the White House knew his America better than T. R. No man has ever responded with more vigor—to the inspiration of its traditions.

He visioned a nation born to strenuous endeavor and ambitious purpose—a nation in which all would strive for the common good,—and when as the head of such a nation he had the power and saw the opportunity to mould its future to its birthright he eagerly, whole-heartedly set himself to the task. Always to do more, to learn more, to progress, were Roosevelt's aims in life, and as President he sought to make those aims his country's aims. His opponents did not dare attack his purpose, so they attacked his energy, his determined effort to accomplish. He wanted government to be purposeful; he wanted an equal share in its benefits for all—no favor, no fear, no power behind the throne. The good and the bad that he found at Washington were used as a skilled workman sorts his materials—he found some good even among the poorest material, and did not hesitate to use it; he found some bad even among the best material and did not hesitate to discard it. Often it was thought that Roosevelt discarded too much, but when the facts came to light it was found that he had made an accurate estimate of the men whom he had thrust aside.

"IMPATIENT FOR RIGHTEOUSNESS"

President Harrison once introduced Roosevelt to an audience by saying good-naturedly:

"He is a young man, impatient for righteousness. He wants everything done before nightfall; some of us can wait until tomorrow."

Elijah Halford, Harrison's Secretary, later corrected this characterization of Roosevelt to read:

"He is a young man impatient with unrighteousness" which to my mind is more fitting.

All this was said of Roosevelt while he was Governor of New York.

Harrison, it may be remembered, gave Roosevelt his first national job—President of the Civil Service Commission. He always had a high regard for Roosevelt. He applauded his earnestness, rejoiced in his integrity, but constantly counselled him against trying to put the whole government under civil service regulation at one fell swoop.

ROOSEVELT'S EARLY DREAM OF THE WHITE HOUSE

Seated on the porch at Sagamore Hill with Roosevelt one afternoon in 1911, our talk went back to the period before

As I Knew Them

1893 while he was serving in the Harrison Administration. I had spoken to him of the possibility of a popular call for him to succeed Taft. "This is the only spot on earth for me," he said. "I am never satisfied away from here. You don't live in the White House. You are only Exhibit A to the country. I've had seven years of it and I know. I admit that I once felt differently about it—very differently.

"I recall that in those Harrison years as I passed the White House every day to and from my office, the thought often came to me that possibly some day I would occupy it as President. Of course it was only a dream. I had no more reason for it than has every other American citizen. Still, it thrilled me even to think of it as a possibility. Well, I did occupy the White House and now I have no feeling but one of gladness that it is over. The thrill was justified in its day; the absence of it is justified now. It has no lure for me.

"It isn't how long you are President that counts, but what you accomplish as President. I've had my chance; I did fairly well with it. I made some kind of a place in history for myself. Someone else might have done better than I did, but I could not, for I did my best. I might not do as well if I were to go in again—unless, possibly, I went in to do some one definite thing, greatly needed by the country. Nothing of that kind is in sight.

"There is no demand for me except possibly the demand of the party for a candidate who can win. There are half a dozen men who come under that heading. No—I've had the title of President once—having it twice means nothing except peril to whatever reputation I achieved the first time."

THE TITLE HE DESIRED IN LATER YEARS

A moment's pause before Roosevelt spoke again.

"Do you know the only title that appeals to me now?" he asked.

"I suppose it is 'Colonel'?" I ventured.

316

As I Knew Them

"Yes,—there's a lot in that title for me," he said. "I like it. But if I were asked what title I would prefer it would not be President nor Colonel; it would be Major General in the U. S. Army in active service. Remember I say active service—no swivel chair for me. Active service, however, is not likely to come in my day, so I suppose 'Colonel' I'll remain to the end. That's good enough.

"After all, what's in a title? A lieutenant—Lieut. Wm. L. Worden—commanded the Monitor when it made that historic fight against the Merrimac. How many people know or care whether he was Lieutenant or Admiral? He had a job to do and he did it well. Ericsson, who designed and built the Monitor, will always be remembered. He had no title. It's the deed and not the title that counts.

THE PATRIOT'S RESPONSE!

"Just keep it in mind though, should a war come while you and I are still around, that the one thrill I shall have will be to be Major-General in active service!"

War did come. The thrill for service took complete possession of him; denial of opportunity undoubtedly was the most depressing disappointment of his life. He could give his four sons to the battle line—but his own service was rejected. I have seen Roosevelt take several disappointments,—things that hurt him deeply,—but not all of them together affected him so deeply as that.

After the last of his sons had sailed for the other side he said to me "there's a chance if the war lasts long that none of them will see me here when they return. There's a greater chance that I shall never see all of them again. One or more is likely to stay over there. I rejoice that they've gone; I wouldn't keep one of them back. But what would I give to know that we are all to be together again some day at dear old Sagamore."

CHAPTER XXXVIII

"MY LAST MILE AS A CAMPAIGNER"

*When Roosevelt Closed His Tour For Hughes, He Declared He Was
Through With Presidential Stump-Speaking—"I've Done My Bit," He
Said—Looking Ahead To 1920 He Declared, "I Shall Not Be The
Candidate!"—His Conviction That He Would Have A Hard Time
Fighting For Health During His Early Sixties—A Midnight Motor
Ride To Oyster Bay.*

"OLD trumps, let me tell you something that will interest
you—I'm finishing with you tonight my last Presidential campaign. I've done my 'bit' for Hughes; I am not going
to tour for any future Presidential candidate; I don't know
how many thousands of miles I had travelled across country
when I closed in Philadelphia tonight, but I know it marked
my last mile as a campaigner. I've done my full share of it;
I am now entitled to go on the exempt list. I am positively
through campaigning forever."

Theodore Roosevelt was the speaker. It was late October
1916—late in every way. He had arrived at the Pennsylvania station in New York city, after midnight, and we were
motoring to Sagamore Hill, reaching there about 3 A.M.
Before his Academy of Music speech in Philadelphia that
night, he had telephoned to George W. Perkins that he was
anxious to get home, that he would insist upon an early speech
so as to catch a 10 o'clock train, if anyone in New York city
would be good enough to arrange for a motor car to take him
to Sagamore. Perkins thought the Colonel should not go
alone.

Turning to me he said he would go if I were game also for

319

a midnight ride. I replied "dee-lighted"—and both of us met the Colonel.

We motored through a Long Island night fog to Oyster Bay.

ROOSEVELT'S DREAD OF HIS EARLY SIXTIES

Almost two years later—in September or October, 1918—I asked Roosevelt if he recalled his talk about no more campaigning, the night we motored to Oyster Bay.

"Of course I remember it," he replied, surprised at my inquiry. "Every word of it. I'll refuse to campaign even should the candidate personally ask me!"

"Well, you will have to refuse yourself then in 1920," I replied, "for you are going to be the candidate!"

"By George, I'm not!"

"There's no one else," I insisted. "The party, in fact the country, is turning to you. It's a unanimous call, Colonel. I hear it now."

"I hear just as much of it as you do and probably more," replied Col. Roosevelt. "It's all right, let it go on. It is well enough to have the anti-Wilson sentiment rally around me. But I tell you again that I shall never make another campaign tour nor shall I be the candidate. Of course, I shall make no public announcement now, but I will do so long enough before 1920 to get out of the way of anyone who wants the nomination."

"Why, Colonel," I insisted. "You are now the leader of the Republican party—you cannot get away from it."

"Yes, I can. I'm a tired man. Let me tell you I shall have trouble 'bucking' my early sixties. If I can get by them I can keep going for a fair number of years. My danger, though, is right in the next few years. At 56 I never should have undertaken that South American trip. It just put the jungle fever into me when I was too old to fight it out of myself quickly. It is in my system yet. I've got to buck it for four or five years before I shall be rid of it. Then I'll be myself again. That is why I am not going to do any more campaigning. Put that down as settled. Let the talk go on, let the party rally around me, if it will, for the present. We must organize to fight Wilson. I'll help in that work. I am not saying anything about 1920. Let 1920 take care of itself when it comes—but I shall not be the candidate."

And he gave a characteristic emphasis to the "not" that led me to understand that back of his decision he had more reason than he was acknowledging.

That was the last talk I had with Roosevelt—the last time I was in his presence until I stood in the Oyster Bay church as his flag-draped coffin was carried up the aisle.

A MIDNIGHT MOTOR RIDE HOME

On that night motor ride in 1916 the Colonel, though tired, was in fine spirits. We plunged through a Long Island fog too fast for safety, while he kept telling stories of campaign experiences. Suddenly our car stopped on the country road so that the chauffeur could clean his windshield of fog. Up stood the Colonel in the car.

"Fellow citizens," he shouted, "fellow citizens of" ——

Then he turned to Perkins and said: "George, where under the sun—no, where in this devilish fog are we?"

"Glen Cove or thereabouts," said Perkins.

"Oh, yes—Fellow citizens of Glen Cove or thereabouts, I am here tonight to say to you" ——

By that time the chauffeur had removed some of the fog banked on his windshield and started the car—the Colonel sat down. In fact, he came down with a crash.

CHAPTER XXXIX

WHEN ROOSEVELT SAID "TAFT"

Loeb Shows Him The Need For Stopping The Drift And Insuring Control Of The Convention—Elihu Root Thanks Roosevelt But Declines To Be A Candidate—Taft, Surprised, Says, "I Must Go In And Thank Theodore For This"—Why Roosevelt Remained Silent—Determined To Be An Effective President To His Last Day—Foraker Demands Of The President Equal Respect For A Senator—"Joe" Cannon Eases A Tense Moment.

ONE morning in January, 1908, President Roosevelt looked up from his breakfast table in the White House to find William Loeb waiting quietly.

"By George, Loeb," he declared, "what brings you here and how long have you been here?"

"Only a few moments," Loeb replied. "I'm here because I want to talk with you before you go over to the office. I want to talk about the national convention."

"What's the matter with the convention—except that it's a long ways off?" asked Roosevelt.

"The matter is that if things drift along as now our friends may lose control of it; if that occurs there will be charges that you would like to have been the nominee but couldn't get the delegates, or that you backed this or that defeated candidate. I don't think that's a good prospect. It puts you in an equivocal position and it should not go on any longer."

"It hasn't impressed me that way," replied Roosevelt, "but you may be right. What do you suggest?"

"Have a candidate," said Loeb. "You are under pledge not to run again. I propose to make people understand that you intend to keep it. Some people believe that a deadlocked

convention might force you to disregard it. Others believe
you will demand a nomination anyhow, and that you are
manipulating things so as to force a deadlock. The air is full
of such talk. The way to settle is to have a candidate."

SEE ROOT, SAID ROOSEVELT

"Do you know the man I'd like to see here as my successor?" asked the President.

"I do not," replied Loeb.

"Elihu Root. He's made a great record over in the State
Department, and would make an equally great one in the
White House. I would be for him against all comers, but I'm
told he couldn't be elected."

"What does Root think about it?" asked Loeb.

"I don't know," replied Roosevelt.

"Well, you have Taft and Hughes to consider, too," Loeb
continued.

"Yes, and Cortelyou as well. He's in my Cabinet and is
anxious to get the nomination. You see it's embarrassing
when there are rivals in your own household. Now, whenever I've talked Taft to our friends I have had a battle. He
is not strong with the men closest to this Administration. I
don't understand it. I think he would run well; they say not.
We must above all else get a man who can win."

"Any nominee can win," replied Loeb, "if you back him—
Taft, Root, Hughes, or Cortelyou. That's my judgment."

"Well, then, you see Root; have a frank talk with him;
tell him what I have said to you, tell him what you think,
and let us get his idea. Of course, if we can't get Root we
must agree on someone else—Taft is the next best, probably;
but see Root."

That same morning, when Secretary of State Elihu Root
walked into his office, he was surprised to find William Loeb
there. Like Roosevelt he asked him why.

"I've been talking with the President about the convention, insisting that we ought to straighten things out," said Loeb. "We ought to have a candidate. He authorizes me to say to you that he would rather see you in the White House than any other man, and that he is ready to endorse you."

ROOT SAYS NO

If Elihu Root is ever surprised by anything he sees or hears his imperturbable countenance rarely shows it. But it did that morning. His face plainly reflected surprise and pleasure.

"That's very fine of him," he said. "Please tell the President I appreciate deeply every word of it, but I cannot be a candidate."

"Why not?" asked Loeb. "This Administration will control the convention and can name the candidate."

"Undoubtedly you can nominate me," replied Secretary Root. "You couldn't elect me—there's the rub."

"This Administration is strong enough with the people to elect the man it gets behind," persisted Loeb. "That's all bunk that you cannot be elected. Your record here will elect you."

"No, Loeb, I've thought it all out. I know the situation. I shall not be a candidate."

"Is that final?" asked Loeb.

"Absolutely final," replied Root. "Thank the President most cordially for me, but tell him I'm not in the running."

Back to the White House and to the President's offices went the diligent Loeb.

He cut short the President's callers, and got down to business.

"Root is out of it," he reported to his chief. "He won't take it—says he couldn't be elected."

As I Knew Them

"I've been thinking it over since you left," said the President. "You have the right idea—we must have a candidate. We had better turn to Taft. He has the experience.' See Taft and tell him of our talk this morning, tell him all of it so he will know my mind all the way through."

An hour or so later, Secretary of War Taft was closeted in the White House offices with Roosevelt's energetic private secretary. He was frankly told of the breakfast table talk, and the President's conclusion.

"The President feels that he wants to settle this nomination matter right away, so far as he is concerned," said Loeb. "He is going to throw the whole strength of the Administration back of you. This talk about his getting into the race is all nonsense. The only way to stop it is for him to declare for a candidate and he has decided to declare for you."

"I must go in and thank Theodore for this," said Taft. "Also I want to send a message to my brother. He's anxious, of course, to know every development in my campaign."

"No messages to anyone," interrupted the cautious Loeb. "Let this thing take its own course. Let us first talk it over with the President. It will be time enough then to settle the next step."

By this time the President had left the executive offices for lunch. Taft and Loeb joined him afterward.

"Yes, Will," said Roosevelt. "It's the thing to do. Our friends should control the convention; we don't want any uncertain note sounded there. We've all talked about candidates long enough; it's time for a decision. I'm for you, and I shall let it be known right away. That's as far as I can personally go. I cannot get into the detail of it. My suggestion to you is to put yourself in Loeb's hands from now on. He knows the politics of this country as well as anyone I can think of; I can lighten up on him, and give him the time so that you two can work together."

That, to state it briefly, is how William Howard Taft came to know definitely that Theodore Roosevelt had ceased to be merely favorably disposed toward his ambitions to be President and had decided to make him his candidate for the nomination.

WHY ROOSEVELT WAS SILENT

For months before the Loeb talk Roosevelt was puzzled as to the best course to pursue. He was not going to accept another term—that much had long been settled. It was settled by the statement issued by him the night of his election in 1904; it was settled as certainly by his own desire, shared most emphatically by his family, to return to Sagamore Hill, there to enjoy a career as private citizen. He knew of the Jonathan Bourne plan in Oregon to nominate him for a "second elective" term; he heard much similar talk from others.

Neither was he unaware of the insistence by his opponents, in and out of the Republican party, that he was killing off other candidacies to insure his own nomination. When I say that he knew of such talk I mean that he knew of it in the shadowy way that gossip reaches a President, unless an alert secretary like Loeb decides that the President should have full information. That is why Loeb had that historic breakfast conference.

Those in Roosevelt's confidence had no doubt of his purpose as to himself. They knew that he felt under no obligation to reiterate what he had said in 1904; in the absence of any public withdrawal or modification he expected his friends to accept his statement as it stood. His opponents would treat a reiteration as skeptically as they were treating the original announcement. So he allowed the record to stand as it was.

THE CROWN PRINCE

As I Knew Them

AS HE SAW HIS FUTURE

He insisted that the more intimate side concerning his own desire to get back home after seven years of the White House did not deeply interest the public. Moreover, it seemed ungracious and perhaps ungrateful to advance his personal desire as a controlling reason for leaving the Presidency.

None the less it was his plan to take himself entirely out of the storm area of life. His strong desire for a public career had always had as a rival his longing for literary renown; he had a passion for both. Having satisfied the first with the rounding out of his term as President, the old love for the pen asserted itself.

He would write, lecture, put into permanent form the experiences of his career, and interpret world-events.

That thought was, in fact, the basis of his arrangement with the "Outlook"—a magazine that was selected by him because it had no partisan ties and stood high in public confidence.

He had thought it all out most carefully during those final days in the White House. There was not a doubt in his mind of his future. For a year or more he was to hide himself away in the African wilderness. By the time he emerged into civilization the new administration would have definitely shaped its policies, most of the patronage would have been distributed and Roosevelt would have escaped the demands which he could not have wholly ignored had he remained within reach. His "Outlook" series and his story of his African hunt would of themselves keep him too busy to think of politics.

Thus he planned while in the White House; thus he dreamed as he trekked across the game trails of Africa; it was not until he reached Egypt that he heard—then only faintly—the first murmurings of the storm that was ultimately to beat so violently about his own head. But in 1908 all that he saw ahead of him was a period at Sagamore during which he was to be a care-free citizen and he rejoiced at the prospect.

DID NOT WANT TO FADE AWAY

Roosevelt had another reason for silence. He was determined not to fade away as President. He wanted his Administration to remain 100 per cent effective until the last moment of his term; he would then be able to hand over a "going" concern to his successor. He knew that as a President approaches the "ex" period, his influence with Congress and party leaders dwindles. Only the old Guard of loyalists for loyalty's sake remain to the end. The dawning day always reveals a majority eagerly scanning the horizon for its new figure.

Many were now waiting for that dawn, eager to seize control of the party organization the moment Roosevelt's hand was lifted from the helm and to thwart him in every way. There were measures pending in Congress that he desired to have enacted into law while he was yet in the White House. Moreover, there was the approaching national convention. He was determined it should give whole-hearted indorsement to his Administration, should declare for a continuance of his policies and nominate a candidate committed to them.

Thus buttressed by platform and candidate, Roosevelt was confident that the effectiveness of his Presidency would remain unimpaired to the end. He would go out of office with a record of seven full years of achievement, and his friends would be in control to "carry on."

In his opinion, that prospect would be imperilled if he silenced rumor as to himself,—in a word if he took himself out before some candidate friendly to the policies of his Administration seemed likely to go in.

As I Knew Them

That was the picture Roosevelt visioned in the early days and weeks of 1908. It was not the picture some of his supporters saw; they painted a different picture to him—some of them so often that he grew impatient over the challenge of his judgment. They didn't believe in silence or in Taft,—to whom he was not then committed—as insurance against the condition he dreaded. Nevertheless he persisted.

The Republican national committee in Washington in December, after fixing Chicago, June 16, 1908 as the place and time of the convention, called upon him in a body, formally. Not a word of encouragement did they get that the 1904 declination had ceased to have force. A modifying word, even a hesitant manner, would have sent them home yelling "Four Years More of Teddy." Some enthusiasts returned to their States uttering that popular cry, concededly without authority.

Southern Republicans were practically a unit in advocacy of another term. They insisted that Roosevelt could carry several Southern States. As Roosevelt admitted in a talk I had with him at the time and printed later in this book, there was a temptation in the prospect of breaking the Solid South. But it did not outweigh other considerations. So Roosevelt's mind dwelt upon Root and Taft.

Governor Hughes was in the field backed by New York Republicans; Vice President Fairbanks was actively picking up delegates in Indiana and neighboring States; George Cortelyou had important backing from national committeemen controlling many delegates; Uncle Joe Cannon, then Speaker of the House, was projecting himself into the situation as an anti-Roosevelt candidate; Philander C. Knox had Pennsylvania, La Follette had Wisconsin and Senator Foraker was disputing Ohio with Taft. But with Roosevelt silent, no decisive strength was possible for any candidate.

As I Knew Them

That was a stirring winter around the Capitol. Cannon in private talk was more and more openly denouncing Roosevelt's policies; insurgent Republican Congressmen were desperately struggling against Uncle Joe's Czar-like grip on Committees and on legislation; the Senate, with La Follette as the insurgent leader, had begun to show evidences of a determination to supplant the House as the place of endless debate. Everybody seemed to be in a restless, impatient mood.

The Gridiron Club dinner typified the spirit then prevailing. The President was the guest of honor; J. Pierpont Morgan, Henry H. Rogers, George F. Baker, and other men of the financial and business world were present. Roosevelt and Senator Foraker had had their falling out, and a good deal of feeling was known to exist between them.

Roosevelt's speech was a lecture to Senators for their lack of respect for the Executive branch of government. As we listened we realized that his words were becoming more and more centered on Foraker, then strongly opposing the Administration. At the beginning of each sentence we felt certain that Foraker would be named before the end. He stopped just short of doing so. Foraker was the next scheduled speaker. His seat was at the far end of one of four tables extending like a gridiron from the presiding officer's table where Roosevelt and other guests of the Club were seated.

Foraker's face glowed with anger while Roosevelt was speaking; he was less stirred when he himself took the floor. At first he spoke in quiet tones, plainly under restraint; step by step he advanced up the aisle toward the guests' table until he stood directly in front of Roosevelt. When within a dozen feet of him—in fact, it seems to me now that only the table separated them—he pointed his finger at the President and with the emphasis of passion said:

"I want to say in this presence that I have great respect for the high office of President of the United States—no American has greater respect for it—but I want to say also to the President of the United States that I demand that he should have equal respect for the chosen representatives in the Senate of the sovereign States of the Union."

Foraker walked slowly back to his seat.

A tense silence followed. All eyes centered on the President, whose countenance by now showed the anger he, too, felt. We wondered what he would do or say. Someone must relieve the tension—but how?

"JOE" CANNON EASES A TENSE MOMENT

The Chairman looked about him as one looks for a life-saver. He saw Uncle Joe Cannon puffing a cigar. Cannon seemed more at ease than any other person. Perhaps he could pour oil on the troubled waters! The Chairman decided to try him. I happened to be seated at Cannon's right. Surprised that he should be called upon, Cannon turned to me and asked:

"What in hell can I say about this mess?"

It was well that he did not wait for my reply, for I could make none worth while. Uncle Joe slowly unwound his long, angular form, bit a little harder on his cigar, and by the time he was standing at full length was ready with his speech.

"Now, fellows," he said, "we all think we're mighty important and that this old globe would stop spinning around if we weren't here to keep it moving. The truth is, though, that if at this instant we should have an earthquake and the earth should open up and should swallow this whole roomful of us, big fellows as we think we are, the morning papers would publish a list of those missing—and the world would go on turning and we would be forgotten. So what's the use of getting excited!"

That ended Cannon's speech and the tension. Everybody laughed and the Chairman resumed the regular order.

CHAPTER XL

THE STRUGGLE TO NOMINATE TAFT

"I Can't Understand This," Said Roosevelt When He Found His Choice Of Taft Criticized—"It's Taft Or Me!" He Finally Declared —Cortelyou Warns Him To Prepare Himself For A Different Life After The Presidency—The Taft Brothers, Eager For Delegates, Raid New York—Roosevelt Told He Will Have Responsibility Without Power—Let The Party Pick Its Own Candidate—The Tafts Always Suspicious Of Roosevelt—A Scene While Taft Was Being Nominated.

IT WAS shortly after the decision for Taft that George Cortelyou, then Secretary of the Treasury, discussing future plans with Roosevelt asked him if he was prepared for the great change shortly to come in his life.

"Next March 4," said Cortelyou, "you will ride up Capitol Hill with all the power of office; a moment later you will ride down that same hill stripped of power. Such a change is a tremendous test for any man, but for you, Mr. President, with your temperament, it is going to be especially hard and I wonder if you are getting yourself in the frame of mind for it."

"I have never thought of it!" exclaimed Roosevelt.

"Better get yourself ready for it," warned Cortelyou. "Once you are out of office, you will miss the opportunities to push policies, you will miss the power of the White House, you will miss all the activities that have made your life here so full. That's a side of your future that you ought to prepare for. If you do it will be easier when you have to face it."

"I intend to live in an entirely different atmosphere when I leave here," replied Roosevelt. "I am not going in for politics. Should I ever do so, it would be only in the broadest sense, entirely divorced from any personal motive. I've made

As I Knew Them

up my mind to go in for the things I like and have neglected.
I've had my day and I know it."

"IT'S TAFT OR ME"

He turned to the task of creating a day for Taft. The
response to that candidacy, following Roosevelt's announcement, was not as anticipated. Protests by letter and in person flowed into the White House. Though Loeb was watching the election of delegates, the President found that, despite
his February statement to Taft that he could not personally
get into the situation, it was necessary for him to do so.
Cecil Lyon, boss of Texas, (whom Taft in 1912 unseated in
the national convention), John G. Capers, of South Carolina,
as well as many western leaders declared against the President's choice.

"I don't understand this," said Roosevelt, puzzled, after
talking with a protesting State leader. "They don't seem to
know Taft as I know him. I've got to explain him to nearly
all of our fellows."

In order to force every possible delegate to Taft, two
courses were followed by the President in his talks. To the
reactionaries he would declare "It's Taft or me," which sent
them scurrying to Taft. To Progressives he would declare
"It's Taft—I'm out!" whereupon most of them reluctantly
accepted Taft.

There was not an act or thought in the White House not
wholly dedicated to Taft's nomination. Unfortunately this
attitude was too whole-souled and unselfish to be compre-
hended in Cincinnati and New York city. In the minds of
Taft's relatives in those two cities, suspicion stalked around
every new evidence of Roosevelt's helpfulness, though one test
after another brought the same response of strength for Taft.

Finally, Taft's brothers decided to raid New York and
take as many delegates as possible from Hughes. William
Barnes and William L. Ward led the bolt from Hughes. Ten

333

delegates for Taft resulted. Candidates seldom go into the home States of their rivals, and Roosevelt did not approve of the policy. In January he had persuaded Taft to address a letter to Herbert Parsons stating that he would not seek to "divide in my interest the delegates from any State which has a candidate of its own." As usual, however, Taft's "court of appeals" overruled him. The raid on New York was made, though Taft then had more than enough delegates to nominate. Roosevelt again cautioned that he should not embitter his rivals. "You will need Hughes in the campaign," he said. "Better let him alone in New York; fight him as hard as you can elsewhere."

This wise counsel for which there should have been thanks to Roosevelt was regarded as a sign of weakening support, and at once the Taft camp was flooded with new suspicion.

T. R. WARNED OF RESPONSIBILITY WITHOUT POWER

I had an encounter with Roosevelt on the matter of candidates about a month before the convention. My newspaper in New York was supporting Hughes, then Governor. I sincerely hoped he would be nominated. After luncheon at the White House one afternoon, the President asked me why I did not switch from Hughes. I had no reason to desert the Governor of my State and my own personal choice, though I knew Loeb had captured some of the New York delegates for Taft.

"Your newspaper ought to be for Taft," said Roosevelt.

"No, Mr. President," I replied. "We're for Hughes. He's our Governor. He would make a fine President. We're going to stand by him to the end."

"Of course you know what the end will be?" asked Roosevelt, with the vigor of impatience in his voice.

"Oh, I suppose you will nominate Taft. There is nothing against Taft. But New York has its candidate, and I think we should stick by him."

WHY DON'T YOU SPEAK FOR YOURSELF, JOHN

As I Knew Them

"There's more red blood in Taft's little finger than in Hughes' whole body," said Roosevelt. "If you knew Taft better you would realize it and switch to him."

"I shall not switch—that is impossible, Mr. President. I am going down with the ship. It's a good ship and if your hand were not on the convention Hughes would land the prize."

"You're wrong," he replied. "Do you know whom we have most trouble in beating! Not Hughes—but Fairbanks! Think of it—Charley Fairbanks! I was never more surprised in my life. I never dreamt of such a thing. He's got a hold in Kentucky, Indiana and some other States that is hard to break. How and why is beyond me. It is easier to win delegates away from Hughes right in New York than to win them away from Fairbanks in those States."

"LET THE PARTY PICK ITS OWN CANDIDATE"

"Mr. President," I said, "I recall that you once told me you liked to hear the truth, even an unpleasant truth, and so I am going to say to you that I do not believe you should pick the nominee of the convention. Let the party pick its own man. It may make a mistake. If it does it will be the party's mistake—not yours.

"If you are going to name anybody name yourself," I added—"You have a clear right to do that."

"I'm not in it," he interrupted.

"Then why not let the candidates fight it out?" I continued. "You are running a risk in naming a candidate. The party has done pretty well up to date in its selections—certainly well enough to be permitted to try it once more. You now take over the function of the convention, and you put yourself in a position of responsibility for the Administration the next four years without the power to see to it that it makes good.

"You will be criticized for every move Taft makes, and ex-

335

pected to correct it. The 'I-told-you-so's' will be the biggest crowd you ever listened to. Better let the convention find its own candidate and take responsibility for his course as President. It may pick Taft. I am not speaking against Taft. I am urging you not to take the responsibility when you are not to have the power. Better leave it to the convention."

ROOSEVELT HEARS THE "I-TOLD-YOU-SO'S"

All this was not listened to without interruptions, without signs of impatience, but I got my thought well into his mind.

"The trouble is that we have no one who fits the bill like Taft," he said. "The fellows don't like Hughes."

"Then the convention will select Taft," I replied. "That will be all right and much better than if you select him for the convention—better for Taft and better for you."

"You're an impossible man today," remarked the President as he ended the talk. "Come and see me after the convention."

[Let me here for a moment jump ahead to 1910. Soon after his return from Africa Colonel Roosevelt asked me if I remembered our talk at the White House about the Taft nomination.

I said I did.

"I do, too," he added. "It came to my mind one night over in Africa. You were right. It would have been better had I kept out of it. The 'I-told-you-so's' are as thick as leaves."]

WHY HE TURNED FROM HUGHES

"Let's talk a little politics," said Roosevelt to William R. Willcox after luncheon in the White House just before the 1908 convention. "I suppose you are for Hughes." Willcox was then chairman of the New York Public Service Commission. He had been Postmaster.

As I Knew Them

"I don't know that Hughes is seeking the nomination," replied Willcox. "Personally, I don't see why you should not be the candidate. I take no stock in that third term talk."

"I could be nominated all right," said the President, "but I do not know that I could be elected. If the third term tradition would not defeat me, my letter would. So that's settled. I have a high opinion of Hughes. He had a fine programme of legislation in his early days as Governor, and for some time I believed he would develop into a splendid candidate for President. So much did I think of him in that way that I said to Mrs. Taft less than a year ago that as much as I thought of Will, it might be that I would feel it my duty to be for Hughes. But Hughes got into the hands of the 'Evening Post' crowd in New York city and he also made public announcement that he did not want any assistance from here. That released me from considering him any longer. So now it's going to be Taft or me."

ALWAYS SUSPICIOUS OF ROOSEVELT

Willcox was not the only visitor at the White House whom Roosevelt found indifferent to or opposed to his choice of candidate. Loeb, however, kept pounding away at every delegate to declare for Taft. As one after another did so, the sigh of relief from Cincinnati was coupled with dread that the next delegate to speak would reveal a subtle Roosevelt plot.

Apparently, Taft himself was the one member of his family capable of believing that any man would relinquish the Presidency to another. The challenge of Roosevelt's sincerity never left the minds of those close to Taft until Senator Lodge as presiding officer of the convention formally declared Taft the nominee.

If Roosevelt learned of these suspicions, he kept his information to himself and went ahead with his plans to make

337

As I Knew Them

Taft certain. He made doubly sure to thwart a stampede in the convention. Few persons ever knew that he had the most expert White House telegrapher stand immediately back of Chairman Lodge prepared to flash a message from Lodge to the White House should a Roosevelt uprising seem imminent. Instantly the President would have imperatively demanded that his name be withdrawn.

I am sure, however, that had a stampede ever begun, it would have accomplished its purpose too quickly even for a telegram to interrupt it. The spirit of the convention was wholly Rooseveltian. Omit the demonstration whenever Roosevelt was named and the convention was distressingly dull. The delegates had no keen interest except in the man in the White House. Lodge, in the chair, knew that in the circumstances Roosevelt should not be named; also he knew the peril if someone put a lighted match to the powder.

One of the greatest demonstrations over Roosevelt came just before the roll call on nomination. Lodge watched closely and was tempted to telegraph Roosevelt for the message agreed upon. Finally, he decided to wait until Massachusetts was called, when the delegation cast a solid vote for Taft. That settled the stampeders. Roosevelt's closest friend and confidant was against them. Ten minutes later Taft was the convention's nominee.

WHILE TAFT WAS BEING NAMED

Joseph Bucklin Bishop, in his "Presidential Nominations and Elections" has an illuminating picture of a scene elsewhere while Roosevelt and Lodge were watching the convention as one watches a dam hard pressed by floods. Here is part of it:

> I remained with the President till about 4 P. M., when I went to the War Department, on personal invitation of Secretary Taft,

and was admitted at once to his private office, in which he was sitting with his wife, daughter, younger son Charlie and a half dozen or more personal friends.

Mrs. Taft sat in her husband's chair at his desk in the centre of the room, while he sat at one side in a group of friends. Bulletins were being received constantly from the convention by telegraph and telephone . . . When Taft was placed in nomination, successive bulletins were received describing the cheering, the length of time it was enduring, its volume and accompanying demonstrations. The Secretary sat calm and composed during this time, but Mrs. Taft was obviously in great agitation. "I only want it to last more than forty-nine minutes," she exclaimed. "I want to get even for the scare that Roosevelt cheer of forty-nine minutes gave me yesterday." The convention had cheered for that length of time for Roosevelt on the previous day. Mr. Taft merely smiled and said: "Oh, my dear, my dear!"

Word soon came that the nominating speeches had all been made, and the convention would proceed to ballot. There was a sigh of relief from the little company, and a brief period of breathless eagerness followed. Then Charlie came in with a bulletin which he handed to his mother. Her face went deathly white, and with visible effort she read (I quote from memory) : "A large portrait of Roosevelt has been displayed on the platform and the convention has exploded."

A silence as of death fell upon the room. Mrs. Taft sat white as marble and motionless. Mr. Taft tapped with his fingers on the arm of his chair and whistled softly. No one said a word or looked at his neighbor. A minute or two later Charlie entered with another bulletin which he handed to his mother, and she read with impassive voice and face. (Again I quote from memory, but the substance is of unquestionable accuracy) : "A huge American flag with a Roosevelt portrait upon it is being carried about the hall, and the uproar continues with increased fury."

That awful silence continued for several minutes, which seemed endless, when again Charlie entered with a bulletin and which his mother, almost leaping from her chair in excitement, read: "Massachusetts gives 25 votes for Taft." . . .

As I Knew Them

Quickly following the Massachusetts bulletin came others, and within a few minutes the nomination was announced. . . . It is needless to add that Mrs. Taft's face had more than regained its normal color. She was the personification of a proud and happy wife.

CHAPTER XLI

THE WRONG ROAD TO CINCINNATI

Taft Detours To Oyster Bay With His Acceptance Speech—There He Had His Last Intimate Talk With Roosevelt—He Faced An Issue And Stuck By Blood—A Silent Boycott Of T. R.—The Acceptance And The Inaugural Speeches Were The Last Heard Of "Roosevelt Policies"— Sherman Replies That The Vice President Is Not a Messenger Boy—A Winter Of Roosevelt Humiliation And Taft Silence—Charles P. Taft Makes An Effort To Get Burton Out Of The Senate And Himself In.

NOMINATED, Taft hurried from his office to express a whole-hearted obligation to Roosevelt. A day or two later he repeated it most profusely when he called at the White House to resign as Secretary of War. No two men could have been in happier mood than were the President and his named successor that afternoon. They gossiped of old times and of the new times ahead. Then it was that the references to his old Cabinet associates were made by Taft—then also it was settled that Luke Wright, of Tennessee, should succeed him as Secretary of War.

His mind cleared of departmental matters, his mood jubilant, Taft left for Hot Springs, Virginia, where he was to prepare his acceptance speech. The President went to Oyster Bay for the summer. No man could have been more confident that events had justified his course, that they had confounded those who had doubted, than was Roosevelt when I saw him a day or so later.

Meanwhile, Taft worked at the acceptance speech he was to deliver in Cincinnati July 29. Ten days before that date, with the speech completed, he left Hot Springs for Cincinnati, announcing, however, that he was going by way of Oyster Bay to discuss it there "and get the President's judgment and his

341

criticism. I have the highest regard for his judgment." He spent the day with Roosevelt, accepted the few changes suggested, and continued on his way.

That visit to Oyster Bay marked the close of the Roosevelt-Taft intimacy. Taft did not talk with Roosevelt again, nor see him, until he called at the White House in December on his way to Augusta, Georgia, five months later.

TAFT STICKS BY BLOOD

What happened in Cincinnati?

I can only repeat the story as told by those who claimed to know, and to which Taft's course gives substance. It is that Taft had scarcely taken his hat off in his brother's house before he was asked rather abruptly why he had come to Cincinnati from Hot Springs by way of Oyster Bay when there was a shorter, more direct route—whether he did not realize that the country would interpret his roundabout trip to Roosevelt as a proof that Roosevelt, not Taft's relatives, had the direction of his fortunes as President. If Oyster Bay side-trips were to be continued his visits to Cincinnati would have the importance merely of rest periods.

Taft was not prepared for this criticism. Until that moment such an interpretation had not occurred to him. He had always gone to Roosevelt with his matters; by habit, he had gone to Oyster Bay. He now saw, however, that he would have to choose between two loyalties—it would not be possible to satisfy both. Those who know Taft best have always believed that he made a reluctant choice. However, he faced an issue and, as always, blood proved thicker than water. He stuck by blood.

A SILENT BOYCOTT OF T. R.

The cordial expressions of gratitude spoken in Oyster Bay died away into silence—silence for one week, then for two weeks, then for the campaign. Speeches were prepared, committee plans matured—but of these Oyster Bay heard only through gossip. National Chairman Frank Hitchcock was polite to his old chief, but after some experiences he decided that when he needed instructions he would travel to Cincinnati for them; also that he would not travel there by way of Oyster Bay.

It may be that in other walks of life men who have worked together intimately and with apparent unity of purpose for five years have separated as abruptly and as silently as Taft

DEE: LIGHTED: OR, THE RINGMASTER, *From The Eagle, Brooklyn, N. Y.*

separated from his former chief, but in politics, at least in American politics, there is no parallel.

No differences in policy or purposes were discussed, no reason whatsoever stated, but a "silent boycott" of Oyster Bay and of all men identified with Oyster Bay went into effect. At first it was confined to Roosevelt, but it widened steadily to others as Election Day approached. Then, with the returns showing Taft elected beyond dispute, the silence slowly developed into whispers,—whispers that led the alert to wonder what had happened, whispers that at once encouraged every Roosevelt opponent to feel confident that Taft as President would follow other policies and other men than those of the Roosevelt Administration.

THE LAST HEARD OF ROOSEVELT POLICIES

Not a word in Taft's public utterances justified such prophecies. Indeed, his speeches were in full harmony with the party platform. At Cincinnati, on July 29,—he had delivered his acceptance speech and had said:

> "The strength of the Republican cause in the campaign at hand is in the fact that we represent the policies essential to the reform of known abuses, to the continuance of liberty and true prosperity and that we are determined as our platform unequivocally declares, to maintain them and carry them on. . . .

> "The man who formulated the expression of popular confidence and who led the movement for practical reform was Theodore Roosevelt. He laid down the doctrine that the rich violator of the law should be as amenable to restraint and punishment as the offender without wealth and without influences. . . . In this work Mr. Roosevelt has had the support and sympathy of the Republican party, and its chief hope of success in the present controversy must rest on the confidence which the people of the country have in its platform that it intends to continue his policies.

> "The Chief function of the Republican administration will be to clinch what has already been accomplished at the White House; to undertake to devise ways and means by which the high development of business integrity and obedience to law which he (Roosevelt) established can be maintained."

> "Mr. Roosevelt led the way to practical reform. The chief functions of my administration shall be to complete and perfect the machinery by which the President's policies may be maintained."

As I Knew Them

These words, coupled later with his inaugural speech, are the last ever heard from Taft in a kindly way about Roosevelt policies; except that he vigorously pressed for and secured from the courts helpful interpretation of the Sherman anti-trust law.

Promptly after delivering his acceptance speech in Cincinnati, Taft had returned to Hot Springs—this time by the shorter, more direct route. There he played golf more persistently and with keener interest than he did anything else. To suggestions intended to enliven the campaign his usual reply, as he rested on a lounge after a golf game, was that they involved too much work. The remark was made at that time that apparently Taft was going to let someone else elect him President just as he had allowed someone else to nominate him.

Possibly that remark seems severe, but no one at Hot Springs at the time—and I was there—challenged its truth. Taft could not have been a more listless campaigner. A feature that was not detected until afterward was that no Cabinet member, no pronounced Roosevelt State leader, was bidden to Taft's presence. The men called to Hot Springs were from the other camp.

It was mid-August before Roosevelt realized that he was under boycott. He kept his own counsel, blinding himself to the separation that, deep down in his own mind, he knew had come. He could make no protest. He could cite no act against him, and Taft's only utterance was in strong support of him. Except by public profession, the candidate had simply forgotten that Roosevelt and his friends existed. Their part in the campaign, if any, had to be voluntary. Roosevelt made his part both voluntary and intense. Hughes stirred the country by his speech at Youngstown, Ohio; Roosevelt followed it with a series of vigorous statements hitting Bryan harder and harder. These were the only memorable incidents of an otherwise lifeless campaign.

As I Knew Them

"The King is dead! Long live the King!" broke out in loud and jubilant tones the moment returns made certain Taft's election. The cry came from those conspicuous in their opposition to all that Taft had supported and that he was to indorse anew in his inaugural. His former associates in the Cabinet waited impatiently to hear from him. They assumed that Taft would send for them and talk with them in the frankness of friendship. He never did. He told his varying purposes to others, who in turn told them to others. Thus, at last, the news reached those who should have been the first to know that they were to go. It was not until it was learned that a successor to Luke Wright was being sought that it was realized that Taft's course was a matter of policy and not merely applied to individual cases. No Roosevelt man was to "carry on" into the new Administration. Those who tried to keep on terms soon discovered that their identity with the old régime was a bar to intimacy with the new.

WHY LOEB WAS HELD

Before allowing this statement to stand in print I have tried to recall one ranking appointment or policy of the Taft Administration reflecting any suggestion from those with whom he had sat around Roosevelt's counsel table. I cannot.

Some reader will probably ask how about William Loeb, Jr., who was closer to Roosevelt than anyone else? The answer to that inquiry is that Loeb was made Collector of the Port of New York because his strategic energies had smoothed Taft's way through the nominating convention. If any man other than Roosevelt is responsible for Taft in the White House, that man is William Loeb. Taft remembered his obligation to Loeb. When appointed Loeb was wise enough to realize that New York city was distant from the White House in more ways than mileage. He never wavered in his loyalty to Roosevelt, but also he never pressed his opinions on his new chief, with a mind made up to new men and new purposes.

VICE PRESIDENT NOT A MESSENGER BOY

How Taft himself veered in those days is illustrated by a statement made to me in December, 1908, at a dinner party given by me to Congressman James S. Sherman, of New York, elected Vice President—"Sunny Jim" as those who knew him well pleasantly called him. Sherman had just returned from Hot Springs, where he and William L. Ward, of New York, had been visiting Taft. Sherman told me that Taft had said to him he did not intend to have anything to do with Joe Cannon, then Speaker of the House, and a candidate for re-election.

"I am going to rely on you, Jim," Taft said, "to take care of Cannon for me. Whatever I have to do there will be done through you."

"Not through me," Sherman quickly replied. "You will have to act on your own account. I am to be Vice President and acting as a messenger boy is not part of the duties of a Vice President."

A month later, Cannon visited Taft by request. Four months later when Taft became President—he and Cannon were in conference at the White House and the Payne-Aldrich tariff was the logical outcome.

CHARLES TAFT'S EFFORT FOR THE SENATE

In that same month of December, 1908, occurred what was probably the crudest effort to grab a Senatorship ever made in politics. It will be recalled that back in 1897 Senator John Sherman was persuaded to become Secretary of State under McKinley in order to create a vacancy in the Senate to which Mark Hanna could be appointed. Immediately following

"UNCLE JOE"

As I Knew Them

Taft's election, Charles P. Taft announced from Cincinnati his candidacy for the Senate. Next came an offer from the President-elect to make Congressman Theodore Burton, of Cleveland, Secretary of the Treasury.

Burton was the leading candidate for the Senate and in the following January the Republicans in the Ohio Legislature elected him unanimously. The sudden ambition of Charles P. Taft for Senatorial honors; the plain implication that he planned to go to Washington as the Mark Hanna of the Administration; the lure to Burton to get out of the way; astounded the country and brought Ohio Republicans closer to disastrous faction strife than they habitually are.

Of course there could be only one outcome. Burton declined the President's offer and the Taft Senatorial candidacy was withdrawn.

Undoubtedly the President-elect realized the damage to his prestige caused by the incident; undoubtedly he bore the inevitable criticism uncomplainingly, for after all, he owed much to the brother who was to be the Warwick of his times.

Probably both men realized later that the humiliation of having failed to sidetrack Burton was easier to bear than the embarrassment of having in the Senate a brother of the President.

ROOSEVELT DEFIED, TAFT SILENT

Nothing more significant forecast the course Taft intended to pursue than his silence throughout the winter of 1908-09 while Roosevelt was struggling to carry out his purpose to remain a 100 per cent President until the last day of his term. It was largely to achieve that purpose that he had declared for Taft. He now found himself thwarted, defied.

Taft himself had once said that an important part of his duties in the Roosevelt Cabinet was to hold on to T. R.'s coattails so as to keep him from going ahead too fast. The time had come when as President-elect he could perform an equally helpful service. The Roosevelt measures in Congress were thrust aside, and it was made plain to him that only his title to office remained.

What such a condition meant to a spirited man like Roosevelt need not be told. One word from Taft would have changed it—would have saved Roosevelt much humiliation. That word was not uttered. In Hot Springs and in Augusta, Georgia, Taft explained his silence by stating that he did not care to begin his Administration with divided party support in Congress. The effect of this remark was to lead the reactionaries in Congress to greater defiance of the outgoing President. They knew then that they had nothing to fear from his successor; more confidently than ever they reiterated their prophecies that the new man would be with them at the proper time.

CHAPTER XLII

"I HAVE BEEN A CRUSADER HERE!"

A Remarkably Frank Talk By Roosevelt As To His Course As President—"There Was Crusading To Be Done And I Didn't Use A Feather Duster"—"We Have Raised The Standards"—"The Country Has Had Enough Of It And Of Me," And "Time For A Man Of Taft's Type"—Give Taft A Chance—We Will Have Four Years Of Up-Building.

TWO or three days before Roosevelt handed over the Presidency to the man he had chosen as his successor, I called at the White House to say goodby. There were so many waiting to see the President that I was determined to limit my call to a handshake and a quick farewell. The Colonel—it is difficult for anyone who knew him to call him by another title—had other ideas. He was in the mood to talk reflectively to somebody, and it was my luck to happen along. "Sit down," he said. "We'll hold up the procession for a while."

I began talking of Africa, but I did not meet his mind until I mentioned that he could have remained where he was, if he had so desired. That was the topic he preferred to discuss. As accurately as I can recall this is what he said:

"I suppose I could have had another term. There was just one lure in it, just one. I was told by Southern Democrats— I don't mean dyed-in-the-wool Democrats but Southern men who have been voting the Democratic ticket because there was no hope elsewhere—that my candidacy would break the "Solid South." They assured me I could carry surely Kentucky and Tennessee, probably Georgia and Texas and possibly Alabama. I felt that if I could do that I would be doing a great service for the country.

"Smash the South's solidarity once and it will be over forever," he continued. "Thousands of Southerners want to break it but they are timid about the first plunge. Once they realize they can vote for a Republican with safety to their local conditions, there will be a break away from the Democratic organization that will make several Southern States as doubtful as are the Northern States.

"They told me that I could cause such a break. I do not know that I could, but I felt that I would like to try. It was the one real temptation to run again.

"THERE WAS CRUSADING TO BE DONE"

"But I don't want four more years here, and there were larger considerations," continued Roosevelt. After a pause, and in a noticeably deeper tone he said: "I have been a crusader here, I have been a destructive force. The country needs a change. There was crusading to do when I took hold. There was something that had to be uprooted. I had to challenge and destroy certain influences or we would soon have had an intolerable condition imperilling everything.

"I have not been deeply interested in the tariff nor in what you call the business problems of government. They have no appeal to me. I know little about them. If the party leaders in Congress had ever come to me with a definite programme on those matters I might have backed it because they wanted it,—but no one ever came.

"If I had occupied myself revising the tariff, there would be another revenue law a little better or a little worse than the present one—and there it would end. The only result might be—a divided party, and possibly 1892 over again.

"Now, we are unified. We have revised government 'up' which is better than a futile effort to revise the tariff 'down.' I have concerned myself with the ethical side. I've wanted to make people in government and out of it realize that it is best to deal squarely by one another—to have a free field and a

As I Knew Them

fair chance for all. I believe I have raised the standards.
We may slip back now and then, but never to the old levels.

"I DIDN'T USE A FEATHER DUSTER"

"The conscience of business had to be aroused, the authority
of the government over big as well as small had to be asserted.
You can't half do that kind of a job; it must be done thoroughly. I think I've done it. I didn't use a feather duster. I
knew I had to hit hard—and be hit hard in return.

"We have had four years of uprooting and four years of
crusading. The country has had enough of it and of me. It is
time for me to go and for a man of Taft's type to take my
place. He's a constructive fellow, I am not. The country
should not be asked to stand four years more of crusading.
There is no reason why it should. The ground is cleared for
constructive work; the man who clears is never the man to
do the upbuilding.

GIVE TAFT A CHANCE, URGED ROOSEVELT

"I know that some of my friends are critical of Taft. They
were critical before his nomination and are even more so now.
But they're wrong to take that attitude. There's nothing to
be gained by being doubtful. Give Taft a chance. He knows
what has to be done here; he knows how it has to be done,
and now he will know how to build on the foundations that
have been laid. He has a legal mind—he can round out and
shape up the policies of the last four years better than if I
were to remain here. He has a big majority in Congress to
back him, and the country is with him.

"Taft will give you four years of upbuilding and I'm going
off to Africa for a real fine time.

"I have done my Sorbonne and Oxford lectures," he continued jubilantly. "I've paid all my political debts. I'm foot-

loose and fancy free, and when I'm back in Sagamore in a year or so as a private citizen I'll be the happiest man you ever saw."

How dimly Roosevelt foresaw his own future!—how dimly Taft's!

CHAPTER XLIII

A PRESIDENT IN A PROPHETIC STORM

Still "Theodore" and "Will," But Not The Same Old Ring—"That Was A Fine Inaugural Address," Exclaimed Roosevelt—It Was A Good Programme Of Policies, But It Never Got Beyond Mere Say-So—Taft's First Conference Was With Joe Cannon And Aldrich—"Carrying Out Roosevelt's Policies" On A Stretcher—Taft Turns To The Old Guard—Every "Insurgent" Marked For Discipline—"I Am Leaving That To Aldrich," Would Be Taft's Answer—Canadian Reciprocity Made Party Unity In Congress Impossible.

WAS there ever a worse March 4 than that on which William Howard Taft was inaugurated President in 1909? Cynical folk could have asserted that the day was made tempestuous so as definitely to mark the transition from Roosevelt to Taft. If so, it marked it well—but whether it was intended as a final clean-up of stormy Roosevelt times or a forecast of what was in store for Taft no one knew. For that matter, there was storm enough to serve both purposes, with still some to spare. Rain, snow, sleet filled the streets of Washington and halted railroads, telephones and telegraphs along the entire Atlantic seaboard. Taft was compelled to abandon the Capitol steps where most Presidents have been inaugurated and to hold the ceremonies in the Senate Chamber.

On the surface, all Republicans were jubilant. Party majorities had mounted high everywhere on election day; newly-elected Republican Governors were around Washington as thick as Southern Colonels; Republican Senators and Congressmen were so many that like a widening Spring freshet they flowed over into the half-empty Democratic side of each chamber.

As I Knew Them

The chief figures in the day's proceedings were still "Theodore" and "Will" to each other; but the old ring of close, unconcealing friendship was gone. Both men were still striving to make others believe that that shadowy something that often separates men when relations change had not been slowly acquiring too substantial form. There were whisperings of trouble but only whisperings. Years later, Roosevelt said to me: "Taft and I knew the true situation and its cause. It did not matter whether anyone else knew or not—best that they should not. There was too much at stake."

TAFT'S TRIBUTE TO ROOSEVELT

Heavily coated, Taft watched the inaugural parade from the White House reviewing stand. He greeted the Taft Club of Cincinnati by waving his silk hat in unison with the incongruous notes of "In the Good Old Summer Time." Meanwhile, a train making slow progress against the storm was carrying his predecessor to Oyster Bay.

Roosevelt had commenced the day by receiving his successor, posing with him for that famous picture of two portly men in the conventional "Prince Alberts" of the time. He had driven to the Capitol with Taft, listened in the Senate chamber to the storm-bound inaugural and before he left for his train said to Elihu Root, "My! That was a fine inaugural address."

Roosevelt had not seen it in advance. The Cincinnati warning had been effective. With his acceptance speech, Taft had gone to Oyster Bay "for the President's judgment and criticism" in July. His inaugural, however, was to be judged by Roosevelt as he heard it with others. He was curious to know what Taft would say and he was well content when he heard these words:

"I have had the honor to be one of the advisors of my distinguished predecessor, and, as such, to hold up his hands in the reforms he has instituted. I should be untrue to myself, to my promises and to the declaration of the party platform upon which I was elected to office if I did not make the maintenance and enforcement of these reforms a most important feature of my administration. They were directed to the suppression of the lawlessness and abuse of power of great combinations of capital invested in railroads and in industrial enterprises carrying on interstate commerce.

"The steps which my predecessor took and the legislation passed on his recommendation have accomplished much, have caused a general halt in the vicious policies which created popular alarm, and have brought about in the business affected a much higher regard for existing law."

A FINE PROGRAMME OF POLICIES

Surely this was a keynote which must have pleased Taft's predecessor. Then Taft recommended relief for railroads from certain restrictions of the Sherman law which were "urged by my predecessor and will be urged by me." He pleaded for reorganization of the departments and bureaus having corporate matters in charge, so that there should be cooperation instead of conflict. Taft declared for tariff revision and announced that he would convene Congress in special session to secure it; he also spoke strongly for conservation of our natural resources "saving and restoring our forests and the great improvement of our waterways."

A good strong programme. Of course in picturesque idiom, "the proof of the pudding is in the eating," but at least here was a fine start.

THE BEGINNING WAS ALSO THE END

Unfortunately the start proved also to be the finish. The hopes aroused by Taft's words wilted like a full-blown rose when the news came that the first important conferees in the White House were Senator Aldrich and Speaker "Joe" Cannon. No two men in Washington had more bitterly opposed

STARTING ON A LONG JOURNEY

the Roosevelt policies to which Taft in his inaugural had paid such tribute, pledging also his own faith, and yet they were the men now selected by the new President to make the maintenance of those measures "a most important feature of my Administration"!

Newspaper dispatches spoke kindly of the conference as an effort to agree on making the Roosevelt policies effective; nearer the truth was a cartoon entitled "Carrying Out Roosevelt's Policies." It showed "My Policies" on a stretcher that bearers were carrying out of the White House.

TAFT TURNS TO THE OLD GUARD

No one in Congress, especially those who were opposing Cannon lost the significance of that conference. It was known for some time that Taft would not help defeat Cannon for reelection as Speaker. There are excellent reasons why a President should keep out of such contests and if Taft had kept out no one could have justly criticized him.

The revolt against Cannon's harsh exercise of his power had broken out in the previous session, and there was now an intense determination to have fair play for all. "Old Guard" Congressmen were the only ones who could get the favor of the Speaker—the only ones not "tainted with Teddyism," as Cannon termed it—and under existing rules unless you had his favor you might as well be in Timbuctoo as on the floor of the House.

Herbert Parsons, of New York, Augustus P. Gardner, of Massachusetts, Victor Murdock and Judge Edmond H. Madison of Kansas, George W. Norris, now Senator from Nebraska, Henry Allen Cooper and Irvine L. Lenroot, of Wisconsin, led in the struggle to revise the rules. In the beginning—that is, just after his election—Taft thought he was with them; then he wanted to think it over; the next heard from him was the news that he was seeking the counsel of Aldrich and Cannon.

PILING IT ON

TAFT TURNS TO THE OLD GUARD

As I Knew Them

Still the insurgents persisted in their battle for their rights. They could not win a complete victory, but they secured a revision of the rules giving every member the right to recognition. The outposts of Cannonism, of Czarism, were captured. But Taft, they discovered, was now in the citadel they were attacking. Here was a battle for justice—the opening skirmish of the fierce contest coming in 1912. Many historic battles have developed from such seemingly remote beginnings; but not until historians later searched for cause has it been revealed that a principle, or a great need, was from the first moment working its way to the fore, and that the final clash was an inevitable sequel of the early and smaller one.

So it proved to be in this situation. The Taft talk with Aldrich and Cannon was not a conference; it was a surrender. The reactionaries in Congress hailed it as such; the progressives accepted it as such. There was no middle ground of compromise. At least, Taft sought none. Steadily, he moved further and further away from the old moorings. "I am leaving that to Aldrich," he would say when asked to discuss some schedule in the tariff bill upon which Congress was then working.

Thus, little by little, progressives came to realize the hopelessness of seeking support at the White House, and the certainty of an unpleasant time there if, by chance, the name or policies of Taft's predecessor were mentioned. They were now not merely insurgents against Cannonism in the House; they were insurgents against the Administration.

Never was there such inept handling of legislation as in framing the tariff bill in 1909. Almost any effort at conciliation would have united all Republicans in Congress back of the new schedules; but conciliation was not what the men in control sought; their purpose was annihilation. Every

361

"insurgent" was marked for discipline, and every suggestion ignored.

Taft knew what was going on, shrugged his shoulders in a helpless sort of way, and gave the impression that he did not care to be burdened with the task of reconciling the warring factions. He must have foreseen what the split, ever growing wider and deeper, would mean to Republicans in the 1910 Congressional elections and later in 1912, but if he did his serenity was undisturbed.

THE CANADIAN RECIPROCITY BLUNDER

The worst was still to come, however. Taft insisted upon reciprocity with Canada. The measure had been refused indorsement in the Republican national convention, and a majority of Republicans, especially those from States bordering Canada were opposed to it. Still Taft persisted. When he forced it to a vote in the House on February 14, 1911, out of the 92 "noes" 87 came from Republicans.

Such extremes as Jonathan Bourne, progressive from Washington, and John Dalzell, a Pennsylvania stand-patter, voted "no"—demonstrating that the opposition embraced all kinds of Republicans. The Senate refused to act—and two weeks later Taft faced the newly-elected Democratic Congress.

PARTY CHAOS IN CONGRESS

Like Cleveland with his silver repeal measure, Taft now looked to the opposition party for votes to pass his bill. Apparently he gauged the popularity of his Canadian proposal by its acceptance by the Democrats—forgetting that any lowering of the tariff bars would have free trade support.

Again, like Cleveland, he called Congress in extra session. The House, now Democratic, passed the bill a second time with practically all the "noes" from Republicans; in the Senate, more Republicans opposed than favored it. With a majority of his own party against his principal legislation, party unity back of the President was thereafter hopeless. A minority of Republicans in both Houses had revolted against his tariff bill; a majority revolted against his Canadian reciprocity bill. Politically, Taft's plight was as bad as Cleve-

"SAY, BOSS, WHY DON'T YER HUNCH OVER A LITTLE TO DE ODDER SIDE? DEN DE
MACHINE WILL RUN BETTER"

land's, and the result worse, for Cleveland stopped the coining of silver dollars. Taft's reciprocity was a dead letter. Canadian voters swept out of office the government of Sir Wilfrid Laurier with which Taft had negotiated. Thus the whole structure collapsed.

CHAPTER XLIV

TAFT'S ONE BIG TRIUMPH

He Won "Decisions That Decided" From The Supreme Court In The Anti-Trust Cases—Our National Policies Take Years To Develop— The Entire Supreme Court Membership Changed While The Sherman Law Was Before It—Only Harlan Stood By The Government From The First.

THE one Roosevelt policy which Taft did not abandon is the one triumph of his administration,—the effort to secure for the government through court decisions complete control of corporation activities. In this effort Taft shows at his best. His heart was in that work, and his mind was trained to the problem. There was need for "decisions that decided" despite the victory scored in the Northern Securities and "beef" trust cases under Roosevelt. They had greatly strengthened the law, but the "teeth" that Roosevelt had so vigorously sought had yet to be provided. It was Taft's task "to round out and shape up" (as Roosevelt had expressed it) efforts which had been made to secure helpful court interpretations. Through George W. Wickersham, his able and forceful Attorney General, this was accomplished.

As a nation and as individuals, Americans have a reputation for moving rapidly toward accomplishing the things they set out to do—much too rapidly, they tell us abroad. The history of our law making does not sustain this charge. Our government moves slowly; it has long periods of swaying back and forth before deciding. First Congress debates for years; then the courts take more years to declare and make effective what Congress really intended. "Half slave and half free," we stood on the brink of a precipice for thirty or forty years before we engaged in civil strife to end slavery. It took us ten years after the war to say that we would redeem our paper-money in coin, it took us a quarter of a century to establish the gold standard, longer to secure votes for women, the income tax and prohibition. Once policies are established we forget the long and doubtful period that preceded their enactment.

A STRUGGLE FOR TWENTY YEARS

So it was with the struggle to confirm the supremacy of the government over industrial enterprises and great wealth. For twenty years every President and every Attorney General had battled with it. The Sherman anti-trust law of 1890 was the corner-stone, but at first it could not be built upon substantially. The entire membership of the Supreme Court changed while, in case after case, the issue was argued before it, and futile decisions came down. In 1895, the Knight sugar case went heavily against the government. Associate Justice Harlan alone voted to sustain. In 1903 the Northern Securities case went in favor of the government by a five to four decision. Among the four dissenters was Associate Justice White who had voted against the government in the Sugar Trust case, and who now proclaimed that the two cases were exactly alike. He insisted that the law should be interpreted in "the light of reason," and not as the government contended.

Still, the Northern Securities case was won, which meant more than Justice White's phrase. Other suits were brought by Roosevelt and in these Taft, back from the Philippines, aided with suggestion. He was, therefore, well prepared to carry on the struggle in his own name. Approximately ninety suits were brought during Taft's Administration. Though not all of them were won, a body of opinion came from the courts that ended the effort of corporate wealth to deny the power of the government to regulate it.

As I Knew Them

Twenty years, however, were needed to establish this supremacy. The only man on the bench from the first test of the law to its final upholding was Associate Justice Harlan. He was also the only justice to vote consistently in support of the government and the law. Associate Justice White voted twice against the government. Not until 1910, in the Tobacco suit, did White change over to the interpretation of the Sherman law that now prevails. It would be tiring to list the number of Justices who sat in the different cases brought between 1895, when the Knight Sugar Trust case was decided, and 1911 when the Standard Oil case was decided with the full membership of the Court in favor of the government, but White and Harlan were the only Justices who sat through all. White as Chief Justice wrote the opinion in the Standard Oil case; and again as in the Northern Securities case he wrote of the "light of reason" in interpreting law. But the same light led him in one case against the government and in the later case in favor of the government—one of the peculiarities of judges that laymen like myself do not understand.

The point I had in mind, however, was not to discuss the attitude of individual Justices but to demonstrate that, despite all the talk that as a nation we hurry into decisions, the record shows that we deliberate long before acting.

CHAPTER XLV

WHY TAFT DID NOT SUCCEED

Two Reasons Why The Smile That Captured The Country Soon Lost Its Power To Persuade—The Comparison With Jackson's Naming of Van Buren—The White House Had Lost Its Real Meaning To Taft —Drift, Drift, Drift—Taft's Real Desire Was For The Bench—An Unusual Conference That Gave Him A Scotch Verdict—Trying To Help Jim Tawney—"God Knows," Said Taft Sympathetically, But Others Took It Differently.

WHY did not Taft get on well in the White House? Many reasons could be advanced but two fundamental reasons were: (1) his nomination did not reflect the party's will but the will of a retiring President; (2) he loved the title but not the work of President.

Whenever Roosevelt's nomination of Taft is discussed, reference is made to the nomination of Martin Van Buren by Andrew Jackson in 1836. Both Roosevelt and Jackson forced their will on their party. Both had the same motive— to insure continuance of their policies—but Roosevelt was by no means so well justified as Jackson. Van Buren was then Vice President; he had been Minister to Great Britain, a United States Senator, Governor of New York, and occupant of several less conspicuous offices. He had submitted himself many times to a vote of the people, and was identified with the issues of the day. In these various positions, he had gained a ripe experience for the Presidency—for the delicate task of knowing how to guide rather than to antagonize public opinion.

Taft lacked that equipment. For nearly thirty years he had held one appointive office after another. In Ohio, early in life, he had been elected to some minor judgeship, but in a broad sense his only experience with elections was as a candi-

date for the Presidency. In that candidacy he did not urge
his election because of anything he had done, but solely on the
ground that he was the standard bearer of the President he
desired to succeed.

His nomination, like that of Van Buren, represented an
unfortunate, unpardonable exercise of Presidential power over
a party convention. Neither nominee represented party sentiment tested by a free roll call in convention. Inevitably in
both cases the result had to be party schism and disaster.

DRIFT—DRIFT—DRIFT

The second reason for Taft's failure became apparent all
too soon. The new Administration was on its way somewhere
but whither it was going no one—not even the President himself—seemed to know. It was drift, drift, drift—little attempted, nothing done. No wonder Republicans grew restive.
No wonder the country began to think it had made a mistake.
There was a sag everywhere in Washington; the old vigor
was gone; none of the familiar sharp calls to action were ever
heard.

Those who went to the White House with suggestions were
seldom welcome, and rarely came away satisfied. Those who
wanted results turned to some department official for them.
The department official usually replied that there was no use
discussing matters until he could see the President "some
time." Nobody seemed to be interested in getting things done.
Officialdom found "the easiest way" was the White House
way; quickly the whole Administration took its color from
the top.

Possibly had this condition not followed seven years of
Roosevelt it would not have excited so much criticism; but
the change from decision to indecision, from action to delay,
was so sudden, the contrast so sharp, that talk of a collapse
of government efficiency soon filled Washington and spread
through the country. The "Old Guard" in Congress promptly

As I Knew Them

took the leadership of the party from the White House, and
Senator Dolliver historically remarked: "Taft is an amiable
man, entirely surrounded by men who know exactly what they
want."

It was the judgment of men who had opportunity to know
whereof they spoke that Taft did not even try to be a success.
Of course, he wanted to make a good record and to be reelected. No man could be in the White House without such
desire. What I mean when I say "try" is to try with every
ounce of effort in you—not once or twice, but until you get a
result. Taft made no such "try." He relied on smiling
through difficulties and finding the easiest way out of them—
usually of course without settling them. They backed up on
him like a mountain stream dammed.

Though no golfer myself, I do not share the criticism of
his golfing or cite it as an example of indifference to his work.
Those hours of relaxation were probably necessary to a man
of Taft's build. He liked golfing and played the course well;
he did not like the grind of the White House—for it is a
grind unless you are temperamentally fitted for it—and he
did not play that well.

THE WHITE HOUSE ONLY ANOTHER WAY STATION

I have always felt that as a member of the Cabinet five
years, and earlier as Solicitor General in the Department of
Justice, the White House had become too familiar to Taft
before he occupied it. Its occupant had been "Theodore" to
him and he was "Will." Crossing its doorsill as President
gave him no deeper emotion than arriving at a familiar railroad station on one of the journeys he was always beginning
or ending.

It had meant no effort on his part; like the engineer of the
locomotive pulling his railway train on his travels, another
person had the power to advance him to the desired place
and did so. The nominating convention, which should have

As I Knew Them

been the power, became merely the vehicle; delegates knew what was wanted of them and did it; so, later did the country. Thus the highest honor that can be gained by an American came to Taft so easily that I question whether it was prized by him at real value. The things you prize are those you struggle to attain.

For nearly thirty years before Taft reached the Presidency, he had been "kicked around," to use a frequent expression of his own. He was on the Ohio Superior Court bench when President Harrison made him Solicitor General; later Harrison appointed him to a Circuit Judgeship. He was on that bench when McKinley asked him to become President of the Philippine Commission.

TAFT'S REAL DESIRE FOR THE BENCH

Taft had three opportunities to go on the Supreme Court bench, and refused all three, before his nomination for President. President Harding's offer of the Chief-Justiceship was the fourth he had received. That one he accepted. No other man has ever had such a tribute.

They show the high opinion held of Taft's judicial mind by all who had opportunity to know it.

Twice while he was in the Philippines, and again in 1906 President Roosevelt vainly sought to place Taft on the bench. The first offer was cabled to him in Manila in 1902. He replied that he had promised McKinley to see the Philippine job through until a settled form of government had been worked out. He wanted to keep his promise.

"I long for a judicial career," Taft cabled, "but if it must turn on my present decision I am willing to lose it."

So far as I know this is the strongest utterance Taft ever made on any subject!

Roosevelt renewed the offer two months later; again Taft declined. In 1903 Roosevelt made him Secretary of War.

370

As I Knew Them

That department has supervision over the Philippines and Taft accepted.

HIS FAMILY WANTED HIM TO BE PRESIDENT!

The revealing declination came in 1906. Again Roosevelt offered him an Associate Justiceship. Again Taft declined—this time not for the excellent reason he had advanced from the Philippines. The new reason plainly stated was that his family preferred that he should seek the Presidency!

This was a commendably frank avowal of his intention to be a candidate in 1908. It could not have been made by a Cabinet officer to a President without an accompanying resignation unless the President was a staunch and genuine friend. If there is anything comparable to it in all the relations of our Presidents with their Cabinet members I have not read or heard of it.

It was an example of the finest kind of friendship possible between two men—how well Taft knew that his superior officer was also a friend to whom he could candidly tell his great desire; how splendidly Roosevelt responded to that confidence!

AN UNUSUAL CONFERENCE

On Taft's request, or at his own suggestion, Roosevelt went so far as to call Secretary of State Root, Attorney General Moody, and Secretary of Commerce Straus, into conference as to whether Taft should go on the bench or not. This most unusual proceeding to determine the future of a man uncertain of which honor he should seek resulted in what might be called a "Scotch verdict."

In the minds of all was a thought which none expressed. Taft had better go on the Supreme Court. One man present did suggest the familiar story of the bird in the hand. The conference broke up when Taft said he would write his brother. In a few days he gave Roosevelt the answer quoted above. Attorney General Moody was thereupon appointed to the vacancy.

Through the next two years Taft travelled and talked the country over. He seemed to be everywhere,—anywhere in fact, except in the War Department. His absences were encouraged by Roosevelt to give him his full chance with the people.

In that friendship Roosevelt saw only Taft. After the message he had received from Taft, he should have seen in the picture not Taft alone but Taft plus the family. For that message carried in it the seed from which all future trouble sprang. Taft was subordinating his own desires to the ambitions of others close to him who could share in the prestige of the White House, but not in the quiet dignity of the Supreme Court. The experience may have satisfied them, but it proved a nightmare to Taft.

A BIG TASK, BUT LITTLE EFFORT

I was one of many Republicans whose loyalty to Roosevelt did not lessen their desire to see Taft get on well. I realized that he followed an unusual man into the Presidency, that in method and temperament he was different. Moreover, I knew the peril of such a heavy vote as he had polled—the largest electoral and popular vote ever accorded. Great expectations were aroused; it was an almost impossible task to meet them. Even such an aggressive and resourceful man as Roosevelt would have found it difficult to keep such popularity at flood tide. Then there was the revolt against Cannon in the House. Try as he might to resist it, the new President was bound to be drawn into that maelstrom. Taft made no effort to resist —he just waded in waist high and was soon in deeper water.

These considerations were in my mind as I listened to criticisms. It was hard to reply. Taft gave no help by doing something, almost anything, that would show that he could master the big job he had undertaken. That something was never even attempted. Instead, there came from the White House either indifference or angry impatience according to Taft's mood for the day. Washington is a place of keen, cold judgment. It quickly judged Taft as a mistake in the White House just as it now has the settled belief that as Chief Justice of the United States he is in a position suited to his abilities and inclination.

Nor was the country long in making the same appraisement. Every evidence of the good will of the people had followed Taft into the White House. His smile had captured the country. But his Administration was less than two years old before it was condemned at the Congress elections of 1910, reversing a big majority into a pitiful minority; and in 1912, four years after he had received the largest electoral and popular vote then recorded for a President, he carried only Vermont and Utah, running behind both Wilson and Roosevelt also in popular vote.

THE WRONG WORD TOO OFTEN

A weighty influence in the wrecking of Taft's Administration and, temporarily, of the Republican party was his capacity for saying and doing the wrong thing politically. I do not wish to be misunderstood on this point, and I cannot emphasize too strongly that I mean no disrespect to Taft. His blundering was in the political field, and in dealing with men. It was largely inexperience. On the bench he is at home, and there, in lesser judgeships and now in the Supreme Court, he has been sure-footed.

In nothing did he differ from Roosevelt more than in his inability to gauge the effect of words. Roosevelt seldom spoke without seeing a picture of how the sentence would look in type, and how it would affect the mind of the reader or hearer. Taft was utterly unable to create such a picture. Before he became President this did not matter, and this Taft was never able to understand—a President cannot soliloquize in public like a private citizen. Every word a President utters is weighed and scrutinized. His words are often more potent than his deeds.

Wilson had some of this Taft trait; he too used words without always calculating their effect. He did not visualize the way "too proud to fight" would appear in print, or what effect it would produce. The angry roar that went up everywhere dumbfounded him. By noon a hurried explanation was issued from the White House to show that the President's meaning had been misinterpreted; too late. So with other phrases, such as "peace without victory," "with the causes and objects of this war we have no concern," and many another.

A TYPICAL CARTOON OF THE DAY

TRYING TO HELP "JIM" TAWNEY

But Wilson was not so frequently unfortunate as Taft. Take Taft's experience with the Payne-Aldrich tariff bill. That law was especially unpopular in the West. In all the West it was most unpopular in the Middle West, and in all the

Middle West it was most detested in Minnesota. And in all Minnesota there was no place where it was more detested than in Winona, where "Jim" Tawney was facing defeat for reelection to Congress.

Taft wanted to help Tawney. So, with unerring instinct for the wrong step, Taft picked Winona as a good place in which to advocate the new law, and journeyed out there to do it. The whole West was immediately vocal with rage. As letters, telegrams, newspaper editorials, began to pile up in the White House, Taft saw the necessity of saying something to meet the criticism. Unbelievable as it may seem, Taft explained the Winona speech by saying that he had "dashed it off hurriedly between stations!"

When people remembered that he had left the golf links at Bar Harbor, Maine, to go to Winona, the original mistake was immediately overshadowed by the explanation. The West was infuriated by the apparent confession that he had played golf rather than prepare carefully what he was to say to it. Everywhere there was dismay over the implication that the President of the United States gave little thought to grave public questions. Furthermore, instead of helping Tawney, the Presidential effort lost him hundreds of votes.

Undoubtedly Taft did himself injustice by his apology. He had certainly given more thought to the speech than he admitted. But he was on record as saying virtually that he was a careless man, postponing until train-time his review of matters vitally important to millions of people for whom he was the chief trustee. Nothing he could say or do afterward would efface the impression made.

ANOTHER UNFORTUNATE "BREAK"

Another of his mistakes came from his habit of thinking aloud and his inability to understand that while anybody else may think aloud, a President may not. Getting off a train in New York city, he was met by reporters who asked him

375

what was to be the outcome of the labor situation. At that time there was a good deal of poverty and unemployment, and the subject was close to the hearts of a great many people not at all interested in politics. Taft mechanically replied with this historic sentence:

"God knows."

In these two words he had provoked a storm. The utterance was not so callous as it sounded. It was really uttered in sympathy—Taft meant it that way. But a President is supposed to be always thinking in definite terms and "God knows" was taken to show that he did not care.

"EVEN A RAT WILL FIGHT"

There is no need to call the roll of Taft's unfortunate utterances, so I will close the list of small but influential incidents with the celebrated one which completed the destruction of any hopes he might have had of carrying a single Republican State primary when he was seeking renomination in 1912. Taft's friends were urging him to take the stump against Roosevelt. At first he refused; no President had ever entered publicly into a contest for his own renomination, and he did not want to create a precedent. But Roosevelt was carrying everything before him with such a sweep that Taft finally yielded. Obviously, apology or explanation for his course was weakness, and so Taft made one. This was his explanation:

"Even a rat will fight when driven into a corner."

In every primary contest the Roosevelt supporters seized on this utterance and rang the changes on it. Taft was satirized as a frightened rat driven into a corner and fighting back hopelessly and unwillingly. The sentence even took the spirit out of his sincerest supporters. One may put some heart into fighting for a lion, but not for a desperate rat.

376

CHAPTER XLVI

CITIZEN ROOSEVELT

Still Sees Himself Out Of The Turmoil Of Politics—Tells Me Of The Greatest Battle Of His Life And How He Won It In Africa—Frank Visitors Rare At The White House—Root Said In London That Taft Had Broken Down—Roosevelt's Royal Welcome Home—Herbert Parsons Uses A William Barnes Interview To Stir Roosevelt To Action—The Colonel Tries To Stem The Anti-Republican Tide, And Names Taft's Cabinet Officer For Governor.

EVERY moment Roosevelt spent in Africa strengthened the resolve announced before leaving the White House to devote himself to things he desired more than he now desired political honors. That vision of a figure remote from faction and personal prejudices still filled his imagination; he saw himself the accepted arbiter of differences, a court of last resort. What an awakening was to follow such a dream!

"I have read what others have written about my battles for health in early life, my battles in politics and my battles with various influences and men," said Roosevelt to me after his return, "but it was in Africa that I won a battle I had been trying for years to win but had never succeeded in keeping won for long. Yet no one ever knew I was fighting it—it was a battle to control my temper.

"I tried to win it in the White House, but you cannot win that kind of a battle while you have the immense power and responsibilities of a President. Trying situations come up, men come to you with unconscionable suggestions, others resort to petty intrigues. The man who speaks out frankly and definitely is a rare visitor, though I can assure you from my own experience he is cordially welcomed in the White House and makes more headway. There were times when I just had

377

to tell such people what I thought of them and, of course, the newspapers would print a story about a scene in the White House. It would never occur to them to print the other side of the story—the side of the President, whoever he might be, forced to listen sometimes to untruths, sometimes to evasions, sometimes to office hunting and bargainings that the public never hears of.

From N. Y. Herald, April 2, 1909.

"THE CALL OF THE AFRICAN WILD"

"I suppose that is part of a President's job, but it tried my patience and my temper. I couldn't win the battle to control it when such matters were pressed upon me to the exclusion of more important things and I realized it. Over in Africa, I had some equally exasperating experiences but it was not difficult to master them. Back in my tent in the evenings I could laugh over them and talk with others about their ludicrous side. It was there that I came to know how to control my temper, and I have been able to do it ever since. It is a great battle won."

ROOT SAID TAFT HAD BROKEN DOWN

This frame of mind fitted the mood in which he had planned his life following his return to Oyster Bay. But other persons were shortly to exert a different influence. Scores of old followers were waiting all along the line home with protests against the Taft régime and insistence that Roosevelt alone could restore popularity to the party. He read their letters and listened to their stories, but his purpose remained unchanged.

In Egypt, Gifford Pinchot, since Governor of Pennsylvania, gave him his version of President Taft's activities and the consequences.

It was not until he reached London, several weeks later, in 1910 that the first definite impression was made upon Roosevelt—and Elihu Root was the man who made it. At least, that is what Roosevelt told me three or four years later. Roosevelt's statement to me was substantially this:

"Root told me that the Administration had completely broken down, particularly the State Department. He expected to see Congress go heavily Democratic, and he regarded New York as hopeless. Root spoke so unqualifiedly that I became convinced the party was in a bad way, but I could not see that I was called upon to throw myself into the situation. Moreover, what could I do? I could not ask the country to elect a Congress to support Taft in the way he seemed to be going, nor could I seek to elect a Congress against him. Root said something about the party needing me, but made no suggestion.

"In a way, his analysis of the situation was more hopeless than that of Gifford Pinchot, but I regarded Pinchot as naturally extreme; his experience with Taft had embittered him.

379

I believed that Taft was justified in dismissing Pinchot;
Pinchot was right in his policies, but he should have resigned
and fought his battle from the outside. His course was dis-
organizing the Department. There was nothing left for Taft
to do but to drop Pinchot."

ROOSEVELT'S ROYAL WELCOME HOME

An emperor could not have had a greater welcome home
than was accorded Roosevelt as his ship entered New York
harbor. A reception committee met him, and a parade up
Broadway followed his landing. It was a satisfying day in
every respect save one—Roosevelt would not discuss politics.
Many sought to get an expression of opinion, but not a word
could be had. His first utterance of a political character was
his telegram a month later from Harvard College to State
Senator Frederick Davenport, of New York, urging the
prompt enactment of the Hinman-Greene direct primary bill.
That telegram followed his talk with Governor Hughes.
After that flash from Roosevelt there came another period
of silence.

Toward midsummer, Herbert Parsons, then Congressman,
national committeeman and boss of New York City Republicans, called at the "Evening Mail's" office, and urged me to
have our ship news reporter meet William Barnes, Jr., on an
incoming steamer from Europe. He wanted Barnes asked
whether he would favor Roosevelt as chairman of the approaching State convention. At that time Barnes was the
acknowledged leader of the "Old Guard" Republicans in New
York.

"Why should our ship news man waste time with that question?" I asked Parsons. "I can write Barnes' answer in advance. He's against it. He is for Sherman," (then Vice
President).

"Of course he is against Roosevelt," came the quick response from Parsons. "I know that as well as you do. I want

him to say so publicly. We have tried in every way to interest the Colonel in this convention, and have failed. He thinks he had better keep out of it. He's our only hope to gain control. A declaration by Barnes against him might stir the Colonel to action. Anyhow, we would be able to press him harder."

So down the bay on the revenue cutter went the "Evening Mail's" ship news reporter charged to induce Barnes to voice his hostility to the Colonel. The reporter did his work too well. That afternoon the "Evening Mail" published an interview with the returning Republican chieftain declaring against Roosevelt for chairman of the convention and in favor of Vice President Sherman. It was a characteristic Barnes talk —frank, positive, straight to the issue.

ROOSEVELT UNDERTAKES A LOSING BATTLE

Of course, I cannot say that the Barnes outburst led the Colonel finally to acquiesce in the movement to make him chairman of the convention and sponsor for the nomination of Henry L. Stimson, Taft's Secretary of War, for Governor. Parsons took the published interview to Oyster Bay, but I never asked how he used it there. All I know is that the Colonel's refusals grew milder. Finally he put aside his own settled purpose and yielded to the persuasion to get into battle. He tried to put hope into a hopeless gubernatorial fight in New York. He was named chairman over Sherman and he nominated Stimson, but the 1910 tide against the Republican party was too strong even for Roosevelt to stem.

It was a struggle that certainly had no promise for him. If he elected Stimson he would be handing the State over to a member of Taft's Cabinet as Governor. That surely was not furthering any political interest Roosevelt might have. If Stimson should be defeated, as seemed almost certain, the cry would go up that Roosevelt had been turned down by his own State in the first battle after his return.

As I Knew Them

The Colonel was advised to look upon that side of the question before identifying himself with such a hopeless prospect, but he refused. The result in New York was proportionately better for Republicans than in other States—(for the Democratic tidal wave ran high everywhere)—but that fact did not prevent the outcry that Roosevelt had been beaten in an effort to capture the Republican organization in the Empire State.

CHAPTER XLVII

THE TAFT BREAK, AS TOLD BY ROOSEVELT

"Preposterous To Believe I Would Want A President To Be Merely A Pale Shadow"—He And Taft Knew The Facts And In Their Own Hearts Could Decide—The Naming Of Luke Wright—"Tell The Boys I Want To Continue All Of Them," Said Taft, But All Were Dropped —All That Roosevelt Asked Was That Taft Should Satisfy The People.

NOW, permit me to recall to the reader my talk with Roosevelt in the White House a few days before the expiration of his term, for I want to reveal here what was deep down in his mind at the very moment he was urging others to give Taft a fair chance.

To tell the story properly I must state that in February, 1916, I was in Trinidad, West Indies, with Colonel Roosevelt and returned home with him on the steamer Matura. We had many talks on deck those twelve or thirteen days at sea. One afternoon I said to him:

"Colonel, all your enemies and a few of your friends think that you broke with Taft because you could not control him, and that you, therefore, are more to blame than Taft. I know that is not true, but I do not know, nor does anyone else know, the facts from your own lips."

"It's too preposterous," he interrupted.

"Maybe it is," I responded, "but you are not fair to yourself to remain silent."

"Taft knows it is not so; I know it is not so," he again interrupted rather hotly. "It does not concern others."

"Yes, it does," I insisted. "It concerns me as your friend; it concerns the four and a quarter million voters who supported you in 1912. They have to defend you against such charges; they do so because of their faith in you but you give them no help in the way of fact. I think you owe it to them to do so."

"It has never come to me in that light," Roosevelt replied. "I have regarded whether faith was kept or not as a matter that only Taft and I knew and in our own hearts could decide. So I have had nothing to say, but if you care now to take down a statement of the facts I will be glad to make one only to be released publicly after you and I agree that it should be."

Other matters engaged attention after our return home, and I never pressed for "leave to print." Here is that statement:

(STATEMENT MADE TO ME AND REVISED BY THEODORE ROOSEVELT ON S.S. MATURA, RETURNING FROM TRINIDAD, H. L. S.)

"There was no one incident on which I broke with Taft. It was a series of incidents, an accumulation of disappointments and of positive evidences of failure to carry out in action the intentions he expressed in words. None of these matters included in the remotest degree anything in which I had a personal interest—that is, an interest in which I as an individual was solely concerned.

"I never asked him to do a single thing; I was deeply concerned that the Republican party should continue to be the party of idealism and of advancing policies. I knew and recognized that it had a period of constructive work ahead of it, rather than destructive work, and I realized that in the evolution of things there would have to be adjustments and changes from the lines laid down in my own administration.

"It is perfectly preposterous for anyone to believe that I would want a President of the United States to be merely a pale shadow of his predecessor, no matter who that predecessor might be.

"In the case of Mr. Taft it must be manifest to everyone

that the only way he could justify the deep interest I had shown in his nomination and election was by making an Administration that would satisfy the people. His relations with me could not be made the test of his success or failure.

"Yes, it is true that before I left the White House I began to see another Taft than the Taft I knew as Secretary of War. When he came to me to go over his letter of acceptance, I gave him the best advice I could regarding it, and to a large extent he acted on it. At that time, he exhausted the English language for words with which to express his obligation to me.

"About that time, I had to name a successor to him as Secretary of War. I told him it was difficult to get a first-class man to take the place for a few months. He asked me if I had anyone in mind, and I replied yes. I wanted to name a Southern Democrat, and had Luke Wright of Tennessee in mind. I added that I did not believe I could get Wright for such a short time, but that if he felt that he would like to have him too, the fact might weigh with him. Taft replied that it would be a fine appointment, and he would be glad to have him in his Cabinet.

" 'Remember that I am not asking this as a favor to me,' I continued. 'I am trying to get a good man in the interests of the department. I would prefer to name a man whom you will continue, but if you do not care to commit yourself I will go ahead and do the best I can without involving you at all.'

"Taft reiterated that he would be more than pleased to continue Wright if I named him.

" 'Then I can tell Wright, when I offer him the place, that I am speaking for you as well as for myself?'

" 'You can.'

"I did so, but Mr. Wright's career as Secretary of War ended when Taft became President.

"About the same time, Taft brought up the subject of his Cabinet. 'I wish you would tell the boys I have been working with that I want to continue all of them,' he said. 'They are

385

all fine fellows, and they have been mighty good to me. I want them all to stay just as they are.'

" 'Why don't you tell them so yourself?' I asked.

" 'No, I don't want to do that. I don't want to make any promises. I want to be in a position to say that I have no promises out. I wish, though, that you would tell them just how I feel and let them know that I want the Cabinet to stand just as it is.'

" 'That cannot be,' I replied, 'and should not be. Metcalf, for instance, wants to go back to California. Root wants to get out of public life unless he can be United States Senator, and I do not believe that you and Cortelyou would get on well together. Those changes must come, I believe. Straus, Meyer, Garfield and Wilson, however, would, I think, be glad to stay on, and if you really want me to talk with them about it, I will gladly tell them of your intentions.'

" 'Yes, I wish you would,' replied Taft.

"I acted on Taft's suggestion within the next day or two, and the matter seemed to be settled until shortly after election the men named heard from several quarters that Mr. Taft was considering their successors. Naturally, they came to me about it, and investigation proved that the rumors were true. All four men were slated to go.

"Senator Lodge, of Massachusetts, interested himself in behalf of George Meyer and persuaded Taft to reconsider his decision. In order to have this new decision hold until the appointment was made, I sent for Meyer one day while Taft was calling upon me, and told Taft that Meyer was on his way over to thank him for the assurance he had given Lodge the day before.

"Perhaps if the matter had been permitted to drift, Taft might have changed his mind again. As it was he and Wilson were the only men continued, although Hitchcock was restored to the place he resigned when he became Taft's campaign manager.

"Now, to go back to the period of the campaign, I found

as we got into September that Taft was drifting more and
more away from the men with whom he had been identified.
I do not refer to myself alone, for I tried hard to keep out of
his affairs except to the extent that he and others with him
believed I could be helpful. But a policy of exclusion of all
the men who had any relation at all with me or what I stood
for seemed to have been inaugurated, under the guidance of
Charles and Henry Taft."

CHAPTER XLVIII

"MY HAT'S IN THE RING!"

The News Stirred The Deadened Party Waters Into Tempest-Tossed Waves Through 1912—Roosevelt's Early Refusals Cost Many Delegates—"Let Taft Take His Spanking," Said The Colonel—Taft Named Because "There's Nothing Else To Do"—"Gentlemen, They're Off!" Said Roosevelt—Walter Brown Urges A Columbus Speech And Promises A Crowd That Will Tie Up The Trolley Lines Of The City—It Does That, And More, Too.

"MY hat's in the ring!"—Roosevelt.

"Death alone can take me out now!"—Taft.

"I'm nobody's cloak. I'll fight to the finish!"—La Follette.

These three declarations in the early weeks of 1912 gave Republicans warning of a more destructive storm than the party had ever been called upon to weather. The Mugwump revolt in the Blaine campaign of 1884 was a summer breeze compared with the typhoon-like character of this new conflict, though in each year the Republican party was split and a Democrat elected President. It was not out of line with the emotional character of the 1912 campaign that, toward its close, the country was startled by the shooting of Roosevelt while in Milwaukee.

Clouds had been gathering over Republican councils ever since the 1910 Congress elections had demonstrated that the Taft Administration was not in favor. The Republican national committee, meeting at Washington in December, 1911, in the spirit of men arranging funeral services, had chosen Chicago, June 18, as the place and time for the national convention. The absurd idea that every President must be renominated, and the known power of a President to force his own renomination, led Republican leaders gloomily to accept

Taft as inescapable and to prepare to take their licking at the polls in November.

"There's nothing else to do," was the hopeless answer to inquiries.

The announcements from Taft and La Follette were accepted as perfunctory campaign literature. Not a ripple disturbed the mill-pond stillness of party waters. A fog-bank of inevitable defeat enveloped everyone. Nothing mattered much.

When later Roosevelt threw his hat in the ring, however, all knew stirring times were ahead; at once the waters lost their calmness.

NOBODY KNEW—NOT EVEN THE COLONEL

Before his announcement there had been rumors, plenty of them, that Roosevelt would be in the field. Many friends had been asserting it, many denying it, many hoping it, many deploring it. *Nobody knew—not even the Colonel himself.* Had he known it and decided it five or six weeks earlier than he did, his majority in the Chicago convention would have been too big to be tampered with; but that's another story.

Some people will always believe that Roosevelt eagerly sought the 1912 nomination, despite all that may be said to them by those close to him and who knew his mind. I realize the futility of endeavoring to change an unchangeable opinion. I have no illusions of that kind. The story I tell is my own experience, my own knowledge and my own interpretation. I must let it go at that.

Roosevelt had the privilege of every other citizen to seek the nomination, and if I believed that he did actually desire it I would offer no apology in his behalf. He was a citizen, a Republican, and out of office; no voters had to support him in the primaries unless they cared to do so. In the long list of delegates elected for him in the tremendous sweep of state-wide primaries all had to win despite the antagonism of a national administration's patronage and influence.

"NOT YET, BUT SOON"

"LET TAFT TAKE HIS SPANKING"

I suppose I talked AT Colonel Roosevelt a dozen times during the last three months of 1911. My voice was only one of many—most of the others being important Republican leaders in different States. All had the same experience—he did not want the nomination. The reader will recall the talk I print on an earlier page in which he stated some of his reasons.

When the National Committee in Washington adjourned the gloom among the members led them to gather in groups discussing the hopeless outlook. One group was composed of Walter Brown, of Ohio, Frank Knox, then of Michigan and now of New Hampshire, and Edward Lee, of Indiana. Each of these men was chairman of his State organization. They agreed that only a Roosevelt candidacy would have any hope of success, and determined to go to New York city to see the Colonel. They telephoned him they were going over to see him. He asked them not to do so. Their visit would be misconstrued.

"Some other members of the committee have said they wanted to see me," he continued, "and I have told them the same thing."

Still they persisted. It was finally agreed that the three State Chairmen would call at Oyster Bay next day.

When they arrived the Colonel did not wait for his visitors to state their views. He began the talk:

"I am not in this situation," he said, "and I am not going to be dragged into it. Taft created it and let Taft take his spanking for it. There is no reason why I should. If I wanted four years more in the White House I would say so and go after it; but I don't want it. I've had enough. I couldn't go back without risking all I gained in the seven years I was there."

NOT THE ONLY MAN WHO COULD WIN

"Colonel," interrupted Frank Knox, "I never knew you to show the white feather, and you should not do so now."

"What do you mean by that?" asked Roosevelt, astonished and angered.

"Why you are basing your refusal on the possibly bad effect another term might have on your reputation," replied Knox. "I contend that you ought to look at this thing from the party's interests and not your own. The party has honored you, and it now turns to you to do a service for it. It is in distress and it needs you."

"By George," said Roosevelt, "that would be a good argument if I were the only man available, but I am not. I agree that Taft cannot be elected. I do not know that any Republican can be elected, but if the party can win I am not the only Republican with whom it can win. I am not ungrateful for the honor I have had, but I think I have repaid in service. When I left the White House every State we had any right to expect was in the Republican column. It is not my job to put them back again."

The three chairmen left Oyster Bay convinced that Roosevelt could not be induced to run.

I knew nothing of this Brown-Lee-Knox interview. I, too, had been in Washington while the National Committeemen were in session; I, too, had returned to New York determined to try to change Roosevelt's point of view. I saw him at the "Outlook" office. It was the same old story,—no, no, no!

George W. Perkins, Frank Munsey, William L. Ward and others urged vigorously and had the same experience.

With the new year, however, came insistent demands from all over the country. Telegrams, letters, visitors crowded in on him. Little by little he began to modify his "no"; little by little he began to ask questions about conditions in one State and another.

"GENTLEMEN, THEY'RE OFF!"

I shall never forget the evening meeting in J. West Roosevelt's home in New York city early in February, 1912, when Roosevelt acquiesced. The house was a typical old New York home. A score of us had distributed ourselves in the nooks and corners of what New Yorkers once called their "back parlor." The hair-covered chairs and sofas with their curving mahogany frames were in keeping. Father Knickerbocker would have rejoiced at sight of them.

The Colonel sat in an arm chair, high-backed and wide, in the center of the room directly under the chandelier, the frosted glass globes of which only dimly-lighted the room. First, Governor Hadley, of Missouri, and other Governors present, talked, then the party leaders from different States; then the three or four editors.

Every man gave his frank opinion as to his own State as well as the nation. The Colonel made inquiries of each of us but expressed no opinion. Finally, we had had our say. There was an interval. Many of us began exchanging views in a low tone, while waiting for the Colonel to speak. He was evidently doing some hard thinking. Suddenly he raised his hands high, outstretching them as though in benediction. Quickly closing them he brought his fists down like a flash, each fist striking an arm of his chair with a bang and in a tone almost a shout, exclaimed:

"Gentlemen, they're off!"

We knew the presidential race had started!

BROWN GETS THE COLONEL FOR COLUMBUS

Walter Brown had come on from Ohio for the meeting and also to persuade Roosevelt to address the State Constitutional Convention then in session at Columbus, Ohio.

"Colonel," he said, "Wilson came out to Columbus and didn't cause a ripple, Taft came out and there was not enough of a crowd to halt a trolley car; if you will come there will be such a crowd that the whole traction system of Columbus will be tied up."

The Colonel was strongly against a speech-making campaign. He thought the contest should be conducted on higher lines. Brown, however, argued that a Constitutional Convention dealt with organic law; it was not an ordinary gathering. The Colonel could accept the invitation of such a body without being compelled to speak elsewhere.

Finally the Colonel said he would go provided certain men would approve. William L. Ward, of Westchester County, New York, George Perkins, Medill McCormick and two others whom I cannot recall were named. I was the sixth member of the group. We met next afternoon at the Perkins

As I Knew Them

house. The final vote stood five in favor of going to Columbus. Ward asked for time to think it over. So far as I know, he is still thinking it over. The Colonel accepted the verdict of the jury and agreed to go.

ROOSEVELT OBJECTS TO TWO-REVOLUTION MEN

Meanwhile La Follette's followers were crowding into New York city, to urge Roosevelt to accept their platform and become their candidate. Governor Hiram Johnson, just then emerging as a national figure, was in the group, which comprised all types of radicals.

La Follette's collapse physically in Philadelphia made it doubtful whether he would ever regain his health, still more doubtful that he would be able to carry on his battle for the nomination.

"I can stand one-revolution men," commented Roosevelt when he heard the names of some of those who were to call upon him, "but two-revolution fellows are too much for me; they want to be revolting all the time. I cannot be their candidate."

CHAPTER XLIX

THAT COLUMBUS SPEECH

La Follette's Lieutenants Sought To Edit The "Recall of Judicial Decisions" Address, But Roosevelt Stuck To The Lines Of His "Outlook" Editorial—Nevertheless, The Country Was Astounded And The Colonel Knew He Had Made A Mistake—It Surely Tied Up More Than The Trolleys Of Columbus—Roosevelt Surprised And Depressed—A Campaign Of Real Spirit—Where Roosevelt Won—Barnes And La Follette As Allies.

IT was unfortunate that the visit of the La Follette men to Roosevelt happened while he was preparing his Columbus speech. They insisted that he should say something to justify them in going over to him in a body. They made a number of suggestions; some he accepted, many he rejected. The big battle between them came over the recall of judges. That was a popular issue in the western States, as dear to the La Follette men as 16 to 1 was to Bryan. The Colonel flatly refused to endorse it. He had them read his signed editorial in "The Outlook" of January 6. Several days of discussion resulted in Roosevelt's concession that the recall of judges might be advocated "as a last resort" but he insisted that the "last resort" was far in the future and not justified by existing conditions. On this basis he resumed work on his speech.

Many others besides the La Follette men saw the first draft of the document and urged their widely differing views. Some did not like the subject, urging other topics; but so far as I ever heard no one foresaw the damaging effect of the speech. The final revision was read by Frank Munsey, E. C. Converse and William L. Ward in the Vanderbilt Hotel, New York

As I Knew Them

City. When the Colonel heard from that group he turned to me and said: "Don't let anyone know you have that speech. Give it to the Associated Press. I don't want to see it again. I want to be able to say that it is out of my hands."

TYING UP THE COLUMBUS TRAFFIC

Meanwhile, out in Ohio, Walter Brown was hustling to make good his assertion that the Colonel's appearance in

From the Cincinnati Enquirer.

IN THE RING AFTER IT

Columbus would tie up the city's traction system. The State seemed to be awaiting his arrival. On his way out, Roosevelt stopped over-night in Cleveland. Of course the local reporters sought an interview; of course they wanted to know whether he had decided to run.

Then came that historic declaration that flashed over the country like a streak of lightning.

"My hat's in the ring! The fight is on and I'm stripped to the buff!"

396

Next morning he went on to Columbus. It snowed hard. Nevertheless the crowd that Brown had prophesied was on hand to tie up the trolley system.

It was not the tie-up of the trolleys, however, that concerned Roosevelt and others next day when they read the newspaper headlines featuring the recall of judicial decisions, and adding interviews with lawyers strongly denouncing the Colonel's utterance.

"It looks to me as though we had tied up the whole campaign as well as the Columbus trolleys," I wired to George Perkins, who had gone to California.

Newspapers and politicians opposed to Roosevelt pounced upon the speech as though it were a new and surprising declaration by the Colonel "to catch the crowd." Yet they should have known that substantially every thought in it was printed in his signed editorial "Judges and Progress" in "The Outlook" six weeks earlier.

THE STORM AMAZED ROOSEVELT

Many theories might be advanced for the explosion that followed this reiteration of his views. Their first publication had created no such consternation. Of course, in January, he had not declared himself a candidate, while only the night before his Columbus speech he had thrown his hat in the ring. Probably that accounts for the different reaction. Whatever the explanation may be the fact is that it was the most sensational campaign utterance since Burchard's "Rum, Romanism and Rebellion" speech in 1884.

Roosevelt, like Blaine, was amazed. Just as Blaine refused for several days to make any effort to repair the damage Burchard had done, so not until a week later, when he visited the Massachusetts Legislature, did Roosevelt look upon the agitation as more than a flurry. In Boston he was staggered and depressed by the fierceness of the assaults upon him.

He had never been called upon to meet such a storm, and he could not understand it.

I do not share the opinion that the speech cost him the nomination. I do not believe that in the net result at Chicago it cost him a single delegate. In the East, the delegates he failed to secure were under "organization" control and would not have been for him anyhow. In New York City, for instance, with or without the Columbus speech, he had no chance against the local machine headed by Samuel S. Koenig. Koenig fought fair, but he fought to win. The West liked what Roosevelt had said.

The Columbus speech hurt because it intensified the opposition not because it cost votes in the convention. It always cut Roosevelt to the quick to be assailed as a reckless radical, and on this occasion the assaults depressed him because some came from men who he thought knew his purposes in life.

ROOSEVELT, FIRST DEPRESSED, THEN VIGOROUS

The letters and telegrams that deluged Roosevelt following his speech and the incidents of a visit to Boston, where he addressed the Legislature, put the Colonel in a frame of mind to abandon the whole campaign.

Such spells of despondency never lasted long with him, however.

He went to work on his reply to the Governors of seven States who had united in a joint request for him to enter the primaries. All his old-time vigor came out in that reply. He knew precisely what he wanted to say and how he wanted to say it, and no revisionists dotted an I or crossed a T. In that letter you will find the real Roosevelt.

Steadily the contest developed. Reluctantly Roosevelt agreed to speak—first in one place, then in another—until at last he was booked for a tour as in a Presidential campaign. He had resisted that kind of a contest, but the appeals for him to speak here, there and everywhere were beyond his control. Had he foreseen them I doubt whether he would have undertaken the fight.

"FIGURE OUT HOW MUCH YOU WANT," SAID MUNSEY

With the struggle in progress, however, he put himself in the hands of Senator Joseph Dixon of Montana, and Oscar King Davis, chairman and secretary of the campaign committee, and like a trained soldier he obeyed orders. When Dixon and Davis came over from Washington to New York in February to be told that they were to conduct the fight for delegates, they asked the obvious question how much they could spend for publicity and where the money would come from.

"Figure out how much you want," said Frank Munsey.

After some discussion Dixon finally said, "We ought to be sure of $50,000."

"I'll underwrite that much if you two will take the midnight train back to Washington and start work tomorrow morning," replied Munsey.

"Done!" was the joint response.

The campaign thus begun brought out every energy and enthusiasm of those engaged in it. If you were interested in it at all you were overwhelmingly interested. Sacrifice of time, of money, of comfort, meant nothing; to win delegates was the one thought. Sacrifices were never made so freely as in the fight for Roosevelt's nomination. Certainly in the subsequent Progressive party campaign for election, individual ambitions were thrust aside as never before. For many persons, their course meant exile from party honors for years to come. All knew it and all accepted.

If the experience was not the biggest thing in our lives it was the finest—the one we knew would be the best remembered by each of us in years to come; there were no doubters, no timid ones; we believed we were engaged in a battle for the right, and we battled with the fervor of the righteous.

As I Knew Them

Of the struggle to elect delegates to the convention, of the fight in Chicago against the steam-roller that ousted enough Roosevelt delegates to give Taft control, the story is too familiar to be told again. William L. Ward, George Perkins and Frank Munsey were the directing heads. It was the first experience in politics for Perkins and Munsey, but Ward, of course, was even then a veteran.

You couldn't pull a trigger faster than Perkins could act. Time and again in the late afternoon he would have a dozen telephone conferences with as many different States, so as to have action everywhere at once. Down in Washington, Senator Dixon and Oscar King Davis were also fighting with tireless energy, for they had Congress as well as the country to look after.

Roosevelt did not lose a State in which a primary was held, except Wisconsin and North Dakota, where La Follette won. Those victories meant that the great Republican States of the nation were lined against the Republican President they had supported four years before. One of the strongest influences in the primaries was a series of articles in Munsey's Magazine by Judson C. Welliver, entitled "Catching up with Roosevelt" —revealing Taft's inability to do so. More than a million copies were distributed.

A vote-making campaigner and a real joy to all of us was Bainbridge Colby. He was never more ready in wit, brilliant in phrasing or vigorous in assault than when he was darting out to fill over-night speaking engagements. Enthusiastic, tireless and determined, he inspired everyone to greater effort. Colby also led the battle for the Roosevelt delegates before the national committee. Had the Southern delegates, chiefly colored, controlled by office-holders been taken out of the Taft column, Roosevelt would have had almost two to one of the convention. As it was, he had two-thirds of the delegates from

Republican States, and a clear majority of the whole convention, but the national committee saw to it that the temporary roll of the convention was made up with a majority for Taft.

Making up that roll was the last work of the committee before it officially ceased to exist. It had been chosen in 1908. As soon as the convention met, each State would name a committeeman and a new committee would thus be formed. Could the contests have come before the new committee, chosen by the just-elected delegates, the Taft forces would have had only a minority of its members, and no unseating would have succeeded.

The absurd custom still prevails that a national committee which goes out of office with the opening of a convention dictates the temporary officers and makes out the roll of delegates. It is a sort of dead man's hand over the initial proceedings. However, in 1912, the dead man's hand had a lively knowledge of its baleful influence, for Bainbridge Colby and other speakers did not spare them.

BARNES AND LA FOLLETTE AS ALLIES

I have always insisted that two men were chiefly responsible for the defeat of progressivism at Chicago—Robert M. La Follette and William Barnes, Jr., then boss of the Republican machine in the State of New York, and field marshal of Taft's working forces in the national convention. No two men in politics were further apart in purpose than La Follette and Barnes. They had not one thing in common except the defeat of Roosevelt. It was an unusual coalition. It exemplified the old saying that politics make strange bedfellows, but never stranger than these two men with heads on one pillow dreaming the same dream—Barnes, a reactionary of the straitest sect, La Follette, progressive.

Barnes, resourceful and daring, directed the ousting of Roosevelt delegates by the national committee. He furnished the brains and the courage. The Committeemen furnished the votes. Barnes' task was to get enough Taft delegates on the temporary roll to elect Elihu Root as temporary chairman. Control of the convention would naturally follow.

La Follette, self-centered and vindictive, declared that the leadership of the Progressive cause belonged to him and to him only. He was determined that no one should displace him. He preferred to have the reactionaries remain in control—even nominate Taft—rather than have anyone but himself come out of the battle as leader. His own candidacy for

THE OLD ORDER—THE LASH OF THE BOSS

the nomination had degenerated from an ambitious hope that he would be named to a vengeful determination not to allow any other Progressive, especially Roosevelt, to be named. North Dakota was the only State supporting La Follette outside of Wisconsin. The delegates from those two States pleaded with him to release them from their instructions so that they could vote for Roosevelt, but he threatened lifelong antagonism to anyone who broke from his column.

Holding his delegates in a detached group, varying from seventeen to forty according to circumstances, was the La Follette way of cooperating with Barnes. He meant just that many less votes for Roosevelt.

As I Knew Them

When the test vote came, Root had 558 votes or a majority of 38 in a total vote of 1078.

Thus, "Fighting Bob's" rule or ruin attitude made him the ally of reactionary forces he had been denouncing for years. He and Barnes made Taft possible. Had Barnes been less daring or La Follette more true to the cause than to his own revenges, Taft would not have been nominated.

CHAPTER L

THE PROGRESSIVE CONVENTION

*Personality, Plenty Of It, Reigned And Rejoiced—A "Call" Or A Plat-
form—Munsey Talks Dieting To Roosevelt—Beveridge Insists On His
Day—"I Want To Be A Bull Moose"—A Great Speech By Beveridge—"We Stand At Armageddon."*

IF YOU did not attend the convention of the national Progressive party in 1912, you missed a thrilling and memorable occasion. Whether or not you agreed with its purpose, you
couldn't help applauding its spirit, its tensity, its honest belief
that it stood at Armageddon and was battling for the Lord.
Its equal has not been held in my day. Every delegate was his
own commander, and delighted in nothing so much as in challenging the right of anyone to stop him thinking and advocat-
ing anything he pleased.

Perhaps this independence was emphasized by the fact that
every delegate and alternate paid his own expenses, and
naturally felt entitled to something out of the usual. Those
not familiar with political conventions may not realize what
it means when I say that every delegate and alternate paid his
own expenses. Such a thing never happens in a regular party
convention. Rival candidates for nomination are anxious to
pay the bills of their supporters. The total often reaches high
figures. We had no rival candidates in the Progressive convention. There was only one man to nominate.

There was a deeper reason, though, for compelling all who
attended to pay their own way. No one knew what kind of
a convention could be assembled in Chicago in midsummer at
a month's notice. We knew that it would tell us, by the size
and earnestness of its membership, whether or not there was a

As I Knew Them

real response "from the bushes" to the revolt from Taft. We wanted that test made on the right basis.

There would be no test if railroad fares and hotel bills were paid in advance. Two convention halls easily could be filled if that were done. A real test could be made only by establishing a rule against providing a dollar for such expenditures, and trusting to luck for a quorum in the convention. At least we would know whether we had a convention or only a caucus. This rule was rigidly adhered to,—even when it was evident that men who had attended the Taft convention could not actually afford a second one. This pay-your-own-way plan proved a success.

PERSONALITY REIGNED AND REJOICED

Instead of lessening the number of delegates as some feared, there were double delegations from many States. A finer body of men and women never were gathered. Personality reigned everywhere,—there was plenty of it and to spare —from Gov. Hiram Johnson, of California, who was in the Seventh Heaven of delight, because he was in revolt; to Charles Sumner Bird, of Boston; "Bill" Flynn, of Pittsburgh; Cuney, the Texas Leaguer unseated in the Taft convention; Francis J. Heney, of California; the suave and eloquent William A. Prendergast, of Brooklyn (who made a brilliant speech nominating Roosevelt); Bainbridge Colby afire with indignation over the national committee's steam-roller; E. A. Van Valkenburg, of Philadelphia; William Allen White and Henry Allen, of Kansas; Oscar S. Straus, Chauncey Hamlin and Paul Block, of New York; and the famous western Governors who had round-robined Roosevelt into running.

You could get a spark, a flash, of hot discussion from a group of delegates as easily as a smithy hammers one out on an anvil. The joy of friction began long before the convention assembled.

It began early in July with the call for the convention.

As I Knew Them

Burdened and perplexed with many other demands, Roosevelt had undertaken to write the call. As usual, he showed the draft to one person; then to another. All had suggestions. The Colonel had his hardest struggle to keep the term Republican out of the new party title. He insisted that Republican

From the N. Y. Sun.

"THE OPEN ROAD"

was a hopeless name down South; with a party having some other title, he could gain thousands of votes there. He might even carry one or two States. Roosevelt thought splitting the "Solid South" would be a great political service.

A "CALL" OR A PLATFORM?

By the time he had accepted many suggestions the "call" was a document of 3,000 words. He sent it to Senator Joseph

Dixon, in New York city, with instructions to lock it in his desk until released next day (Sunday) for the Monday newspapers. Dixon put it in his desk but failed to lock the desk. I happened along while Dixon was out to lunch; seating myself at his desk I looked around for something to read until he returned. There lay the call! Without any thought of its contents I picked up the manuscript, and began to read it. Frank Munsey came in at that moment and asked me what I had found to interest me so deeply. I told him and began to read it aloud to him. I had not read far before he stopped me and said, "That's not a call, it's a platform. We don't want to send out anything like that."

"It's all interlined with T. R.'s handwriting," I replied, "and I guess it will have to go."

While we were talking, Dixon returned with Perkins. His eyes fell on the document in my hands, and if he were not a Quaker I am sure he would have used unprintable language. Munsey insisted on cutting more than half of the "call." I agreed with him. For an hour we discussed it. Then Perkins telephoned the Colonel that it wouldn't do. What was said I do not know. Perkins laughingly said he did not care to be shot; he would not go to Oyster Bay to discuss it. He left for home. Finally, another telephone talk, and Munsey and I were asked to go to Oyster Bay, to supper—and discussion.

When we got there, a hot July night, we found the Colonel in anything but a placid mood. "There are ño two men I would ordinarily welcome here more cordially than you two," is the way he greeted us, "but tonight, in view of your mission, there are no two men I want less to see."

MUNSEY TALKS DIETING TO ROOSEVELT

At the evening meal, Munsey sat on the Colonel's right and I sat on his left. Every moment I felt there would be an explosion, for Munsey had been studying dieting and he kept telling the Colonel how wrong it was to eat cold roast beef and

baked Idaho potatoes. Roosevelt was taking a plentiful helping of both. Nor did Munsey believe in salt, which the
Colonel indulged in heavily. The peril of heavy eating and
the benefits of light eating were told us with the deadly
earnestness of a revival preacher. Still the Colonel kept on
eating. He would look—almost glare—at Munsey and then
take another mouthful; look again, listen a moment, and then
go at the roast beef with renewed gusto.

All the time our threatened revision of the "call" was also
on Roosevelt's mind—and nerves.

Several attempts were made by others at the table to divert
the conversation to other topics than dieting. But Munsey
was always deeply in earnest in anything that interested him,
and it was difficult to get him away from a subject until he
felt that he had enlightened and convinced his listeners. On
that occasion he was doing almost everything but convincing.
He did not lessen by an ounce the Colonel's meal. My own
appetite went unsatisfied because I kept trying to decide on
what I would do when the Colonel would blurt out his impatience. The Colonel, however, stuck to his food and his
patience.

Soon, we were in the library discussing the "call." It was
midnight before the document was cut to half its original
length.

"Now, gentlemen," said the Colonel as we left for New
York city, "we have had our battle tonight and you have
won. You were right. It would have been a mistake to have
allowed that call to go as it was."

That was a typical Roosevelt surrender,—frank and complete.

BEVERIDGE INSISTS ON HIS DAY

The Progressive convention was called for August 5 at
Chicago. Senator Albert J. Beveridge, of Indiana, who was
slated for temporary chairman, was also to make the opening

address. Roosevelt was anxious that every delegate should know at the outset precisely what the new party meant. It was arranged, therefore, that he was to speak immediately after Beveridge. When the Indiana Senator learned that he and Roosevelt were bunched in the same afternoon, there was an outburst that threatened for a time the whole convention schedule. Beveridge declared, quite properly, that the papers would publish the Roosevelt speech and minimize his. Two stars could not shine in the same firmament. Beveridge telephoned from York Harbor, Maine, insisting upon a day to himself or no speech.

Gov. John N. Parker, of Louisiana, who was scheduled for permanent chairman, was entitled to his opportunity on the second day, and there were a score of orators for the third and last day. Thus the task of arranging speakers was as delicate as arranging the precedence of diplomats at a dinner. There were not enough days to go around. The Colonel had prepared what he called a "Confession of Faith." It contained 20,000 words, even after Oscar King Davis had edited it down to a point at which the Colonel stoutly demurred. But Roosevelt still insisted upon speaking the first day, and so did Beveridge.

Finally, in the Colonel's library, Davis evolved the theory that a big 16 inch gun should follow and not precede a little gun. Roosevelt should have the second day, provided Parker would yield as permanent Chairman. Parker generously yielded—and Beveridge and the Colonel each had his day.

Such were two of many incidents in that gathering destined to make political history. They tried one's patience and one's nerves, but they were the outcroppings of intense earnestness, and finally melded into a great enthusiasm that swept us along through three months of hard, up-hill campaigning until the last ballot was cast on election day.

We did not win the election, but we had been in battle, and the zest of conflict, the thrill of a stubborn fight for what we believed was right had stirred us more deeply than any other political contest ever had before or is likely to do again.

The convention was in the mood for a jubilant, heroic time. Every State delegation entered the hall in marching order cheering and being cheered. Governor Hiram Johnson marched at the head of the Californians, whose banner read:

> "I want to be a Bull Moose,
> And with the Bull Moose stand
> With Antlers on my forehead
> And a Big Stick in my hand."

The Michigan men got the whole convention parading to the tune of their song:

> "Follow, follow,
> We will follow Roosevelt,
> Anywhere, everywhere,
> We will follow on!"

And the New York delegation, headed by Oscar S. Straus, marched through the aisles singing "Onward Christian Soldiers!" Surely, we were all set for a fine, care-free time;— in just the mood to greet Senator Beveridge's opening sentences as Chairman: "Knowing the price we must pay, knowing the sacrifice we must make, the burdens we must carry and the assaults we must endure,—knowing full well the cost, yet we enlist for the war!"

The Beveridge speech was one of the strongest ever delivered in a political convention; had it been made in a regular party convention, it would have been accorded a place in political oratory with the Conkling, Ingersoll, Garfield and Bryan speeches.

No wonder Roosevelt greeted him afterward with the exclamation "A great speech, Albert! I'm glad you insisted on your own day. It's worth two days!"

As I Knew Them

The speech was a splendid summary of Progressive purposes. These extracts give an indication of its trend:

"We stand for a nobler America. We stand for an undivided nation. We stand for a broader liberty, a fuller justice. We stand for social brotherhood as against savage individualism. We stand for an intelligent co-operation instead of a reckless competition. We stand for mutual helpfulness instead of mutual hatred. We stand for equal rights as a fact of life instead of a catchword of politics. We stand for the rule of the people as a practical truth instead of a meaningless pretence. We stand for a representative government that represents the people. We battle for the actual rights of man.

"For the party comes from the grass roots. It has grown from the soil of the people's hard necessities. It has the vitality of the people's strong convictions. The people have work to be done and our party is here to do that work. Abuse will only strengthen it, ridicule only hasten its growth, falsehood only speed its victory.

"The root of the wrongs which hurt the people is the fact that the people's government has been taken away from them. The government must be given back. And so the first purpose of the Progressive Party is to make sure the rule of the people. The rule of the people means that the people themselves shall nominate as well as elect all candidates for office, including Senators and presidents of the United States. What profiteth it the people if they do only the electing while the invisible government does the nominating?

"The first work before us is the revival of honest business. For business is nothing but the industrial and trade activities of all the people. Men grow the products of the field, cut ripe timber from the forest, dig metal from the mine, fashion all for human use, carry them to the market place and exchange them according to their mutual needs, and this is business.

"Present day business is as unlike old time business as the old time ox-cart is unlike the present day locomotive. Invention has made the world over again. The railroad, telegraph and telephone have bound the people of modern nations into families. To do the

411

business of these closely knit millions in every modern country great business concerns came into being. What we call big business is the child of the economic progress of mankind. Warfare to destroy big business is foolish because it cannot succeed and wicked because it ought not to succeed. Warfare to destroy big business does not hurt big business, which always comes out on top, so much as it hurts all other business which, in such a warfare, never comes out on top."

Beveridge concluded:

"The Progressive Party believes that the Constitution is a living thing, growing with the people's growth, strengthening with the people's strength, aiding the people in their struggle for life, liberty and the pursuit of happiness, permitting the people to meet all their needs as conditions change.

"The opposition believes that the Constitution is a dead form, holding back the people's growth, shackling the people's strength but giving a free hand to malign powers that prey upon the people.

"The first words of the Constitution are 'We the people' and they declare that the Constitution's purpose is 'to form a perfect union and to promote the general welfare.'

"To do just that is the very heart of the Progressive cause."

"WE STAND AT ARMAGEDDON!"

The same turbulence lasted throughout the three days' session. Roosevelt's appearance on the platform the second day led to an hour's demonstration, which was repeated when he closed with these words:

"To you men who have come together to spend and be spent in the endless crusade against wrong, to you who face the future resolute and confident, to you who strive in a spirit of brotherhood for the betterment of our nation, I say now as I said here six weeks ago, we stand at Armageddon and we battle for the Lord."

It was in the color of such a convention that no one should ask a formal roll call on any question or demand a ballot for candidates. We were voting enthusiasms, and they could neither be counted nor divided. It probably is the only na-

tional convention of which it can be said that it never had a roll
call or cast a ballot.

The great climax came when the two nominees, Roosevelt
and Johnson, appeared on the stage, walking side by side

THE SPIRIT OF 1912!

to the front, while a banner was unfolded from the rafters
above them reading:

> "Roosevelt and Johnson!
> New York and California
> Hands across the Continent!
> For there is neither east nor west
> Border nor breed nor birth,
> When two strong men stand face to face
> Though they come from the ends of the earth."

Naturally, that convention has a tender place in my memory.
I shared its spirit fully, and I prize the recollection of every
moment of those three days as a lifelong treasure. If the
earnestness and high purpose of those delegates could be put
into the conventions of the regular party organizations, there
would be no need for protests such as that of 1912.

CHAPTER LI

WAS 1912 A MISTAKE?

An Earnest Purpose, Even In Politics, Is Never A Mistake—An Endeavor To Save The Republican Party From Defeat With Taft—No Other Thought Back Of The Roosevelt Movement Until The Theft of Delegates—La Follette Would Not Do—Taft's Weakness, Not Roosevelt's Strength—A Result That Might Have Been Secured—Norman Mack's True Forecast.

WAS 1912 a mistake?

To many persons a lost battle is always a mistake. Historians then call it a revolt while if the battle had been won they would call it a revolution.

It is not what you say when you buckle on your sword that counts; it is what you are able to say when you take it off.

An earnest purpose, however, is never a mistake, even in politics. Those who strive honorably to achieve it and fail may well regret defeat, but they have no reason to regret their effort.

There is one place above all others in which to justify yourself—that place is in your conscience—

> Yet still there whispers the small voice within,
> Heard through Gain's silence and o'er Glory's din,
> Whatever creed be taught or land be trod
> Man's conscience is the oracle of God!

It may be that of the 4,150,000 voters who followed Roosevelt in 1912 there are some who in their own conscience—call it their political conscience if you care to do so—now believe they were unwise in doing so. I have not happened to meet many who take that view and personally I am not of the

414

number, whether large or small. My impression is that it is small.

If a refusal to see the Republican party go down to defeat, without endeavoring to save it, is a mistake, then the struggle to prevent Taft's renomination was a mistake.

If a refusal to condone the unseating of elected delegates to force the nomination of Taft after he had been clearly defeated in the primaries—particularly the primaries in all Republican States—is a mistake, then the Progressive party was a mistake.

It is conceded, I presume, that no one who opposed Taft's renomination had any thought at the outset that the movement would result in the organization of the Progressive party.

It may not be conceded, though it is none the less a fact, Roosevelt was made the candidate in the primaries not because he desired the nomination but because no other candidacy was likely to insure Republican success after the collapse of 1910.

It may not be conceded, though it is none the less a fact, that until the wrong decisions of the Chicago convention made it impossible for the anti-Taft delegates to do anything else, a bolt was not contemplated.

A FIGHT TO INSURE PARTY VICTORY

These points should be kept in mind by those who, either from prejudice or from lack of knowledge, insist that the protest against Taft's renomination was primarily an effort to put Roosevelt back in the White House. It was not. It was an effort to insure a Republican successor to a Republican President who could not be reelected.

The unpleasantness of opposing a President of your own party, the difficult task of overcoming in a nominating convention the power of presidential patronage, led many Republicans of the "organization" type to reconcile themselves to

Taft and defeat. Many justified their stand by the fact that they held office, or as patronage dispensers had secured office for others. Loyalty to the Administration controlled them, though it meant disloyalty to the party. Others insisted that a political organization must stand by its men in office and their record whether they have carried out its pledges or not. They

1912—THE RETURN FROM MOSCOW

declared that it meant defeat if they failed to renominate, and defeat if they renominated. Hence they favored renomination.

LA FOLLETTE WOULD NOT DO

Other Republicans beyond the influence of those two theories believed a candidate should be found. Throughout 1911 efforts were made to find one. The only candidacy that met with response was Senator La Follette—"Fighting Bob," of Wisconsin. Between defeat with Taft and possible success with La Follette, however, the bulk of Republicans, at least in the East, would have taken defeat. Ten or twelve years later, as the 1924 vote suggests, they might have accepted La Follette rather than defeat—but not in 1912.

Until Roosevelt threw his hat in the ring there was hope that someone else could be developed who would be strong enough, despite Taft patronage, to win the nomination. I know Roosevelt had this hope.

When he finally abandoned it, and became a candidate, it looked as though the Republican party would be able to crawl from under the Democratic avalanche of 1910. Its only chance to do so was by nominating Roosevelt. I do not believe there was one Republican leader, whether in the Taft column or out of it, who in January, 1912, honestly thought that Taft could be reelected.

TAFT'S WEAKNESS—NOT ROOSEVELT'S STRENGTH

The State-wide and district primaries for delegates to the convention reflected this Taft weakness. Substantially Roosevelt carried all of them. His delegates came from Republican territory while the Taft delegates came largely from doubtful or Democratic States, and from Congress districts controlled by Presidential patronage. Taft's weakness, not Roosevelt's strength, showed in the long list of Roosevelt delegates.

Had that condition been other than a guess before the primary tests, had it been realized that Taft's hold on his party was as feeble as his seven electoral votes from Vermont and Utah in November indicated, there is every probability that such a man as Herbert S. Hadley, then Governor of Missouri, would have been the anti-Taft candidate. Hadley might have secured almost as many delegates as Roosevelt. But contesting a nomination with a President in office is no holiday undertaking, and even some who were not over friendly to Roosevelt supported him finally because they believed he could be nominated over Taft and they were certain he could be elected over any Democrat.

As I Knew Them

Take a glance at the situation.

I repeat the statement I made as to the opinion of Republican leaders early in 1912—that Taft could not be elected—and assert that every delegate who voted for Taft's renomination in the Chicago convention knew he was nominating a candidate certain to be defeated, even were Roosevelt to support him. Most delegates candidly admitted it.

Some reader may ask here how I know the mind of every delegate in that convention inasmuch as I did not poll each delegate. Since they were all more or less in politics, they had the 1910 defeat in mind; they had in addition the indisputable evidence of the primary contests that that weakness continued to exist in 1912; in fact those contests showed Taft weaker. Assuming, therefore, as I do, that the delegates were competent to judge the situation, they must have known that a Taft candidacy was hopeless.

One might justify the Taft nomination by insisting that his defeat would be preferable to Roosevelt's election. Delegates had a right to that belief and to vote that way; but the exercise of that right carried responsibility for the consequences to the party on election day.

I do not contend that they should have turned to Roosevelt. I do not contend that they should have disobeyed telegraphic orders from the White House, and from Attorney General Wickersham and other Cabinet officers, to vote for Taft and defeat. I do insist, however, that any considerable number of them could have united on a compromise candidate and forced his nomination. This they talked about doing, but never did.

Just before the convention Taft was quoted as having said, "Whether I win or not is not the important thing; I am in this fight to perform a public duty—to keep Theodore Roosevelt out of the White House." Unfortunately, he kept out Roosevelt, the Republican party and himself. It was in his power to keep the party in, by keeping both Roosevelt and himself out, but he made no effort to do so.

NORMAN MACK'S TRUE FORECAST

I remember that Norman E. Mack, then chairman of the Democratic National Committee, said to me in New York City a week or so before the convention:

"We can beat Taft hands down if you nominate him; I am not so sure about beating Roosevelt but I think we can. You fellows will be split up if either man is named. If it is Taft we will nominate a liberal Democrat and get the liberal Republican vote; if Roosevelt is your candidate we will nominate a conservative and get the conservative Republican vote. That is why our folks believe we have you beaten."

"Suppose we don't nominate either man?" I asked.

"Then the Democrats will have a harder battle," replied Mack, "but you won't get away from Roosevelt and Taft. Neither of those fellows will give up."

This experienced Democratic authority gave a true picture of the possibilities of the Republican convention. His opinion that a new man would give the Democrats a hard battle was a correct analysis. Obviously, the suggestion of a compromise candidate could not come with controlling strength from the Roosevelt camp. After the adoption of the temporary roll, Roosevelt delegates were in a minority in the convention. Responsibility rested with those in control. They shrugged their shoulders at defeat and took Taft.

That determination was responsible for the change in political history that occurred in November; the Progressive party emphasized but it did not cause Taft's defeat. Had Roosevelt acquiesced in the Taft nomination, he could not have persuaded voters to follow his example. The tide was too strong. Taft seemed to have lost the power to interest the people—to interest even the partisans who vote at party primaries, for they had declared against him.

NOT A SUNDAY-SCHOOL

No one expects a political convention to be conducted like a Sunday-School. It is a battle ground and those engaged in combat know that the hardest blows are the only blows that count. Hard blows were anticipated at the 1912 convention, but not the kind of blows that would have ruled out any contender who delivered them in a fair fight. The unseating of delegates has been practiced in nearly all conventions. The contests usually reflect merely local factional dissensions. Occasionally they mean a handful of delegates for one or two out of half a dozen candidates for nomination; they seldom have broad significance. In 1912, however, the unseating was done to control the convention, its candidate and its platform. It was a duel. The 4,125,000 votes polled by Roosevelt are the best answer to those who ask which side in the convention voiced the spirit of the Republican party, which side was striving to do what Republicans wanted to have done. Those 4,125,000 votes also answer the question whether 1912 was a mistake.

CHAPTER LII

GEORGE PERKINS AND FRANK MUNSEY

Two Men, New to Politics, Whose Pledge Made Possible the Pro-
gressive Contest of 1912—as Strange as Any Friendship That Ever
Existed—Perkins Liked Politics and Kept On, but Munsey Sought
to "Amalgamate"—Perkins Tireless in Welfare Work.

GEORGE PERKINS and Frank Munsey influenced the
politics of this country in 1912 more than any other men
with whose activities at that time I am familiar. And, of
course, the events of 1912 had their marked influence on national politics until 1920.

There certainly would have been no national Progressive
party but for those two men; there probably would not have
been a Roosevelt candidacy for nomination in the convention
against Taft but for them. Perkins had executive ability,
great energy and money; Munsey, in addition, had his newspapers and magazines. Governors, State chairmen and local
leaders aplenty were urging Roosevelt into a contest with
Taft; but I doubt whether he would have acquiesced had he
not known that Perkins and Munsey would organize and
finance his battle. He realized that, without organization, his
forces would not be effective.

Six months later, in Chicago, when the decision was made to
bolt the regular party convention, they were the men on
whose word Roosevelt depended to insure a proper campaign
management.

Deliberately, I have used "probably" as to the battle for
nomination and "certainly" as to organizing the Progressive
party. I speak with full knowledge of the facts as to both.
Had either Perkins or Munsey faltered in Chicago, the call

for a national Progressive party convention would never have been issued. Therefore, I repeat that Perkins and Munsey influenced the politics of this country in 1912 more than any other two men.

The amazing feature of their activities that year was that neither of them had ever figured in politics before, and that Munsey had an intense dislike for politics and politicians. He avoided both whenever possible. Perkins, on the other hand, liked the activities and the excitement, and got deeper and deeper into the game. They had no other motive in urging Roosevelt to become a candidate for nomination than to save the Republican party from defeat with Taft.

In Chicago, they resented the theft of Roosevelt delegates and in that frame of mind refused to abide by the decisions of a convention that in their firm opinion had been stolen.

THE FRIENDSHIP BETWEEN THE TWO MEN

As strange as any friendship that ever existed between two men was the friendship lasting thirty years between Perkins and Munsey. They differed in temperament and in many characteristics. Both were positive individualistic men, each had to dominate in whatever he undertook; both were quick in temper and quicker still in action. Seldom a day passed that they did not meet. They knew each other's traits, and guided themselves accordingly. I knew both men intimately, sat with them often in discussion of public men and measures, and I never heard either of them advocate a course for a wrong motive or for his personal gain.

Frank Munsey, sitting alone in his apartment before a blaze of Maine maple logs, had a rare talent for seeing into the future, for analysis of a situation. It was there that he habitually sought the solution of all his problems and there that he made his plans. The day's work was merely carrying out those fireside decisions.

As I Knew Them

Once his course was thus determined, only actual experience would change him. He would insist upon a demonstration; no change was possible until it was proven that he was wrong. Then he would quickly change and admit his error. But he was not wrong often, though he frequently had to wait long to be justified. Let me cite one example.

I spent an evening with Munsey while Woodrow Wilson was returning from Paris acclaimed at home and abroad as a world leader. Wilson had his League of Nations covenant with him; opposition to it seemed small in number and less in hope. "The Senate will never ratify it," said Munsey, "and if it ever gets before the American people they will vote it down two to one. Every year that goes by will make us more and more thankful that we never entered the League."

I did not accept Munsey's prophecy—but it has come true.

PERKINS DEEP IN WELFARE WORK

Perkins was not so sure of himself as Munsey. He liked to confer with others and to search for facts. Once his mind was made up, however, he was never timid. I have known many men generous with their wealth but I know of no one who equalled Perkins in giving time, thought and money to the welfare of others. When he resigned from J. P. Morgan & Co., he told me he had all the money any man should possess; henceforth he would devote himself to public affairs—not public office. I know that he did so with a devotion that meant many sacrifices—in fact that really cost him his life.

Roosevelt as Governor had put him at the head of the Palisades Park Commission, some years earlier. He took hold of the enterprise as though it were his own, and made it the wonderful playground it now is for thousands of people unable to meet the cost of outings elsewhere. When the right man was needed to go to France, in 1919, to straighten out the

423

As I Knew Them

Y. M. C. A. tangle there, Perkins was chosen—and in that work he so exhausted himself that he was never well again.

Perkins and Munsey, so strongly united in friendship, never had a business transaction together; each sought and gained fortune in his own way. And they knew that their friendship would endure longer if business transactions were not involved. The one exception was the National Progressive Party of 1912. Perkins managed that battle, but Munsey agreed to share the deficit. Just the word of one friend to another, without a line in writing, was good enough for those two men to undertake a national campaign.

MUNSEY WANTED AN "AMALGAMATION"

True to his habit of abandoning experiments that did not work out Munsey abandoned the Progressive party promptly after the 1912 election. The figures, great as they were, proved that the party could not displace the Republican organization; division meant that the Democrats would continue to win. He made an elaborate analysis of the vote cast by the Republicans, Progressives and Democrats in each State, and showed that, by uniting, the Republicans and Progressives would control two-thirds of the States, as well as the Presidency and Congress.

Munsey promptly urged them to unite—an "amalgamation," as he called it in the terms of the day. In his signed appeal to "get together" Munsey cited the success of industrial amalgamations as an example, and insisted that political parties could be merged with similarly good results. In politics, however, two and two do not always make four, and the Munsey amalgamation did not gain the confidence of politicians.

However, other forces were slowly uniting the two wings of the old party, though it was not until 1920 that Time had accomplished what Munsey had so keenly visioned in 1912 as the real thing to do.

PERKINS STUCK IT OUT

Perkins did not accept the Munsey viewpoint. He did not believe in amalgamation. He had gone wholeheartedly into the Progressive party; he had seen it poll more electoral votes and more popular votes than the Republicans; his confidence and enthusiasm were not lessened because the party had come out second instead of first. He was for fighting on—and he did. Perkins, unlike Munsey, was an idealist. He gave much of his time to the Progressive organization, and abandoned it in 1916 with great regret for the same reasons as those that controlled Roosevelt. Criticism that Perkins was dominating Roosevelt through the years following 1912 did not affect the intimate, confident relations between the two men.

Perkins was not dominating—he was doing. While others talked, Perkins acted. The thing was done before others had started. Roosevelt saw that quality in Perkins and admired it. When the possibility of Roosevelt's return to the Presidency was discussed, a question often came up regarding his disposition of Perkins. Many thought Perkins would insist upon being Secretary of the Treasury, but Roosevelt told me that Perkins had notified him that he would never accept office. He did not care to be tied to a desk. The one office with any attraction for him was Secretary of Commerce and Labor—there he might help work out some welfare measures for labor. Nevertheless, he believed he could do better work out of public office than in it. So he freed Roosevelt of all obligation.

CHAPTER LIII

ROOSEVELT'S ONE PURPOSE: BEAT WILSON

Never Had Any Other Desire In 1916, But His Name Stalked Through Republican Committee Meeting Like Banquo's Ghost—Sails For West Indies To Avoid Situations—My Voyage To Trinidad And The Resulting Message To The Country To Get Into An "Heroic Mood"— A Letter From Elihu Root That Never Got To The Public—T. R. Hits Hard From Trinidad—Wilson Wanted Roosevelt As Opponent.

ROOSEVELT'S name and purpose attended like Banquo's ghost the meeting of the Republican National Committee in Washington, December, 1915, when the 1916 convention was fixed for Chicago, June 16. The same rumors of a Roosevelt candidacy heard at the meeting four years earlier disturbed the councils of the party chiefs.

In 1912 the rumors had been listened to with hope that they were true; now with dread. The committeemen knew that in the minds of the people Roosevelt was the only sharp contrast to Wilson, but 1912 was too close. Many Republicans were unwilling to accept a Roosevelt leadership even though it might lead to victory. Nevertheless, they were fearful of another contest in Republican primaries, and of another campaign of divided opposition to Wilson. Who could command unity? The committeemen looked inquiringly to the U. S. Supreme Court, where the sombre robes of an associate justice were an uninviting prospect for politicians; when they turned from that picture and looked upon other possible nominees the figures seemed so pale and thin that the Roosevelt apparition assumed substantial form; the committee meeting adjourned with many members confessing their inability to find a candidate so strong as the man they would not have.

ROOSEVELT'S ONLY CONCERN: BEAT WILSON

How little they knew that man!

More intent even than they to have Wilson defeated, moved by patriotic impulses to make every sacrifice that would insure unity and success, Roosevelt had no thought of a primary contest, and no desire except to find a candidate, who, if possible, would unite all Wilson opponents.

He, too, had vivid recollections of 1912. While he believed that there was common ground on which Republicans and Progressives could stand to fight Wilson there was still much ground that, in his opinion, they could not then occupy together. Therefore, while he was not concerned over their attitude toward him, he was concerned as to whether they would name a candidate that Progressives could accept. Whatever differences of opinion may exist as to Roosevelt's desires in 1912, there can be no honest belief that he had any purpose in 1916 other than to find the man most certain to beat Wilson. And his supreme reason for desiring Wilson's defeat was his conviction that the President's timid policies were forcing the nation on the rocks.

Far back as October, 1915, Roosevelt said to me: "At best this war will be a stalemate for the Allies unless America gets into it. I don't say that Germany will win, but I do say that the Allies cannot. They may check Germany, but not more. For us the question to determine is whether we will get into this war with the Allies cooperating with us, or go into a later war against Germany without help from the Allies. Wilson ought to see that we must make a choice. I wish he would realize stern facts and not keep up in the clouds. I don't want to be constantly criticizing him; I would like to stand shoulder to shoulder with him—if he ever takes a stand I shall be with him."

427

As I Knew Them

It was not difficult that year for Roosevelt to prevent independent Republicans from using his name as a candidate in the party primaries; he promptly stopped the first efforts. It was difficult, though, to determine an attitude toward the Progressive National Convention. Should it precede or follow the Republican Convention? Should it be held at all? Many Progressives were against a convention. They argued that it would end all hope of unifying the anti-Wilson forces. It would put new life into an organization that if left alone would disappear before campaign time. Other Progressives argued that a convention was necessary as a club to force the Republicans to an acceptable nomination; they believed that agreement on such a nominee could be brought about.

In that belief the convention was called for the same time and place as the Republican Convention. It was a mistake that led to the most humiliating episode in Roosevelt's career. He would have been wiser had he promptly faced the inevitable and allowed the Progressive organization to drift out of existence, as it was doing, for delay only made his position more difficult. But Roosevelt was controlled by loyalty to old friendships; he did not want to be charged with abandoning a cause. He was confident that when the convention met he could persuade it to his view.

With that course settled, he began holding conferences, beginning with one in the apartments of William Hamlin Childs, with Horace Wilkinson, George W. Perkins, E. A. Van Valkenberg and others. All agreed that the nomination of a "reactionary" by the Republican National Convention would compel a Progressive ticket, but there was more than one interpretation of "reactionary." The divided opinion then expressed should have warned the Colonel of the spirit that would surely prevail in the Progressive Convention, but it did not. He never lost faith that it would see the situation as he saw it. He had to notice, however, that others did not share that faith.

AN UNPUBLISHED LETTER FROM ELIHU ROOT

Finally, in January, to take himself out of embarrassing political situations, he sailed for a tour of the West Indies. It was agreed that he was to remain silent while away. Before his steamer had reached its first port of call, it was stated in New York City by someone who claimed to have seen it that Elihu Root had written a letter to be read a month hence, at a meeting of Republican leaders in Chicago, in which, while he declared he was not a candidate for President, he outlined a sort of platform for Republicans that was substantially a summary of Roosevelt policies.

It was alleged that despite his refusal, Root was providing a platform for himself. Some Republicans opposed to a Root candidacy urged that the Colonel should anticipate the Root essay by a new statement of his own views. The Root letter was addressed to Frederick C. Tanner, then Republican State chairman. Its fate is a political mystery. It was not read at the Chicago meeting, nor, so far as I know, has it ever been made public. The discussion in New York city regarding its contents led to a series of cables to Roosevelt, which in turn led to a suggestion from him that I should catch up with him in Trinidad, and explain what was desired of him in such a hurry and in view of the understanding that he was to say nothing.

Germany's sub-marines were then making ocean travel anything but a pleasure trip, but it seemed to me that if Colonel Roosevelt could risk a tour of the Atlantic with Mrs. Roosevelt there was no reason why I should hold back. The steamer leaving next day carried Mrs. Stoddard and myself to Trinidad. There I met the Colonel and from there I cabled his one thousand word statement—a statement that stirred Republican politics. It took nearly two days to give the proper tone and phrasing to the document. I was impatient to get it on the cable, and the delay in preparation left me in no mood to meet with equanimity the slow processes of the English censor in satisfying himself that no secret conspiracy in behalf of Germany lay concealed in Roosevelt's words!

It seems incredible that a statement from an ex-President of the United States, especially from one who at the moment was being fêted in Trinidad, should be held up "for consideration." Nevertheless I had to abandon a trip to the asphalt lake with government officials and the Colonel, to waste time persuading the censor that there was no hidden help to Germany in the document. I sat by the cable operator's side until the last word had gone, so as to be ready for any new objection from the censor.

"UNLESS THE COUNTRY IS IN HEROIC MOOD"

A few days later we were amazed to learn from home dispatches that the statement was regarded by some Republicans as a bid for the nomination. This feeling was reflected at a banquet in Trinidad, where the Colonel was greeted as the next President of the United States. He tried to explain the situation, but they would not see it. Nevertheless, he told the banqueters that his sole purpose was to arouse the country to the peril of a pacifist mood, and that he regarded his own nomination as too unlikely to be discussed seriously.

In that statement the Colonel said:

> "I am not the least interested in the personal fortunes either of myself or any other man. I am interested in awakening my fellow countrymen to the need of facing unpleasant facts. I am interested in the triumph of the great principles for which with all my heart and soul I have striven and shall continue to strive.
>
> "I will not enter into any fight for the nomination, and I will not permit any factional fight to be made in my behalf. Indeed, I will go further and say that it would be a mistake to nominate me unless the country has in its mood something of the heroic;

unless it feels not only like devoting itself to ideals, but to the purpose measurably to realize those ideals in action.

"This is one of those rare times which come only at long intervals in a nation's history when the action taken determines the life of the generations that are to follow. Such times were those from 1776 to 1789 in the days of Washington, and from 1858 to 1865 in the days of Lincoln. . . .

"Nothing is to be hoped from the present Administration. The struggles today between the President and his party leaders in

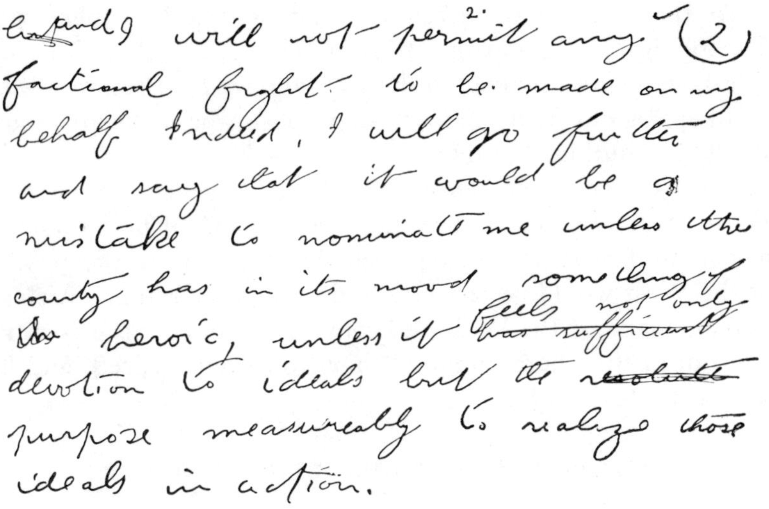

[handwritten manuscript page]

A PAGE WRITTEN BY ROOSEVELT FOR ME AT TRINIDAD

Congress are merely struggles as to whether the nation shall see its government representatives adopt an attitude of a little more or a little less hypocrisy and follow a policy of slightly greater or slightly less baseness."

"THAT WOULD BE A CRIME," SAID T. R.

As the date for the Republican and Progressive conventions drew closer, it seemed more difficult to avoid another division of Republican voters. Another division meant handing the Presidency over to Wilson a second time.

"That would be a crime!" exclaimed Roosevelt. "It is unthinkable that I could be a party to such a result."

It was in that spirit of intense disgust for Wilson's policies that Roosevelt worked to have one nominee come out of the two Chicago conventions, and it was in that effort that he met his most humiliating defeat. Neither convention responded.

"HE KEPT US OUT OF WAR"

At that time, too, incredible as it now seems, there was developing throughout our West a feeling that America's interests were not involved in the war, and that a President who had kept us out of it, and whose purpose was to keep us out, should be continued in office.

Gov. Glynn's "he-kept-us-out-of-war" speech nominating Wilson was not indorsed by the President until he had satisfied himself that, if a sharp issue could be raised the people of the West would reelect him to do that very thing. A close canvass made of the West had convinced him that the country was not in the "heroic mood" that Roosevelt desired, and he was ready for the test.

WILSON WANTED ROOSEVELT AS OPPONENT

Just before starting for the Chicago convention from Washington I met Samuel Untermyer, as he left the White House.

"What are you fellows going to do in Chicago—Roosevelt or Hughes?" he asked.

"Roosevelt," I replied, to get his reaction.

"Well, that will suit the man in there exactly," said Untermyer, indicating the White House. "He can lick Roosevelt on the war issue, and he wants to do it. If Wilson could name your candidate he would name Teddy."

The Democratic national convention knew exactly what it wanted in candidate and issue; the Republican convention did not. The Republicans made their first blunder when they called their convention to meet a week in advance of the Democratic convention. The Democrats were in power; they had held the government for four years and wanted four years more; under all the rules of politics they should have been the first to state their case and ask the judgment of the people; then issue could be joined by the opposition.

The Republican managers unwisely determined to lead off. They fixed an early date—June 7—deliberately, to show their disregard for anything the Wilson convention might do or say. When they got to Chicago, their platform committee discovered that, aside from the ordinary partisan condemnation, they had no target at which to direct their fire; "He-kept-us-out-of-war" had not yet emerged from Democratic councils. The result was the weakest platform ever written in a Republican convention.

CHAPTER LIV

1916—A CONTRAST IN CONVENTIONS

The Republican Gathering Colorless, The Progressives Loaded With Pyrotechnics—A Conference Committee That Knew It Could Not Agree—Lodge, Aroused From Sleep, Visions The Presidency—Roosevelt Refuses The Progressive Nomination And Centres His Efforts On Defeat Of Wilson—The Severest Trial Of His Career.

THE convention itself was as colorless as the platform. It had no real rivalries for nomination since Hughes was at all times the obvious nominee. Its proceedings, never exciting the slightest enthusiasm, forecast the campaign and the result.

With one exception that was the dullest convention held within my recollection by either party. The one exception was the 1888 Democratic convention in St. Louis at which Cleveland was re-nominated, only to be defeated. The St. Louis convention was so listless that the correspondents were forced to write of the muddy waters of the Mississippi, and of the old-timer river steamboats that Mark Twain immortalized.

In Chicago in 1916, they would have been compelled to do likewise but for the Progressive convention. The Progressives furnished the pyrotechnics of the week; let me say that they had quite an assortment of explosives, and used them furiously, especially at the close. As in 1912, it was a crusaders' gathering—and Roosevelt was still their leader, though now convinced that union not division was a duty.

In the big Coliseum five or six blocks away from the Progressive gathering, the Republicans went through their convention proceedings as though it was a mail order catalogue. Warren Harding, then Senator, made a long speech as Chair-

434

man; not a note sounded by him or by any other speaker had the vibrant quality of definite purpose. Many delegates would have preferred to go elsewhere for their candidate than to Hughes but there was no elsewhere.

A conference committee of the two conventions had sought for two nights to agree upon a candidate whom the Republicans and the Progressives could support. The Republican conferees were former Attorney General Charles J. Bonaparte, Senator Murray Crane, Senator William E. Borah, Nicholas Murray Butler, and Senator Reed Smoot. The Progressive conferees were Gov. John N. Parker, of Louisiana, Hiram Johnson, George W. Perkins, A. R. Johnson, of Ohio, and Horace Wilkinson, of New York. There, two immovable forces met.

"We'll take any one you offer but Roosevelt," were the first words spoken by the Republican conferees. Reed Smoot uttered them.

"We don't believe in barring any man," was the response from Wilkinson. "Let us put all the cards on the table and discuss which one is the best to play."

The one name the Republicans crossed off their list so arbitrarily was the one name that made up the whole Progressive list. It was soon found that unity on any candidate was impossible—1916 was too close to 1912. In factional politics memories are prejudices and they disappear slowly. Hiram Johnson gave up the conference. Then Gov. Parker gave it up.

Somewhere in the midnight hours, with a decisive ballot certain to be cast the next day in each convention, Roosevelt was telephoned, to suggest a possible nominee. When his telephone rang, the Colonel was engrossed in writing an article on birds, promised to his publishers that week. He had stayed up late to finish it. He asked Chicago for time to think it over. Soon the reply came, "Lodge." It astounded the conferees on both sides. They knew Lodge could not be nominated in either convention. Yet they felt it a duty to inform the Massachusetts Senator.

LODGE, SEATED ON BEDSIDE, VISIONS HONORS

A committee went to Lodge's hotel room and awakened him. Seated on the bedside, clad in his pajamas, his eyes blinking with sleep, he listened in astonishment, and took it seriously. He thought Roosevelt's indorsement would bring his nomination in the morning.

"Oh! that this honor should come to me at my time of life!" was his first utterance.

He exaggerated Roosevelt's strength at that time with a regular convention, and utterly misunderstood his motive. Roosevelt knew that Hughes would be nominated, but he did not care to indorse Hughes to the convention and have it charged that he had nominated another presidential candidate. This time he was evading, not seeking, responsibility for the nominee. What a change eight years had brought! He believed his message would bring Lodge some prestige and some votes—as it did—and that the Massachusetts Senator would understand the strategy. But Lodge did not see it that way. His mind was thrown completely out of balance.

I have seen other men while their names were before conventions lose their good judgment, but Roosevelt's telephone message surely should have been too slender a hope for a man who had presided over three conventions. How the strong light of the Presidency dazzles the most experienced! The committee talked with Lodge about the possibilities, and then retired. They made a report to the convention, as they were bound to do, presenting Lodge's name. It met with no response. By noon that day Hughes was the nominee.

As I Knew Them

While Roosevelt could thus easily dispose of the Republican convention, so far as he was concerned, he faced the severest trial of his career in the Progressive convention. He sincerely believed it was his patriotic duty to refuse another Progressive party nomination and to indorse the Republican nominee. It was a hard decision to make—his country or his party?

That broader view was not shared by the Progressive convention. Most of the delegates were emphatically in favor of another campaign. All the wonderful spirit of the first convention four years before was reflected in this second gathering. Despite the unwisdom of its insistence upon a third ticket, it merited a better fate than that which came to it when it named Roosevelt only to have him decline.

I shall never forget the scene of dismay, anger and defiance, with their old leader, in those closing hours. They little knew how deeply he felt back there in Oyster Bay, or how poignantly he regretted that the party of his creation had to be sacrificed for his country. The Colonel bowed his head, and unprotestingly accepted the condemnation of those who did not see the real issue as plainly as he saw it.

That was Saturday night; the following Tuesday Roosevelt dined with Hughes, the Republican nominee, in New York City, and pledged his full support.

CHAPTER LV

HUGHES: THE OFFICE SEEKS THE MAN

No Career In American Politics Compares With That Of Charles E. Hughes—Never Sought Honors, Never Asked Support, Never Expended A Dollar For A Nomination—The Archie Sanders Incident That Separated A Governor And A President—Hughes Would Never Use Patronage To Pass Legislation—Root's Arraignment of Hearst, "By Authority Of The President"—A Candidate Who Gave No Help —Roosevelt Urged Hughes For Governor In 1908—Some New Facts About Hughes And Roosevelt In The Struggle For Direct Primaries.

MY earliest recollection of Charles Evans Hughes goes back more than twenty years to the time when he was a citizen of New York City, not known outside of his profession. He lived on the upper west side of Manhattan Island; my home was in the same neighborhood. Hughes liked to walk—with quick, vigorous step, his thick heavy cane tightly held. On cool breezy afternoons his rapid pace against the wind would carry the tails of his unbuttoned light overcoat fluttering far out behind him. You could see in his stride that he was a purposeful man, who at all times knew where he was travelling. Not many of his neighbors were personally acquainted with him, but the brisk walker morning and afternoon was a familiar figure.

It is common-place to say of any man that there are none like him, but it is so true of Hughes that I cannot help saying it. You may search the careers of all the men in our public life for a century and a half and you will not find a career like his. He has never sought public office; he has never asked any individual to speak for him, or to work for his advancement. He publicly repudiated the announcement in 1908 that Hughes headquarters had been opened in Chicago, to secure his nomination for President; his silence while on the Supreme Court in 1916 was broken before his nomination only to disavow responsibility for Republican leaders who sought to create the impression that they had his consent to seek delegates for him.

In a word, Hughes has been Governor, Associate Justice of the Supreme Court, Presidential nominee and Secretary of State without ever having expended so much as a postage stamp and without ever having uttered, or authorized others to utter, a single word in his behalf. Here is a remarkable record. It is not one of indifference—for I am sure Hughes is not indifferent to the honors he has had. It reveals a determined purpose to let the office seek the man, uninfluenced by personal appeals or manipulation of delegates.

We have had men in our public life who believed in that policy, but the temptation of new honors proved too strong for them. Hughes, however, has adhered to it so consistently, so firmly, that the man who would announce that he spoke for Hughes on any subject would have to show credentials stronger than his own say-so, whoever he might be.

AN INCIDENT WITH LASTING CONSEQUENCES

Once Theodore Roosevelt while President acted, as he declared, to aid Hughes, then Governor of New York, in his struggle to enact anti-racetrack gambling laws. Archie D. Sanders, Internal Revenue Collector at Rochester, New York, and since Congressman, was believed to be the influence holding "on the fence" the votes of two Rochester Assemblymen. Sanders' term was expiring. At the suggestion of Congressman Stevens, an enthusiastic Hughes man, the President refused to reappoint Sanders unless he first brought the two Assemblymen into line. The White House frankly explained the purpose; the sincerity of Roosevelt's desire to help was never questioned. When the news was brought to Hughes at Albany, he stated that he was not interested in Sanders' fate, had not requested the President's action and knew nothing of it.

The significance of this incident was large and lasting. Hughes as Governor always refused to use patronage to pass legislation. When legislation came before him for official action, he never inquired whether friend or foe sponsored it. He looked only to the proposal. Several times while Governor he astounded his factional opponents by naming one of them for office, because he believed him to be the best man for the place. He as freely refused to appoint from his own supporters unless they could furnish a man as capable as he could find elsewhere.

With his policy in this respect unbroken by any act of his own, Hughes felt even more strongly that he could not accept support secured for him by another, through patronage. He could not acquiesce in having the President do for him what he would not do for himself. Hence his prompt denial of any interest in the matter. He wanted the votes of the Rochester Assemblymen, but he did not want them that way. Hughes always has been a stickler for maintaining what he calls "the integrity of his position," and to the dismay of his friends he has sacrificed much in the way of immediate gain rather than break through the line. The real gain has come later.

ROOSEVELT FELT REBUKED

You can imagine the effect on Roosevelt. He felt that his friendly offices had been rejected in a most unfriendly way; he expected thanks rather than what he considered a rebuke. From then until 1916, he and Hughes travelled different paths.

I am not prepared to say that except for the Sanders incident Roosevelt would have supported Hughes in 1908, but I am certain that it led Roosevelt to feel that Hughes was

As I Knew Them

almost the last candidate he cared to see nominated as his successor.

I use the Sanders case because of its undoubted influence in separating Hughes and Roosevelt politically; even though the Presidency may not have been directly involved, their inability to work together was unfortunate for the party and the country.

"BY AUTHORITY OF THE PRESIDENT"

The world of politics knew nothing of Hughes until his nomination for Governor in 1906. He was a stranger to it and was not thought of for public office. He owed that nomination to his success as counsel for the legislative committee investigating the big insurance companies in New York. I understand that his name as counsel was suggested by Bradford Merrill, then associated with the New York World, which newspaper was largely responsible for the investigation.

Hughes made good as an investigator and the Republicans turned to him to save New York for them. Their grip on the State was slipping and Tammany had nominated William Randolph Hearst for Governor in the belief that he would add to the Democratic strength enough politically unattached votes to win. It did not turn out that way, but there was a hard, uncertain fight until the last returns were in.

The feature of the campaign was a speech in Utica, New York, by Secretary of State Root, made "by authority of the President," in which he arraigned Hearst unmercifully. This most unusual proceeding was full of boomerang possibilities. I never understood why the Democratic leaders did not seek to arouse the people on the issue of presidential interference in State affairs. There have been many demonstrations of the sensitiveness of voters on that point. However, the Democrats thought it best to drop the matter as quickly as possible. When elected, Hughes announced himself as "counsel for the people" in all that he was to do as Governor, and acted accordingly.

A CANDIDATE WHO GAVE NO HELP

Party machines are never enamored of Governors inclined to do much thinking on their own account, and the New York Republican machine did not like that characteristic in Hughes. The people did, however. By 1908, Hughes had grown to Presidential size; the State machine reluctantly responded to the strong Hughes sentiment by accepting him as the State's choice for national honors. They gave him no real support, however. Nor did Hughes help himself. He gave no encouragement to those who really wanted to see him nominated. What might have developed into a formidable candidacy had New York's Governor followed the ambitious course of other men, was stunted in its growth because it could make no headway with a candidate who discouraged rather than encouraged. That is why, as Roosevelt told me in a White House interview, it was easier for Taft to win delegates away from Hughes than from other candidates. He had 67 votes in the Chicago convention.

ROOSEVELT INSISTS UPON HUGHES' RENOMINATION

Another two years of Hughes as Governor was not what the "organization" in New York wanted after the delegates returned from nominating Taft. New York was certain to return a heavy Republican plurality on President, and the swing could be depended upon to carry almost any Republican candidate for Governor with it. Conferences were held to agree upon a nominee, and for a time it seemed likely that Hughes would be dropped. Roosevelt, however, took a broader view, though he was still smarting over the Sanders matter. His attitude is revealed in the following reply I

received to a letter I had written him urging Hughes'
nomination:

Oyster Bay, N. Y.
August 29, 1908.

My dear Stoddard:—

   I share entirely your view. I think it will do damage to nominate Mr. Hughes, but that it will do far more damage not to nominate him. I think he has given just cause and offense to decent
men engaged in active political work, and that he has shown grave
ingratitude to men like Parsons; but nevertheless I am convinced
that the popular feeling about him is exactly what you describe, and
that, therefore, he ought to be renominated, inasmuch as there
is nothing to be said against his personal integrity.

Faithfully yours,
Theodore Roosevelt.

As usual, Roosevelt followed word with action. He made
the New York leaders see the folly of turning down Hughes,
and a second term for the Governor followed.

THE HUGHES STRUGGLE FOR DIRECT PRIMARIES

At once, Hughes went into a struggle for direct State-wide
primaries. The party "organization" opposed the legislation,
and the winter's development was the familiar story of conflict between executive and legislative branches. In the midst
of it came Taft's offer to Hughes to become Associate Justice
of the Supreme Court. The "organization" rejoiced that
Hughes would now be put out of the way, but the Governor
out-generalled them. He accepted the appointment with the
proviso that he would not be called upon to take his place on
the bench until the Legislature had adjourned. That meant
a finish fight.

Roosevelt was homeward bound from Africa while the
battle was in the final stage. Albany was full of rumor that
he was not in sympathy with the Hughes programme. There
was no truth to such talk, for he knew nothing of the conflict,

but the rumor served its purpose of stopping the bills until Roosevelt could be heard from.

Then came a letter from the Colonel, dated London, inviting Hughes to Oyster Bay when convenient after Roosevelt's return. Hughes would have gone there but both men discovered that they were shortly to attend the Harvard commencement exercises and their meeting was postponed until then.

I have always regretted that the conference was not held in Oyster Bay. Roosevelt, in London, must have had something in mind beyond a social engagement with Hughes, something big enough for him to write about it weeks in advance. Its political significance would have been beyond the power of the two men to explain away.

Moreover, there would have been no stories that they had met unexpectedly at a college commencement and that Hughes had there persuaded Roosevelt to undertake to win a battle which, without Roosevelt, was lost. Not knowing the facts, those stories were accepted as true. Neither Roosevelt nor Hughes ever attempted to silence them by making known that their Harvard meeting was a substitute for an Oyster Bay visit, and that both men went to Cambridge knowing that the New York situation was to be discussed. If the facts here related have ever before appeared in print I have failed to see them. The direct primary bill was, of course, the most important measure pending. Hughes had hardly mentioned it before Roosevelt interrupted with a short:

"I have determined to remain silent."

"I am not urging you to get into the struggle," said Hughes, "but your silence is used by the opposition as evidence that you are against the bill."

"They say my silence means opposition to the bill?" queried Roosevelt. "Of course it means nothing of the kind. I am for the bill. I'll wire Fred Davenport now telling him I think it should be passed."

And within a few moments the oft-quoted telegram was on the wires to the State Senator from Utica, now Congressman. The fight was ended, the bill became law, and in October Hughes took his place on the Supreme Court.

He was through, or thought he was through, with politics. In truth, however, the work on which his fame is to rest had not begun.

CHAPTER LVI

A SURPRISED AND SILENT JURIST

Though Lost To The World Of Politics For Six Years, Hughes Was Found And Made A Candidate For President—He Knew Politicians Did Not Like His Ways—His Real Desire Was To Return To His Law Practice—Finally, Allowed Fate To Take Its Course—His Campaign For Election Was Emphatically His Own—Crocker, Not Johnson, Responsible For Loss Of California.

THE remarkable feature of the demand for Hughes' nomination for President in 1916 was that there was not a word or an act on his part for six years to arouse new interest in him. As a justice of the Supreme Court, absorbed in its duties, he was lost to the world of politics. No one was more surprised than he that his name was mentioned. It was a long time before he believed that those Republican leaders who were declaring for him really meant it, or that they had any considerable public opinion back of them.

Crowded with court work, unable to make inquiries without encouraging the belief that he was seeking the nomination, Hughes blinded himself to newspaper talk, political talk and even the talk of friends lest he be misinterpreted. It seemed to him that any move he might make would be inconsistent with his rule about "maintaining the integrity of his position" —his position at that time being that of a judge too deeply immersed in his work to concern himself with what was going on outside his court room.

There was just one move he could have made that would not be misinterpreted—to take himself out by a flat declaration that he would not accept. This he did not do. His position was much the same as that of the young lady willing perhaps to marry but not willing to disclose her mind until

As I Knew Them

formally asked. He was not a candidate and was not seeking to influence the convention's choice; he was under no obligation to assume in advance that there was anything for him to accept or reject. Statements by party leaders seemingly involving him were met with a brief public announcement disavowing them, but he steadfastly refused to anticipate the possible action of a convention not yet in session.

I know that the thought dominant in Hughes' mind that winter was that he should resign from the court and return to New York City, resuming his place there as a citizen and practice law. Two terms as Governor and six years on the bench had materially reduced his income, and he felt that longer public service meant continued denial to his family of the comforts to which they were entitled.

WOULD NOT ENJOY WHITE HOUSE TURMOIL

Another consideration that tempted Hughes to stop the talk of a possible nomination was the strong feeling that he then had that politicians did not like his ways, and that in the White House he would have to deal almost entirely with politicians; the prospect of unity of purpose was not bright. He had not forgotten his troubles at Albany and four years of similar contention at Washington were not alluring. He liked to deal with public questions on their merits, not on their political aspects. His experience on the bench had strengthened this tendency.

"Your friend Roosevelt can handle the work of the White House and enjoy it," Hughes said to me at one time when the Presidency was under discussion. "It would take me a whole day to dispose of matters that he could get rid of in an hour. The Presidency is the greatest honor that could come to any man; it is also the greatest burden."

More than once during that winter of 1916 when his silence made him the mystery of politics the considerations I have mentioned weighed heavily on Hughes' mind. They led him

447

close to an emphatic declaration, as he had declared in 1912, that his name must not be used politically while on the bench.

But the Presidency is too big for an American to turn his back upon. Confronted with what seemed like a certainty that he would be nominated and elected, he must have decided to let Fate take its own course. It did—and the silent jurist became the nominee of his party.

ONE FACTOR THAT DEFEATED HUGHES

No one will ever write the history of the campaign that followed without challenge of his analysis of its changing phases and its surprising result. I realize that my opinion cannot escape that fate, but I may say on behalf of it that it is based on familiarity with the day-to-day developments while the struggle was on,—a knowledge that led me early in September to doubt the election of Hughes despite my confidence in June that he would surely win.

Looking backward, it is my judgment that the seeds of Republican defeat were sown in the Republican and Progressive conventions held in Chicago in June. The Republicans adjourned in a deadened calm of over-confidence; the Progressives adjourned in a riot of defiance of Roosevelt. They had nominated him for President with all the enthusiasm of 1912. Then came his telegram that he would think it over and let them know later whether he would accept or not. Bainbridge Colby's quick response "we, too, will think it over" voiced the resentful spirit that swept over the convention, changing it in the last hour from an intensely Roosevelt gathering to an intensely anti-Roosevelt gathering. Had the delegates been polled then on their choice for President as between Hughes and Wilson, I am certain that a majority would have declared for Wilson. Antagonism to Roosevelt, not to Hughes, would have influenced that choice.

The delegates carried that feeling back to their homes, where, finally, it found its way into the November ballot box.

THE SPHINX AND THE CANDIDATES

It made no impression on the heavy Hughes majorities in the East, but in the West, where the Progressives had their greatest strength, it was probably responsible for the loss of the two Dakotas, Oregon and Washington. No man could control it. Roosevelt in particular could not. It was the feature of the campaign that Chairman Willcox always feared. There was also, of course, through the West the kept-us-out-of-war issue that brought States like Kansas into the Wilson column. That, of course, was the talked-of issue west of the Mississippi, but the Progressive bolt to Wilson was also a real factor.

HUGHES PLANNED HIS OWN CAMPAIGN

Hughes' campaign was emphatically his own affair. That is to say, that while he did not interfere with what other campaign speakers might say in public speeches, Hughes had his own conception of what he should say and do. He was also resolved to have no entangling alliances made by the national committee. To insure this policy, he made his friend William R. Willcox chairman of the national committee.

His across-the-continent tour was undertaken because of his desire that as many voters as possible should see him and hear him. He had been on the Supreme Court for six years; he had not concerned himself with public questions nor appeared in public places in that long time. He was only a newspaper name to thousands who were now asked to vote for him; they had a right to look him over, and to hear what he had to say. He did not want their vote merely as a name.

That was a fine position to take, but even an experienced campaigner would have regarded it as perilous. It was certainly extremely perilous for a candidate unfamiliar with the varying moods and temper of the people in different parts of the country, especially for one not given to setting his sails to catch every breeze. Hughes did not realize how completely the West had been deceived by the Democratic platform plank about the "splendid diplomatic triumphs" that had "kept us out of war." He knew the opinion of the East, but western Republican leaders did not enlighten him as to a different opinion across the Mississippi. His speeches show that he did not join issue with the "kept us out of war" propaganda until his return to the east. Then he denounced it vigorously, but too late to change the trend of the West.

The failure of the western Republican leaders to sense the opinion of that section is without parallel in political history. It cost a Presidency. I have known national committees to feel too certain of one State or another; I have known State chairmen to judge poorly the drift of voters in different counties; but I have never known so many State leaders so wholly unaware that their opponents had stolen a march on them and had captured the mind of the people.

The Republican effort was confined to a futile attempt to win back the rebellious Progressives, and election day was at hand before it was realized that, deeper than the Progressive bolt to Wilson, was the feeling of the West that Hughes meant war and Wilson meant peace.

I was permitted to read many of the reports received daily at national headquarters. I also had frequent talks with Murray Crane and John W. Weeks, both experienced campaigners, who, with Willcox, were directing the battle. Those daily reports and those talks prove that eastern headquarters had no advices indicating the real situation in the West.

THE DEMOCRATS RELIED ON THE WEST

The strategy of the Democrats was masterful. President Wilson and Col. House planned it and to the end remained its directing mind. The East was abandoned as "the enemy's country," as Bryan had termed it in 1896, but, more shrewd than Bryan, the 1916 campaigners did not advertise the fact. Wilson staked his hope of election on his ability to persuade the West that war sentiment was an Atlantic seaboard affair and that Hughes was its candidate. He linked Hughes with

Roosevelt as certain, if elected, to plunge us into war, a charge bound to make an impression, for the two men could not disavow each other.

I must not give the impression that better than others I knew the weakness of the Republican cause. But the remark made to me in Washington by Samuel Untermyer that Wilson would prefer to have Roosevelt as his opponent rather than any other man stuck in my mind. It gave me clearer light on some campaign developments. I repeated it to the Colonel.

"I refuse to believe that the people out there are pacifists," he declared, "or that they will indorse Wilson's flabby policy."

"But, Colonel," I persisted, "Wilson's people have studied the situation carefully and really believe it. They believe it so much that they would rather have had you nominated. They feel certain they could defeat you."

"That would be the keenest humiliation I could suffer," replied Roosevelt, "but Wilson would have a fight on his hands before he licked me."

CROCKER, NOT JOHNSON, CAUSED HUGHES' DEFEAT

California, of course, furnished the sensation of the campaign. Hughes' across-the-continent tour extended to the Golden Gate State where he failed to meet Governor Hiram Johnson. That failure is supposed to have cost him California's electoral vote. The newspapers made much of that unfortunate incident, but back of it was a situation of which that incident was only a part.

Anyone experienced in Pacific Coast politics could have warned Hughes of the peril of touring California. Johnson not only controlled the Progressive party but the Republican primaries as well. The old Southern Pacific Railroad crowd, led by William H. Crocker, ousted six years before, were in continuous battle with him to regain power. It was a duel, and no one can safely step between duellists. It was well known in the east that Johnson regarded the State as his bailiwick. He assumed responsibility for it, and the election figures year by year show that he always made good.

Hughes knew something of the situation, but he did not know its intensity. He did not know, either, that, when at the San Francisco meeting he greeted Crocker as California's leading citizen, and emphasized his error by failing to ask why California's Governor was not present, he overlooked the real political power of the State—a power unusually jealous of its due. In such cases, explanations seldom catch up with the offense.

When the election returns showed Johnson elected Senator by nearly 300,000 plurality and Hughes defeated by 3,773, Johnson was arraigned everywhere as the man responsible for continuing Wilson in the White House another four years. Such a wide discrepancy in the figures gives apparent support to that charge, but the figures are not the true guide to the cause of the disaster. I am of the opinion, and my view is shared by others close to the situation, that National Committeeman Crocker is the man who made Hughes' success in California impossible. The records of the Republican National Committee confirm this statement.

THE SITUATION IN CALIFORNIA

We can all recall the anxiety with which the country waited the day after election for the final returns from California. Hughes and Wilson alternated in the lead by a margin too close for comfort until finally it was settled that Wilson had it. The story leading up to the result has not been told, so far as I know, in the new light of the national committee records. I think it worth telling. Let us start at the beginning of the campaign.

Johnson, then Governor, was a candidate for the Senate, and undoubtedly the spokesman for two-thirds of the voters of his State. He attended the Progressive National Convention in Chicago, in June, where he urged Roosevelt's separate nomination, and the continuance of the Progressive party. When that body adjourned, with Roosevelt refusing to run, Johnson went to New York City, to determine his course. In New York City he conferred with Hughes. "He's my man for President," he declared with enthusiasm to National Chairman Willcox as he left for home.

Now, what was the situation at home—in California? It was different from that existing in any other State. Hiram Johnson as a Republican had been elected Governor several times over the opposition of the Crocker faction and controlled the state organization. He carried most of the California delegates for Roosevelt in 1912. In the election that year 283,000 votes were cast for Roosevelt and only 3,914 for Taft. Taft's total vote in 1912 was approximately the Wilson plurality over Hughes in 1916. After the 1912 campaign, Johnson entered all Progressive candidates in the regular Republican primaries, and won indorsement for them over the Crocker candidates. In 1916 he undertook to repeat that success—and in fact did repeat it—in the primaries by winning the nomination for Senator for himself. Both sides were hotly engaged in that Senatorial fight when Hughes toured the State.

WILLCOX APPEALS IN VAIN TO CROCKER

Such facts make it impossible to dispute Johnson's complete control of the Republican as well as of the Progressive voters of the State. Certainly he was a force not to be ignored. In other States, and particularly in Illinois in 1916, warring factions dropped their antagonisms while the Presidential candidate was within their borders. Honors were divided as equally as possible. All factions had representation in meetings and receptions.

Crocker, however, would not have it that way. He was

the regular Republican national committeeman for his State and he insisted upon all the prerogatives of his office.

But Chairman Willcox, in New York, was anxious to bring Progressives into helpful cooperation, and had added representative Progressives from several States as campaign associates to the National committee. The California Progressive chosen was Chester H. Rowell. Naturally Crocker should have shared authority with Rowell in arranging all national meetings, particularly those for the presidential candidate.

One cannot read the telegrams passed between National Chairman Willcox and these two ostensible collaborators, and believe that Crocker regarded the success of Hughes in California as equal to him in value to the success of the Crocker candidate against Johnson in the Republican primaries. The telegrams from which I use extracts have never been published.

WILLCOX VAINLY ASKS CROCKER TO DESIST

The first of the series of dispatches (July 8) was sent by Crocker's chairman, Keesling to Willcox, and pledged Hughes a "cordial reception" under the auspices of "a re-united party." It soon developed, however, that the Crocker idea of a "re-united party" was of a party to which the Progressives were to be like the young lady of Niger and at the end of the campaign the two factions were:

> ". . . return from the ride,
> With the lady inside,
> And a smile on the face of the tiger."

Evidently Chairman Willcox had heard of Crocker's real attitude for he sent him this telegram:

"Disquieting rumors are current here of lack of co-operation looking to the general support in your State of all forces opposed to the Wilson nomination. We feel that every effort should be made to harmonize all differences. . . . Will you kindly give this matter your personal attention?"

Progressive committeeman Rowell suggested that Johnson preside at the San Francisco meeting, and the Crocker candidate for Senator at the Los Angeles meeting, "although," he added, "my suggestion of Johnson considers him as Governor and not as a candidate."

This proposal seemed a fair division of honors between the two factions, but Crocker would have none of it. Apparently he appealed to Murray Crane to head Willcox off from urging peace. In a telegram dated July 16, Willcox refers to Crane and adds: "I sent the telegram as I did for I feel very strongly that in those States where there is a fight on for United States Senator, if continued until election, will work harm to the national ticket."

CROCKER'S REAL PURPOSE

Under date of July 19, Crocker reveals his purpose to control the Hughes visit in the interest of his candidate for Senator and against Johnson. He telegraphed among other statements "California must have Republican (meaning Crocker candidate) Senator. My efforts will be judiciously and unreservedly so directed."

On July 28, Rowell telegraphed: "In any other State the Governor and Hughes supporter would be obvious chairman and to refuse Johnson recognition will be taken by voters as indication of ostracism of Progressive participation. I shall therefore insist upon my suggestion of Johnson. I have no objections to postponing Hughes meeting until after primaries, but maintain Governor should preside if meeting is held on original date."

On July 30, Chairman Willcox telegraphed: "I might say personally and not officially that I think there is force in the Governor of a State who is supporting a presidential candidate having the privilege to preside at one of the meetings.

This is a courtesy that usually should be extended. . . . It does seem to me that during the two days that Hughes is in California all hands should pull together in an effort to make the meetings successful both for the interests of the national candidate and for themselves, thus removing local complications."

Finally, August 2, Crocker wired: "We believe we can handle the situation," which meant, as Rowell telegraphed on August 6, that Progressive participation in the two meetings was excluded and that only those Progressives whom Crocker invited as guests were included. Rowell asked that something be done "to prevent calamity to Hughes which Crocker's proposed exclusion of Progressives will produce. These plans if unchanged will arouse such widespread resentment as to render California a doubtful State for Hughes."

CROCKER REIGNS AND TAKES SOLE RESPONSIBILITY

On August 10, Willcox telegraphed Crocker: "I desire to record my earnest protest against any reprisals being placed on those who are supporting Hughes and who may not have supported our ticket in past years. . . . I state as emphatically as I can that if there are any grounds for Rowell's complaints they should be speedily removed."

Crocker's reply to this telegram was brief. He wanted no more argument. He curtly wired: "Replying to your telegram all arrangements for California meetings have been completed."

The series of telegrams ended as they had begun with Crocker insisting upon his own way regardless of consequences to Hughes. He presided at the San Francisco meeting, as he had always intended to do, and he named one of his lieutenants to preside at the Los Angeles meeting, leaving the Johnson forces out in the cold.

The Governor of the State was thus deliberately denied formal notice of the presence in the State of the presidential candidate he was supporting. An organization capable of delivering only 3,914 votes to its presidential candidate in 1912 took sole responsibility for Hughes; receptions, dinners and meetings were held with Crocker as the one directing authority.

Naturally Johnson resented this affront; naturally, his followers resented it even more deeply. They saw a presidential candidate for whom they were asked to vote completely surrounded by their factional opponents; they lost interest in him. In every speech Johnson continued to urge support of Hughes; had he not done so Hughes would not have come within 3,773 votes of winning the State.

It may be true, that aside from speaking for Hughes, Johnson concentrated his campaign efforts on his own election as Senator. What else could he do? Crocker had taken over responsibility for Hughes' political fortunes in the State. Despite the protests of Chairman Willcox, he used his place as national committeeman to treat the Johnson forces as outsiders. The latter had no responsibility in the campaign after Crocker's decree. Planning a return to control of the State under a Hughes Administration,—Crocker was determined that Hughes should understand that he, and he alone, had fought the battle. His mistake was that he could not wait until after election to make his purpose known. He had to dominate at once, he had to put his own ambitions ahead of Hughes' interests as a candidate—and California voted with Crocker more in mind than Hughes. The surprise is, that under such conditions the Hughes vote was so large.

HUGHES AS SECRETARY OF STATE

Of course, the honor of the Presidency is too great to lose without regret, and Hughes must have felt the blow keenly. No shock-absorber will blunt the sharpness of it for any man —not even Time, for most men. But Hughes has now resumed the place he really had in mind before the call of the

Chicago convention—his place as a citizen and in his profession—and as I see him on public occasions I get the impression that the four years he missed as President have been more than made up by his satisfaction with his six years as Secretary of State.   Undoubtedly those years are the hap-

From the Glasgow News.

A FINE HAUL FOR HUGHES

piest of his career.   In that office he did the work on which his fame will rest.   Both Harding and Coolidge gave him a free hand.   He was Secretary of State in fact.   It was an atmosphere to his liking, and he quickly impressed the country and the world.   He was as far removed from the political currents that swirl around an Administration as it is possible for a Cabinet officer to be.   Aside from the World Court and the recognition of Russia he had no political phases to consider seriously.   It is not my province to contrast the records made by the Premiers of various Administrations, but it would be difficult for me to name one who achieved

As I Knew Them

greater renown than Hughes, who has to his credit so many treaties ratified, or who can point to a Department reorganized on a basis that offers a career to those who enter it. Every policy was thoughtfully studied, frankly declared, and vigorously pressed. There were no hasty judgments, no subtleties of language or of purpose, no timidities.

An earnest desire to be on good terms with other nations, to exert the good offices of this government in the after-war chaos of Europe, was translated into performance. It will never be known how frequently our State Department was called upon immediately after the war to adjust minor but irritating differences between other nations solely because there was confidence that the man at the head would see to it that right prevailed. It was in giving that character of exact justice to his administration that Hughes performed his greatest service to other countries as well as to his own, and made a record of substantial achievement.

Today he is our ranking citizen without title—what I call our first citizen for emergencies. Every big occasion needs him. Coolidge as President is spokesman for the nation, but when a voice from our untitled citizenry is desired, the people turn to Hughes.

CHAPTER LVII

HOW WILL HAYS BECAME NATIONAL CHAIRMAN

WHEN William R. Willcox in 1918 decided to resign as chairman of the Republican national committee, Senator Boies Penrose, ex-Senator Murray Crane and others agreed upon John T. Adams, of Iowa, as his successor.

The committee was called to meet in St. Louis, February 12, 1918. The election of Adams seemed settled. Ten or twelve national committeemen of the progressive type, however, did not like the choice. George Perkins finally became active in this minority movement, and the newspapers gave it attention. A week or so before the meeting Murray Crane telephoned me to take breakfast with him at his apartment in the Biltmore Hotel, New York city. After breakfast, he suddenly asked me, "What is the use of stirring up all this muss about the chairmanship? Perkins cannot defeat Adams. I wish you would tell him so."

I replied that I had no interest in the matter—that a newspaper editor had no business in purely "organization rivalries."

"We have from 36 to 40 sure votes in the committee for Adams," continued Senator Crane. "There isn't a ghost of a chance to defeat him. Try to see Perkins today and make him see that he is up against a stone wall."

I talked with Perkins, as requested, and a check-up of the national committee showed the "Old Guard" strength about as Crane had stated.

"They have the votes," replied Perkins, "but possibly we can produce something else. Walter Brown has just been here from Ohio. He says we are going out to St. Louis with only a pair of deuces to draw to, but if we can draw the other two deuces we will have a strong hand. I'm after the other two. Better come out to St. Louis with us, and help in the good work."

"No," I replied, "I've attended enough funerals the past six years and I don't care to go to any more. You and Brown can be the whole show."

I learned later that the other two deuces Perkins was seeking were a series of letters written from Germany by Adams in the summer of 1914 (just after the outbreak of war) and printed in Adams' home-town paper in Iowa. They were distinctly pro-German. Perkins believed the committee would not dare to go to the country with a chairman who had expressed such opinions. He had sent a man to Iowa to dig up the letters. Three days before the St. Louis meeting they had not been found. Nevertheless, he and Walter Brown started for St. Louis.

SOME LETTERS ARRIVE AND ADAMS RETIRES

There was just one hour to spare when the documents arrived in St. Louis. The committee was about to meet. Apparently the Adams candidacy had no serious opposition. Perkins showed Senator Calder, of New York, the Adams publication.

"I'm for Adams," said Calder, "but these letters, if true, make him impossible."

They proved to be true enough. Adams frankly acknowledged their authorship when Calder read them to his astonished colleagues. You never saw a body of men so startled. In less than ten minutes the Adams candidacy was withdrawn, and the Committee recessed in a chaotic search for a new chairman. Murray Crâne always insisted that had he been present the committee would have ignored the letters and elected Adams. The Massachusetts Senator, usually so thorough, had assumed that Adams was certain of election, and had remained at home. He thus lost control of the situation;

he vainly tried to rally the members by telephone, but he found that the water was over the dam. The next problem was to find a man whom both Murray Crane and Boies Penrose would agree was not "the other fellow's" candidate. He .was hard to find.

SULLIVAN, INDIANA, PRODUCES ITS LEADING CITIZEN

Back in the little town of Sullivan, Indiana,—said to be somewhere near the geographic centre of population in this country—there lived a young man whose unusual ability in politics had been recognized for several years by Vice President Fairbanks and other Hoosier Republicans. He was unknown to fame beyond the banks of the Wabash but for a year or more he had been the working head of the Indiana Republican organization. He had represented Fairbanks in the 1916 convention and had persuaded him to accept a second nomination for Vice President, despite reiterated refusals. In Chicago that year he met Republican leaders from other States—and, in particular, he met George W. Perkins, who at once shared the Indiana faith in the young man from Sullivan.

The young man was Will H. Hays. That was the name suddenly thrust into the situation in St. Louis. His strength was that he had no political ties outside of Indiana; he was young, tireless and able. He seemed the man of the hour, and the committee turned to him as to a life-saver. Not a vote was cast against him. Hays was speaking before a Presbyterian Church meeting in Indianapolis that afternoon, when the presiding officer asked him to stop for a moment and announced that he had just been unanimously chosen chairman of the Republican National Committee. A national career clean, honorable, forceful and achieving was thus begun—and has not yet ended.

CHAPTER LVIII

WHEN ACQUAINTANCE, NOT ISSUES, WON

The 1920 Convention Had Many "Ifs" To It But Harding's Acquaintances Carried The Day—Hiram Johnson Refuses To Go On Ticket—Oregon Interrupts The Lenroot Boom With Calls For Coolidge, and Delegates Insist Upon Naming Him For Vice President.

SO MANY "ifs" could be used in the story of the 1920 Republican national convention that it is still possible for any candidate before that body to believe that he would have been the nominee "if" any one of several particular things had happened as he had planned.

Of course the big "if" in everybody's mind was—if Roosevelt were alive, could he, or would he, have stopped his own nomination? Undoubtedly, he would have liked to see his return to the leadership of the Republican party authenticated by the vote of a national convention indorsing his views if not his candidacy. But I cannot forget his emphatic "no" not many months before his death when I told him he would be the unanimous nominee. In 1912 I never abandoned hope that he would finally acquiesce, but I had a different feeling about him after my talk in 1919. He was then beyond his sixtieth birthday, the strain of a persistent illness was telling on him, and I knew that he was in no condition for the return of other days and their burdens. His passing away was so sudden that he left no word to indicate the man of his choice, if he had one.

So we had another "if"—would Roosevelt have urged Leonard Wood? The General's supporters insisted yes. They declared that the mantle of Roosevelt had fallen upon his shoulders—others said no.

As I Knew Them

If Saturday had not arrived with the delegates anxious to avoid further hotel bills, would they have continued balloting instead of making a hasty choice so as to get away? If they had continued, would the steady increase of votes for Leonard Wood have gone on?

There was still another "if." Had Senator Warren Harding insisted, as at one time he was inclined to do, upon "filing" for reelection as Senator from Ohio on Thursday night (the last lawful date) he would have fallen out of the Presidential race next day. If that had happened, who would have been the nominee?

HIRAM JOHNSON REFUSES SECOND PLACE

Without dwelling upon other "ifs," however, or summarizing the rivalries for nomination, let me divert and speak of an "if" that as matters turned out really would have made a President.

If Senator Hiram Johnson, of California, had agreed to Warren Harding's personal request that he go on the ticket as Vice President, he and not Calvin Coolidge would have succeeded President Harding in the White House. Not many persons know that Johnson refused such a request, but he did. It came to him just as the delegates were "breaking" and Harding's nomination was assured. The Harding group of managers went hurriedly into conference to consider the man for second place. Harding himself suggested Johnson. Not all of those present could wholly forget 1912, however. Some argument was required to overcome their factional objection. The convention was moving fast toward its decisions. Any settlement on Vice President had to be made quickly. Johnson therefore was selected.

The California Senator was informed of Harding's wish. He promptly replied that if he could not be named for President he preferred to remain in the Senate. On several ballots Johnson had polled close to 150 votes; like other candidates he resented the hurry-up programme of the Harding supporters; he was against forcing a nomination on the plea that the convention should adjourn before Sunday. Other tactics by the Harding managers had also displeased the California Senator. His visitors, therefore, heard some rather strong words from the man they wanted to make Vice President— and Johnson knows how to be emphatic. In fact the Harding men felt uncertain as they left him whether he would support the convention's nominee and the ghost of California in 1916 came to their minds. But Johnson delivered a handsome majority to the ticket of which he might have been a part and thus two years later achieve the eager ambition of his life.

ACQUAINTANCE, NOT ISSUES, CONTROLLED

I have heard the 1920 convention referred to as a convention in which acquaintance rather than issues influenced the choice of the delegates. And that is as good an appraisement of it as any other, for the Harding nomination had no deeper significance.

He stood for no particular issue. He was a party man, ready to do whatever everybody thought best. All that week in Chicago he was smiling and buoyant throughout the usual ups and downs of convention manipulation, apparently the least concerned person in town. He had more acquaintances in the convention than any of his rivals, and in a real sense he put himself in the hands of his friends. They did the work and the worrying.

I believe that Harding was the most astonished man who ever sought the Presidency when Harry Daugherty and others convinced him Thursday night that he could safely ignore his last opportunity to file for reelection as Senator. He had signed his nominating papers for the Senatorship, and they were ready for filing in Ohio. Reluctantly, he allowed the last moment to go. Then, and not until then, did he take an active interest in the convention result. He had to get the nomination or go back to Marion as Editor of the Marion "Star" after March 4, 1921.

The Lowden candidacy at the outset had the most votes on roll-call, though it never had a strong hold on its delegates. Hiram Johnson was a definite figure among the candidates. But among seventeen men formally nominated for President, Leonard Wood had the longest identity with public affairs. As against the Wilson Administration, he meant something in the public mind. So did Calvin Coolidge, whose candidacy was based on the issue raised by the police strike in Boston. While the strike was a local affair the issue was national.

NATHAN MILLER THE ONLY MAN WHO EVER BEAT "AL" SMITH

Another candidacy that had greater possibilities than the roll-call indicated, was that of Herbert Hoover, now Secretary of Commerce. His name was presented by Nathan L. Miller, soon to be Governor of New York. Miller has the honor of being the one man who ever defeated "Al" Smith for Governor. Smith turned the tables on him in 1922, but not before Miller had made a record as one of the ablest Governors of the Empire State. It was a record that appealed to Harding in the White House, for he offered to make Miller an Associate Justice of the Supreme Court—an honor that Miller, for financial reasons, reluctantly declined.

Had the move to Harding failed Saturday forenoon, the convention surely would have adjourned until the following week. There would then have been only three candidates in the "likely" list: Calvin Coolidge, Herbert Hoover and Leonard Wood. The Lowden column had broken, but the Wood column did not weaken until Harding was too far ahead to be overtaken. There were rumors that the Lowden delegates were to turn to Wood. They might have done so had there been time for negotiation but the convention leaders refused a recess and forced a nomination.

THE NAMING OF COOLIDGE

The one surprise of the convention came in a most dramatic way when Chairman Lodge asked for nominations for Vice President. Failing to persuade Hiram Johnson, the Harding people had no candidate for second place. Senator Medill McCormick of Illinois, got recognition, and walked to the platform to make a nominating speech. To reach it he had to pass my desk in the press section.

"What are you going to do, Medill?" I asked.

"We're going to put over Lenroot," he replied.

"The hell you are!" broke in a correspondent seated at an adjoining desk.

McCormick glared at him in surprise, and as he climbed up the ladder steps to the platform, called back, "Watch me and see."

A Senators' ticket—top to bottom—Harding and Lenroot! It seemed a narrow structure for a national appeal. However, that was the slate, so I awaited developments.

McCormick had not uttered fifty words before a voice from the rear delegates' seats interrupted with "Coolidge! Coolidge!" It was not a heavy voice, but it penetrated the convention hall. All kinds of voices and all kinds of interruptions are heard in a convention. They are accepted as part of the proceedings and merely swell the volume of noise. This voice, however, had a different sound—it seemed to say something worth heeding.

Senator McCormick went on with his speech to the next period. Again came that voice from the rear benches—"Coolidge! Coolidge!" Once more it filled the hall. This time it was echoed by other delegates. From individuals in a dozen State delegations came an echo to the cry "Coolidge!"

McCormick closed by naming his candidate, Lenroot, but from the delegates and galleries came insistent calls for Coolidge.

Probably two-thirds of the Republican Senators were delegates. Most of them rose to shout for Lenroot. Edge, of New Jersey, Calder, of New York, Brandegee, of Connecticut, just in front of me, jumped upon their seats and hurrahed as though they were cheering a home run by their local base ball team. But the Senators could not out-cheer the ordinary delegates, who by this time had grown into a substantial group demanding Coolidge.

OREGON NAMES THE BAY STATE GOVERNOR

The voice that had started the Coolidge demonstration was a voice from Oregon—truly across the whole continent from Massachusetts; the Pacific calling to the Atlantic. At once all eyes turned toward the Oregon standard to see the man who had broken in on the Senatorial slate. Delegates asked his name, and wondered how it happened that far-off Oregon —the pathless wilderness that Daniel Webster preferred in 1848 to let England own rather than have America burdened with it—had become so deeply interested in the Governor of Webster's State. Conventions are often moved by their great orators but rarely by men unknown beyond their own State lines.

In one of Bernard Shaw's comedies, the critics, when asked to give their opinion of a play they had just witnessed, responded by asking the name of the author. "How can we tell whether it is good or bad unless we know who wrote it?" So it is in large assemblages—the crowd mind seeks a big name to guide it. In this instance, however, the convention only knew that a man from Oregon was insistently calling for Coolidge, and that on every call he was getting a louder response. Perhaps in those final hours the delegates were glad to be free after three dreary days of balloting for President, under the restraint of "organization" decrees.

As I Knew Them

On the Vice-Presidency, the bars were down, and the delegates streamed out of the old, beaten, follow-the-leader path into new pasture like colts turned out on June grass. There were calls for "Oregon," calls for "platform," but the man whom nobody knew modestly stood on his chair and nominated for Vice President a man whom shortly the whole world was to know. Wallace McCamant made no long speech. He merely said that the Oregon delegates had come to the convention to nominate Calvin Coolidge for President. Since they could not get him in first place, they now wanted him in second place.

By this time the Coolidge boom was everywhere. The delegates themselves were in control of the convention; leaders—especially Senators—did not count. Not since Garfield was nominated in 1880 had there been an uprising so entirely "from the floor." Senator Joseph S. Frelinghuysen, of New Jersey, moved to make the nomination of Coolidge unanimous before Lodge, surprised and chagrined, could put the motion.

469

CHAPTER LIX

"DON'T LET'S CHEAT 'EM!"

Harding Always Anxious To Tell The Whole Story In His Speeches—My Visit To Harding's Home Town And A Breakfast Prepared By A Statesman—A Last Talk with Harding Before He Left for the West—"You've A Better Job Than I Have"—He Was "Warren" To The Whole Town—Fighting Illness To Do His Duty—"It Must Not Be Again! God Grant It Will Not Be!"—His Last Act Was To Gain An 8-Hour Day For Iron And Steel Workers—A Fine Record Through The Chaos Of War.

I SHALL never forget my first visit to Harding a week or so after his return to Marion. With Senator Coleman Du Pont, Harry Daugherty, and two others, I went down on the night train from Chicago, reaching Marion before six o'clock in the morning. There was no one "at home" so early in the Marion Club, but nearby we found a bakery and a butcher shop open. Du Pont fried the ham and eggs, heated the rolls and boiled the coffee. Others set the table, I acted as waiter. Never was a breakfast better cooked or more thoroughly enjoyed.

About nine o'clock we walked over to call on Harding. There in one of those modest village homes that are the greatest asset of American life we found the candidate—physically a splendid type of manhood. He asked my opinion as a newspaper editor as to how long an acceptance speech should be. Spread out before him were proofsheets that would fill a newspaper page.

"About half that much," I said.

He looked surprised.

"Candidates try to say too much at one time," I continued,

"and the people will not read it all. Give it to them little by little; then they will read it all."

"You're right from one point of view," he said, "but an acceptance speech is a sort of confession of faith; it's a record. The folks ought to know it all in one story. They expect it that way and we mustn't cheat 'em. Let them know it all, and then let them decide. Don't let's cheat 'em; let's make the record full and fair."

The speech when published filled almost two newspaper pages, or sixteen columns.

"DON'T LET'S CHEAT 'EM!"

After the campaign I learned that "Don't let's cheat 'em!" was a usual phrase with Harding when discussing the completeness of his speeches. Richard Washburn Child was one of those in charge of Harding's speaking engagements. Every morning they would have a conference about the speech for that particular day. Harding would ask for the data that had been gathered and listen to arguments about emphasizing or omitting different features. Invariably he would end discussion by saying: "Well, boys, let's tell them the whole story. Don't let's cheat 'em! They'll like us better."

Whenever there was doubt around the Harding headquarters in Marion as to what to do in public utterances, the candidate's "Don't let's cheat 'em!" became the guide. Finally, it spread to national headquarters, where Will Hays began using it in talks with campaign spell-binders.

Frankness was a strong Harding trait. And he always meant what he said. When the adjusted compensation bill —the "bonus bill"—was before him for approval or rejection in September 1922, he had decided not to sign it. He knew, however, that he had made a number of campaign speeches on the subject. Obviously, he could not recall every word he had said, but he wondered whether he had ever made any statement that could be regarded as a pledge to favor such a measure. He sent for Will Hays, then Postmaster General, who had managed the campaign.

"Will," he said, "you know my campaign speeches. Did I ever say anything that would lead anyone to charge me with breaking faith if I should refuse to sign this bill?"

"I think not," replied Hays, "but I would have to look it up to be sure."

"Then I'll give you two days to have it looked up," replied the President. "Put enough men on the job to read every word I ever uttered. I am sure my record is clear, but make doubly sure, for if I'm pledged to sign it I'll sign."

The speeches were gone over, no pledge was found, and the bill went back to Congress with a Harding veto.

A LAST TALK WITH HARDING

"This is the most distressful decision of my life," said President Harding to me in the White House as he held up before me the contract, just signed, for the sale of the Marion "Star." "It tears at my heart. But what else is there for me to do? I do not expect ever to live in Marion again, and there is no joy in running a newspaper from a distance. Besides, every community is entitled to a resident editor for its newspapers. It is hard for me to think that my days as editor are over. An editor has the finest job in the world— I envy all you fellows. You've a better job than I have."

For nearly two hours, we talked "shop." It was a day or two before the President left on the trip from which he never returned. He was in a strange mood. I have since frequently recalled his tone, his words and his attitude that afternoon and as I have done so it seemed to me as though something hovering over him led him into a sort of spiritual mood.

I did not suspect that he was a sick man, for only his closest intimates knew that he was ill, but it was plain that something was sapping his strength and taking the color out of his face.

As I Knew Them

I realized as I left him that I was saying good-bye to a man who needed rest. I made up my mind also that Harding was not happy as President.

The austerity of the White House, the separation from companionships that meant much to him, created a void in his daily life that the honor of his title did not fill. This was reflected in his face the afternoon in July 1921 when he went to the Capitol to plead with the Senate not to pass the first bonus bill. Before making his address he sat with his old group at lunch around the familiar corner table in the Senate restaurant. Senator Frelinghuysen accompanied him from the White House.

"Don't make any early dates for me this afternoon," Harding called to his secretary. "I want to feel free."

And, as I watched him step into his motor car, I remarked that I had never seen him look so happy. That day, he told the Senate frankly what that particular bonus bill would mean to the finances of the nation. To the surprise of all observers, it was sent back to committee, and another year elapsed before the adjusted compensation bill succeeded it.

HARDING—HIS HOME TOWN'S "WARREN"

Fate was unkind to Warren Harding. It made him President almost against his will and certainly without his urging; it gave him the greatest popular and electoral majority ever recorded in a national election, and then, as he was growing into the bigness of his office, it robbed him of the opportunity to make good on the larger conception of his responsibilities that had slowly come to him out of the burdens and anxieties.

To get an accurate line on Harding you must go back to his days as Editor of the Marion "Star." He was the best known man in town. His office was the gathering place for all seekers after favor—the favor of publicity and the greater favor of no publicity. At the club, in the shops, everybody called him Warren, and he called every fellow townsman by his first name. For him, the intimacies of a small town made life worth living; their boundaries marked the world of his desires.

He drifted into county conventions, state conventions, national conventions—always a popular figure. Then his road led to the Legislature at Columbus, to the Lieutenant Governorship, and to the Senate at Washington.

Even with these honors ambition did not stir him greatly. He remained "Warren," with all that that implied. With every advance he carried wholeheartedly the load of old associations. Each period back in Ohio had had its group of them. Slowly, without full appreciation of the changes he had outgrown them; but they clung to him and he clung to them. He was the last man in the world to realize their embarrassment to him when he entered the White House, also the last man to turn from them because they were embarrassing.

It seemed the task of gratitude, and the test of loyalty, to stand by them, and he did stand by them. He could see no wrong in their ways or their purposes, could see no reason why the ways of Marion and of Columbus as he knew them could not be the ways of the White House.

HARDING LOVED LIFE AND HIS FRIENDS

There was gratitude, there was friendship, there was a comradic warmth about Warren Harding that in every presence made him less a Senator, less a President, and more a genial understanding companion; life had finally turned its pleasant side to him and he tried to make it do the same for everyone he knew. He greeted every dawn with the sunny, cheery smile of the man who loved life and his friends, and whose record is made up only of kindly acts. It was so back in Marion days, so in the Ohio Legislature, so in the Senate, so in the White House, and so to his last breath in San Francisco. Truly a consistent record, for it was flesh of his flesh, bone of his bone.

As I Knew Them

Harding did not make a burden of his work, but he was an earnest President. He had Hughes in the State Department, Mellon in the Treasury, Hoover in the Interior, Hays in the Post Office, Weeks in the War Department, and Dawes at the Budget. What stronger group could be assembled, to relieve a President of perplexities, and to aid him in a wise solution of his problems? He knew he was in safe hands when he trusted them; he believed as confidently that he was in safe hands when with equal faith he trusted others who did not prove so dependable.

Then too, Harding was an undisciplined man in his day's work. The old times of care-free printer and editor were still coloring his cordial nature. Method rather than purpose stood in the way of rigid organized effort. But those who criticise must face the fact that Harding labored for a year with a blood pressure exceeding 180, defying the orders of his doctors and silencing those who had to know of his peril and might speak of it to others.

While the newspapers were publishing reports of Mrs. Harding's illness, they could with equal truth have published reports of the President's defiance of death, day after day, in order to attend to the affairs of the nation. The calm courage with which he endured that strain is shown by the way in which he kept it his own secret, shared only by his Cabinet, until finally, it was revealed to the world by his collapse in San Francisco.

FACING AFTER-WAR PROBLEMS AND CHAOS

A colossal task faced the man who became President in March 1921. Returning the country to a peace basis—(to "normalcy," as Harding described it)—was quite as difficult as directing it on a war basis. The spirit of united effort left the people when war ceased. Every nation was in chaos. We had our railroads emerging, almost bankrupt, from government control; we had ships by the score that had never sailed the seas, and scores of others destined never to sail again; we had millions of men demobilized from the army, but not yet gathered back into industry; we had industrial and farm over-capacity and over-production that finally forced a deflation period through which the country staggered but did not fall. In our great agricultural States more banks closed than remained open. In truth all the chaos of war in our own country as well as its terrific ravages abroad came to Harding for adjustment.

THE RIGHT MAN FOR EACH TASK

He was a newspaper editor and a politician. He had no experience equipping him for the situation he had to deal with. He could not be a Mellon, but he got Mellon; he could not be a Hughes, but he got Hughes; he could not be a Hoover, but he got Hoover; he could not be a Hays, but he got Hays. The experience he lacked was to be found in those men. Yet in their selection, except with Hays, he ran against the narrow views of his party leaders. They could see no politics in the choice of such men, but Harding had a larger conception of the country's need.

There was the unemployment conference with Hoover and Davis at the head, with leading employers of labor gathered together in Washington to find a way to put men to work. That, too, was not politics, but it was service for the country. A railroad strike was settled, a coal strike was settled, farmers were financed as well as possible through the War Finance Board, Dawes was brought on from Chicago to budget government expenditures, and the one big constructive after-war measure upon which all nations agreed—the limitation of naval armament—was carried to success. I have no exact figures, but my guess is that that agreement has already saved taxpayers close to a billion dollars which would have been spent for war ships.

SOUGHT THE RIGHT WAY AND RIGHT MAN

Sum it all up from the record of Harding's two years in the White House and it will be found that he proved greater than his conceded limitations; and that in every large policy and task the intuitions of a deep patriotism led him in vital matters to search for the way and the men that would accomplish most. His judgment was not infallible; some mistakes were inevitable. But when suspicion reached him, he corrected two mistakes in men. The scandals attaching to those men are discussed by scandal-mongers as though Harding had not moved in the matter, though the date of his action, in each case, is easily available.

HIS VICTORY FOR THE 8-HOUR DAY

Harding found approximately 200,000 men in our iron and steel mills working twelve hours a day. He made no public announcement, but a few months before he started west he took up the subject with Judge Elbert H. Gary and Charles M. Schwab. As he was leaving for Alaska, he made public the written pledge of the iron and steel companies to change from a twelve-hour to an eight-hour day. Harding did not live to see the change made. But he died knowing what he had accomplished for labor. The eight-hour day in that industry is a Harding day. He told Judge Gary that he would regard it as the greatest triumph of his Administration.

"IT MUST NOT BE AGAIN"

I witnessed that scene on the long Hoboken pier when the first bodies of our soldier dead were brought home for burial. I followed behind Harding as he walked the length of the pier, viewing the long row of coffins, visibly agitated by the sight. In the speech he then made he brought tears to many eyes as well as to his own as he said:

> "They have served, which is the supreme inspiration of living. They have earned everlasting gratitude, which is the supreme solace in dying. . . .
>
> "There is ringing in my ears like an admonition eternal, an insistent call—'It must not be again! It must not be again!' God grant that it will not be, and let a practical people join in cooperation with God to the end that it shall not be."

And the same sentiment ran through his speech later, at the naval limitation conference in Washington when he declared to the assembled statesmen of the great nations:

> "The United States welcomes you with unselfish hands. We have no fears; we have no sordid ends to serve; we suspect no enemy; we contemplate or apprehend no conquest. Content with what we have we seek nothing that is another's. We only wish to do with you that finer nobler thing which no nation can do alone."

Of war, he said in the same address, "How can humanity justify, or God forgive?"

OUR PROTECTION IS OUR FRATERNITY

No better picture of Warren Harding, man of sentiment, of friends and of patriotism can be painted than his own words. And he spoke no finer sentiment than is to be found in his address at Vancouver, British Columbia, on July 26— only a week before his death. Here is an extract well worth reading:

> "Thousands of your brave lads perished in gallant and generous action for the preservation of our Union. Many of our young men followed Canadian colors to the battlefields of France before we entered the war and left their proportion of killed to share the graves of your intrepid sons.

As I Knew Them

"When my mind reverts and my heart beats low the recollection of those faithful and noble companionships, I may not address you as fellow citizens, as I am accustomed to designate assemblages at home, but I may and do, with respect and pride, salute you as 'fellow men' in mutual striving for common good.

"What an object lesson of peace is shown today by our two countries to all the world! No grim-faced fortifications mark our frontier, no huge battleships patrol our dividing waters, no stealthy spies lurk in our tranquil border hamlets.

"Only a scrap of paper, recording hardly more than a simple understanding, safeguards lives and properties on the Great Lakes, and only humble mile posts mark the inviolable boundary line for thousands of miles through farm and forest.

"Our protection is our fraternity; our armour is our faith; the tie that binds more firmly, year by year, is ever increasing acquaintance and comradeship through interchange of citizens; and the compact is not of perishable parchment, but of fair and honorable dealing, which, God grant, shall continue for all times."

CHAPTER LX

WHO *KNEW* WOODROW WILSON?

No One Convinces Others That He Knew Him—A Many-Sided Man—Would Never Get Anywhere If He Listened To Suggestion—No Use For Cabinet Or Senators—Write And Wait For Your Type-written Answer—A Solitary Figure, Battling Alone—The School Master Sure Enough.

I WISH that I could say I *knew* Woodrow Wilson. I have never met anyone who makes that claim and who at the same time validates it in any mind but his own.

Of course, you can always hear two contrasting opinions about our Presidents, usually more than two, but never were so many diverse opinions heard as could be heard of Wilson in his day. Such a thing as being in his confidence deep enough to know beyond challenge the real man, to understand his moods and impulses, seems to have been impossible.

"A cold intellectual," some folks said; "an inspiring, stimulating companion," others said; "the most curt, opinionated man of all I know," another said; "a man of superb ability and the most workmanlike man I was ever associated with," is another direct quotation to me from the leader of a group.

These utterances, though from different sources, echo the estimate made to me, seven or eight years ago, by one who knew Wilson intimately at Princeton and for some time thereafter, "a many-sided man, so many sides that there is room for a variety of honest opinions." There were those who found in him much to admire, and with good reason; there were those who found in him much to deplore, and with good reason. There were those who were baffled by his swift, pitiless, unexplained changes from friendly relations to cold dismissal, and with good reason.

480

As I Knew Them

Those who saw the good in Wilson acclaimed him with Islamic faith and adulation; those who saw the other side were equally intense in their condemnation. The in-betweens were not so numerous during his first term as either of the extremes; during his second term, the idolaters were not so many as in the earlier years of his Presidency, but they grew more emotionally devout as their ranks grew thinner.

The groups I have quoted were in the Cabinet, in Congress, among the leaders of his party, and among those who though not in politics had contact with him on public matters.

Sifting these varied opinions plus my own observation of the man, my guess is that Wilson held himself from you unless he felt you had something to bring him that he lacked, and that there was not much that in his own opinion he lacked for long. He had few around him whom he regarded as on a level with himself, and to whom he felt it worth while to listen.

NEVER GET ANYWHERE IF HE LISTENED TO OTHERS

During his first year as President one of his intimates urged him to establish better relations with his party leaders in the Senate and House, to ask for suggestions, and discuss contemplated policies with them.

"Utterly futile," he quickly replied in decisive voice. "A waste of time. I would never get anywhere if I should do that. Every fellow has his own views; I would be swamped."

"Even if they have no ideas worth adopting, Mr. President," persisted this visitor, "you would get their cooperation in things you want to accomplish. They would feel that you at least had given their views consideration."

"Futile! I tell you, futile!" again replied Wilson, "I can make better headway by giving consideration to my own ideas, whipping them into shape, testing them out in my own way, and insuring their adoption by their own fairness and merit. I waste no time while I am engaged in such work."

481

It was not Congress alone that was thus held at arm's length.

One night I found Franklin K. Lane, his Secretary of the Interior, sitting on a hotel corridor lounge deeply absorbed in reading an address just delivered by the President. "Great stuff," he said to me, "great stuff that is. I like to have him talk that way."

"Didn't you know he was going to say it?" I asked.

"Not a word of it," he replied. "I haven't seen the President for a month, and don't know when I shall."

NO USE FOR CABINET OR SENATORS

From that talk and from others I learned that Wilson's Cabinet officers rarely saw his public addresses until they read them in the newspapers; they were not privileged, either, to have an advance reading of his messages to Congress except such portions as concerned their individual departments. Wilson was not distrustful or suspicious of people; he ignored his Cabinet and Senators because he did not regard them as his equal, and wanted to hear their views only when he asked for them. Cleveland maintained the most cordial relations with his Cabinet and he gave his confidence to those Senators and Congressmen he trusted. The latter were few, it is true, but they were a crowd compared with Wilson's intimates.

Yet it was this same Wilson who in his inaugural address in 1913 had said:

"I summon all honest men, all patriotic, all forward-looking men to my side. God helping me, I will not fail them, if they will but counsel and sustain me."

AN INCIDENT IN TRENTON

Wilson's curtness and unwillingness to listen to discussion were attributed sometimes to the inability of men to "get" him, to understand how to approach him and the arguments

As I Knew Them

that would appeal to him. I have had cited as an illustration
an incident at the State House in Trenton while he was Governor of New Jersey.

Wilson was then jamming his famous "Seven Sisters" bills
through the Legislature. The measure attracted nation-wide
attention and was heralded as a cure-all for corporation evils.
Its only result in fact was to give Wilson a place in the public
mind, and to lose New Jersey several million dollars in taxes
on foreign companies.

Wilson was not pleasing Jersey Democrats with his distribu-
tion of patronage. A group of legislators determined to hold
up the "Seven Sisters" bills until they could have an understanding. They called upon the Governor, but their line of
argument quickly showed no meeting place for their minds and
Wilson's.

Presently they began to hint that his legislation might suffer.
The light blue of his eyes when in friendly conversation deep-
ened at once into the dark blue of the ocean when tempest
tossed. He got up, took a quick turn about his desk (a habit
of his when excited to anger), and cut them off in a series of
short, savagely contemptuous answers. They went out silent
and bewildered.

WRITE—AND WAIT FOR YOUR ANSWER

In a larger way, the same incidents frequently occurred at
Washington. They strengthened his distaste for "conference" and for meeting people. Some in anger, some in admiration, all in silence, left him at his bidding to his own
thoughts. More than once, when reminded of his abruptness
he seemed surprised. He would curtly say, "Well, I can't
make myself over."

This practice of "self-determination" grew with Wilson as
he found himself with the dazzling power of a President. He
listened reluctantly, if at all, to oral suggestions; he gave as

his reason that he did not want his mind swayed by the personality of the proponent. You were asked to present your views in writing. He insisted that in that way only could he consider them dispassionately, and without regard to the source. Even Cabinet officers were forced to do this, and to wait, sometimes for weeks, the famous typewritten memo from Wilson's study in reply. This much must be said for that memo—it always bore evidence that he had thoroughly considered your paper.

But a President cannot carry on a government on a typewriter. Most essential to him is the open conflict of many minds, searching for the best conclusion—the enlightening contact of a round-table discussion. A product of the cloister cannot escape its rigid environment, and our ocean-to-ocean continent is too big for one man, unaided, to grasp its needs.

A SOLITARY FIGURE BATTLING ALONE

In that sense, Wilson became almost a recluse after his second election. Constantly he would reiterate that he had no time for discussion. More and more angrily he resented efforts to change his mind, more and more he stripped himself of old friendships—eventually even of Colonel House—and stood a lone, slim, pallid figure on an eminence as unapproachable as Mount Everest—

——such a man, too fond to rule alone,
Bears, like the Turk, no brother near the throne.

If you will look over the Wilson friendships, you will find that they were ever-changing. He took none of his associates out of Princeton into public life; he took only Tumulty out of Jersey political life and left only antagonisms behind him; and after his eight years in the Presidency the men remaining close to him in private life were Bernard M. Baruch, Norman Davis and Bainbridge Colby, who were of the last not the early vintage of his friendships. The separations were his choice; not the choice of his early supporters. Even Tumulty was dropped, his wonderful loyalty spurned. Wilson is the only President of the last half century who failed to honor in a conspicuous way some friend or friends of other years. In his view, friendship meant service to him and not by him; friendships were bridges burned behind as he himself moved on, a solitary traveller.

While writing this chapter I asked one of Wilson's most loyal supporters in his last days how he accounted for this marked absence of long-time associates in his Administration. "In pursuit of what he believed to be right Wilson was as relentless as time," he replied. "Public office was to his mind most emphatically a public trust and he acted as a trustee. It might and would grieve him deeply to refuse to appoint a man whom he liked immensely but he would surely refuse unless he believed the man was capable. He had the stern sense of duty that would lead him to send his best friend to the scaffold, though it would break his heart to do it."

ANOTHER WILSON IN PRIVATE LIFE

The Wilson in private life, in social intercourse, was an entirely different man. He was genial and witty; he could tell a story magnificently, and he had a highly developed sense of humor. He was not the cold unresponsive overlord but a lively companion. His sense of his own dignity was less than Roosevelt's; he did not seem to value it, while Roosevelt sometimes over-valued his. Wilson did not get himself across the footlights, though. He was pleased beyond words when, while stumping in 1912, some one in a crowd called him "Woody." His face was one big smile whenever he talked of that greeting and he took it as an indication that he was putting over with the people the Wilson of his own mind. But he was not, and never did.

485

As I Knew Them

During the early days of Wilson in the White House it was said in Washington, chiefly by those politically opposed, that he was a schoolmaster in public office, and that no event or experience would be powerful enough ever to take him out of the rôle. At the national Capitol one is accustomed to cynicism and criticism and I tried not to allow that particular estimate to take hold of me. It was to be expected that some of the atmosphere of the school-room would cling to him, but I believed that the wider outlook and contacts of the Presidency would quickly dissipate it. That belief was to be slowly shattered. As the months rolled by I heard the early opinion echoed by members of his own party. But not until the memorable night of April 2, 1917, when he appeared before Congress to deliver his war message, did Wilson seem to me to justify his critics.

As he entered the crowded House of Representatives through a narrow stage-door back of the Speaker's rostrum, he was the schoolmaster beyond all question—the perfect product of the conventional mould. His pale, immobile face, his protruding chin, his long thin nose firmly supporting eye-glasses, his carefully brushed hair, his slender figure seemingly elongated by a close-fitting frock coat, his dark gray trousers painstakingly creased, his ease, the manner of one conscious of his commanding place and of the importance of what others were now to hear from his lips;—yes, he was the schoolmaster from head to foot.

When he looked out upon the faces in front of him, he saw the revered justices of the Supreme Court seated in semicircle around the "well"; back of them were ranged the somewhat less revered members of the Senate; in their seats were the Congressmen, whom no one seems to revere. Diplomats and their wives crowded their assigned gallery, important folks from all parts of the country filled the public spaces to over-

486

WOODROW WILSON IN CHARACTERISTIC POSE WHILE SPEAKING

flowing. We knew war must come and its brutalities and tragedies even then cast a shadow of solemnity over the brilliant scene.

THE COOL AND COLLECTED WILSON

I studied Wilson from the press gallery. As he advanced to the space in front of the Speaker's desk I searched his face and manner for some emotion responsive to the vital importance of that moment. Not a sign! No man ever was more at ease. To the correspondent who sat next to me I remarked that Wilson took his manuscript from the pocket of his frock-coat and began his address with the calmness of a clergyman announcing the evening meetings of the coming week before service; he read it with as little emphasis. If his manner was deliberate restraint it was a masterpiece; if it was just Wilson, he certainly was the coldest man I ever looked upon.

He got from that great audience what he gave it—the coolness of an academic address.

Oh, for a Roosevelt! the thought came to me as I listened to paragraph after paragraph without a handclap, without a change in the placid faces of the audience, without any noticeable depth of feeling in the speaker's tone.

Perhaps Chief Justice White had much the same thought, for after vainly waiting for someone else to punctuate the President's speech with applause, he dropped on the floor the felt hat he had been holding on his lap, and started a vigorous first round. Wilson was then half way through. Of course, at the close, there was a wave of enthusiasm, for the peroration was thrilling, but nothing in his manner or tone gave encouragement to go much beyond respectful hearing and courteous response.

And no one did.

CHAPTER LXI

SAW HIMSELF THE WORLD'S ARBITER

Wilson Sure At First That He Was To Be Arbiter Of The World War—Other Methods Would Have Brought Us Into The League Of Nations—An Amazing Secret Agreement "Probably" To Go To War —"You Know My Mind And How To Interpret It" He Told House— Kitchener's Words "Worth Serious Consideration"—"We're Just Backing Into War" Said Senator Stone—Wilson's Liking For "13"— "How Far From Paris To Versailles?" Asked Senator Martin.

FROM the first beat of the drums abroad, the World War drew Wilson into a wider field than any President was ever called upon to work in—as wide as the world itself. It was not given to any man alone to foresee its tremendous scope, to know and appraise its developing phases, or wisely to guide a nation desiring peace, but being steadily drawn into war. Wilson undertook to do it—alone. It seemed to him an opportunity almost as great as came to Washington and Lincoln to make himself immortal, and it was in his nature to want no rivals for that fame.

The dimensions of the picture gave him no concern; he never doubted he could measure up to them. He had always worked alone; he was now President of the most powerful nation. Alone he stood at the peak of fame; with the poet his one thought was:

> "What shall I do to be forever known,
> To make the age to come my own?"

The prospect fascinated, controlled him. His great power coldly, dispassionately, held aloof from the intense conflict seemed to him certain to make him the chosen arbiter of the fate of nations. Many strange and baffling situations were to arise, but Wilson never lessened faith in his ability to master them, nor in his purpose to be the central figure; rather he emphasized both. He lost his opportunity to leave deeds instead of words as his record because it was not possible for one mind to force every other mind to its single point of view; and he lost his life because, physically and mentally, it was not possible for one man alone to carry the burdens and solve the problems of a 100,000,000 nation at war.

There were three distinct periods in Wilson's career as it relates to the World War.

The first period was dominated by his early determination to keep America "ready to play the part of impartial mediator, not as a partisan but as a friend"; "neutral in thought and deed."

The second period covered our participation in the war.

The third period was dominated by his re-awakened purpose, after having gone through war, to make himself the peacemaker of history. Alone so far as America was concerned he outlined the terms of a world settlement; alone he sat at the peace table in Paris; alone he passed on the wisdom or unwisdom of every line of the treaty; alone he carried the treaty back with him to Washington, personally submitting it to the Senate and demanding that that body ratify it precisely as it stood because, in his judgment, it was the embodiment of the sum of human hopes.

WHY WE ARE NOT IN THE LEAGUE

The result of this unyielding attitude is that the United States is not a member of the League of Nations, and that Wilson, his personality and his policies still remain in controversy.

When the historian analyzes Wilson's course, he will find that the Versailles Treaty in all probability would have been ratified by the Senate without a serious fight over the League of Nations, had Wilson sent to Paris a peace commission representative of America, with power, purpose and ability to negotiate with other nations, even with Wilson present.

Again, when the historian reads the series of Wilson notes to Germany and England covering more than two years and sees how the two nations at war persisted in their own way— one with sub-marines and the other by seizing our ships and taking them to port—he will be astounded at the claim of the 1916 Democratic national platform of "splendid diplomatic triumphs" that had "kept us out of war."

He will search in vain for diplomatic triumphs; the record shows an unbroken line of diplomatic turn-downs and evasions. The response from Mexico in 1914 to our demand to salute our flag was a pattern later for the responses of both England and Germany to our notes of protest. Mexico never saluted, England continued to search our ships and Germany sub-marined more ruthlessly than ever. Toward all three countries we adopted a policy of "watchful waiting" for something that never came—and that everybody but Wilson knew would never come.

Three days after the torpedoing of the "Lusitania" Wilson proclaimed an "America too proud to fight." With that sentiment crossing the Atlantic to Germany simultaneously with our note of protest, the Kaiser knew, as indeed the whole world knew, that the head of the American government had other aims than war in mind. No matter how loud we might thunder, "too proud to fight" was accepted by Germany as a roving commission for her sub-marines; the subsequent warning that we would hold her to "strict accountability" did not stop a single attack; nor delay or change a single German purpose.

WHEN THE GERMANS ERRED

Von Bernstorff and other Germans had studied their Wilson and they thought they knew him; then came the 1916 triumph of his kept-us-out-of-war platform. That result confirmed them in their wrong assumption that the President could not be dragged into war, whatever Germany might do. The defiant "unrestricted" sub-marine policy shortly announced by the Kaiser was a consequence of that judgment. It held good so long as war events failed to arouse Wilson's patriotism to the peril of his pride of opinion. For no one can truly say of Wilson that he lacked intense love of country; he was deeply patriotic. But his supreme confidence in himself created a certainty that his own purposes were best for the nation and he did not hesitate to let others know it. Nothing was so precious to him as his own opinion, his own future; nothing so valueless as what others might say or think to the contrary.

A SECRET AGREEMENT "PROBABLY" TO WAR

Has anyone ever explained the staggering fact that at the moment Wilson was giving his O.K. to Governor Glynn's keynote utterance in the 1916 Democratic National Convention, "He-kept-us-out-of-war," there was lying on the desk of England's War Minister, Sir Edward Grey, awaiting England's approval, "at an opportune moment," a secret document (signed of all days on the calendar for a foreign alliance by America, February 22nd) and approved by Wilson, reading as follows:

> "Confidential. Col. House told me that President Wilson was ready, on hearing from France and England, that the moment was opportune, to propose that a conference should be summoned to put an end to the war. Should the Allies accept this proposal and should Germany refuse it, the United States would probably enter the war against Germany.
>
> "Col. House expressed the opinion that if such a conference met, it would secure peace on terms not unfavorable to the Allies, and if it failed to secure peace the United States would leave the conference as a belligerent on the side of the Allies if Germany was unreasonable. . . ."

Only within the last year, through "The Intimate Papers of Colonel House" and Sir Edward Grey's "Memoirs" has this document become public; had it been known to exist at the time the Democrats were hurrahing in convention over the Glynn speech, or had it become known during the campaign while western voters were convinced Wilson would continue to keep us out of war, a tornado of protest against secret war agreements would have swept the country.

The only change Wilson made in the original House memorandum was to insert the word "probably" before "enter the war against Germany." "Probably," of course, was a saving clause that ordinary precaution suggested.

HOUSE AS THE PRESIDENT'S SPOKESMAN

House had sailed for Europe on December 15, 1915, with the definite understanding reached between Wilson, Lansing and himself that he was to supersede all Ambassadors and represent the President directly. Wilson thanked him for consenting to make the trip, and provided him with a "To-Whom-It-May Concern" letter as his trusted and confidential spokesman. In effect, those in Europe to whom the letter was intended to be shown realized at once that House reflected the President's mind. It is now in Yale University Library but it properly belongs on the files of the State Department at Washington, for no man ever went abroad to pledge this country in any circumstances to war, authorized only by a private letter. Only an Emperor of the most autocratic type would make the fortunes of a great nation his sole personal concern.

Thus in considering Wilson before the war we have a Wilson "neutral in thought and deed," "ready to play the part of an impartial mediator," a Wilson nominated for reelection because his avowed purpose was to keep us out of war, and in contrast at the same moment a Wilson with an outstanding pledge to go to war if "Germany proved unreasonable." I leave it to the reader to judge had England accepted Wilson's condition what chance there was for America to escape war under the terms of that memo—the only document in existence in which this government was ever committed even remotely to a foreign government to engage as its ally in war. House insists in his diary that this was an effort for peace, but he concedes that if England had accepted the result would have brought us into war.

Of course, the Grey memo was in fact a Wilson document; but how Wilson could go through a Presidential campaign as a kept-us-out-of-war candidate with that we-will-go-in document lying around like a ton of dynamite is beyond me. Every morning he must have given a sigh of relief when he found that the newspapers were still without information of the most daring negotiation ever carried on in the name of our government. Fortunately for Wilson's political fortunes the newspapers never learned of it. Downing Street proved rumor-tight.

KITCHENER'S WORDS WORTHY OF CONSIDERATION

Here, indeed, we see the many-sided Wilson his friends described—so many sides, as one friend had said, that there is room for a variety of honest opinion. It was at this time, too, while the Grey memo still awaited England's "opportune moment," that Wilson frankly stated that he was impressed by a voice from England—that of Lord Kitchener. Only a short time before Kitchener sailed on his fatal voyage, he had said to House, "God forbid that any nation should become involved in this war, but if the United States should feel compelled to come in, it would shorten the war, save an untold number of lives, and lighten for the world the burden that will otherwise crush it for years."

Of all the soldiers and statesmen of the world Kitchener alone in 1914 sensed the duration of the struggle just begun. By 1916 events had confirmed his conception of it and when Wilson that summer heard Kitchener's words as to our own

From London Punch 1916.

BRINGING IT HOME.

"TUT! TUT! GERMAN SUBMARINE BLOCKADING NEW YORK? IMPOSSIBLE!"

participation he promptly accepted them as "worth serious consideration."

Reelection, however, turned Wilson's thoughts back to his rôle of "an impartial mediator"—more suited to him than any other. Again he visioned the monument he was building for himself with the grateful inscription by his countrymen "He kept us out of war" and he went to work at it with new determination. The Roosevelt onslaughts, vigorous, scathing and persistent, only hardened him to his course. He continued to speak of war as an Atlantic seaboard affair with which people west and south had no sympathy. He insisted that they believed with him that it was "no concern of ours" and that the election had proved that they wanted him to continue "neutral in thought and deed."

Wilson's message to Congress in January, 1917—three months later we were at war—that "this country does not intend to become involved," and later his plan for "peace without victory," were a logical sequence to his December letter to the belligerents that they should declare their purpose in war and seek an adjustment. Never was Wilson so strongly against our getting into war, never so resentful of reminders that events were making our entrance into it inevitable, as during the months immediately preceding our war declaration. His own judgment was against it—hence it could not be. Orders became more rigid against any preparation of our army and navy, and Cabinet officers whose unexpressed views were known not to agree with the President's found themselves ignored.

"WE'RE JUST BACKING INTO WAR!"

A President has facilities for learning the true situation available to no individual, but the only facts Wilson sought were those that seemed to sustain his position. His course recalls a statement made after the 1912 election by one closely associated with him at Princeton: "He will make a fine President so long as he is right, but God help the United States should Wilson be wrong!"

While the perplexities and uncertainties were reaching their climax in the winter of 1916-17, Senator Stone, of Missouri, —"Gum Shoe Bill," as he was commonly called,—then Chairman of the Senate Foreign Relations Committee said to me in a tone that reflected the existing chaos, "We're just backing into war."

"I'LL DO MY DAMNEDEST!" SAID WILSON

War had to be; Wilson had to abandon his dream. When he faced the reality he went whole-heartedly to his new task. At their first conference, the Allies told him of their exhausted condition, of the imperative need for haste. Wilson's instant reply was "Gentlemen, I'll do my damnedest!" And he did. He shunted his Cabinet to the side lines and picked men in whose organizing ability he had more confidence. They formed his "War Cabinet" and with them he sat in conference every Wednesday. In that circle were Newton D. Baker, Bernard M. Baruch, Charles G. Dawes, William G. McAdoo, Herbert Hoover, Vance McCormick, Edward N. Hurley and Dr. Harry Garfield, president of Williams College. There Wilson listened to criticism as he listened nowhere else, but he insisted upon having suggestion with it. An illustrative incident occurred when one of the War Cabinet said that a certain member of a leading commission was incompetent.

"All right," said Wilson, "get me a successor who will do better and I'll appoint him. Put up or shut up."

Two weeks were spent in vain search for the better man. Everybody who was sought professed to be too busy. Finally the Cabinet officer abandoned the effort and reported to Wilson.

"Now you have had your chance to put up," said the President, "and you couldn't. So it's your duty to shut up."

As I Knew Them

THE PENALTY OF BEING UNPREPARED

But with all its man-power, its spirit and its factories, America could not hide its unpreparedness for war. Wilson did his best to make up for this humiliating consequence of his peace dreams; the whole country went to work with a will; yet the sad record is that not an American cannon of real power was ever placed on the battle lines of France, not an American aeroplane ever flew over enemy country, not a wooden ship ever felt the splash of an ocean wave against its prow.

Wilson's damnedest, however, did give the Allies something most effective—his speeches and addresses. Lord Northcliffe had them printed in German and from aeroplanes covered Germany with pamphlets as with a blanket of snow. Such propaganda outdid the Allies' cannon in breaking down the morale of the German army; it led the German people to doubt, for the first time, whether their Kaiser was right, but particularly whether they could win the war. That kind of fighting appealed to Wilson; he was at home with words and phrases; he could produce them without the aid of factory or furnace, or farm. He did it well.

THE PEACE TABLE ALWAYS WILSON'S GOAL

Never for an instant during the nineteen months we were engaged in war did Wilson regard the conflict as his place of opportunity; the peace council not the battlefield was always his goal. And when the peace-making came we had again the two Wilsons—the Wilson sincerely intent upon making the world "safe for democracy" and the Wilson determined, alone, to dictate and control the manner of doing it. He could see no difference in the aims of the two Wilsons, so sure was he that, better than any or all others, he knew what was best.

As I Knew Them

In his letters and speeches from the moment of the armistice you will find many appeals for support for what he was undertaking to do, but never a suggestion that he desired cooperation.

When he announced to Congress that he was going to France he gave as his reason that the Allies "very reasonably desire my personal counsel," though there is no record of such a request; he asked for "undivided support," and then assured the listening legislators that the cables would make him "immediately available" for any aid or counsel *they* might desire of him. Not a word in that address could even by inference be accepted as indicating that he felt in need of counsel from the coordinate branch of government. He wanted support—not advice.

SEEKS, THEN IGNORES, ELECTION VERDICT

Yet at the time he was on notice definitely from the country that world peace was neither a one-man affair nor a one-party affair. Two months earlier, just before the Congressional elections of 1918, he had amazed the people by his letter addressed "To My Fellow Countrymen" asking them to express themselves unmistakably by returning a Democratic majority to Senate and House, "if you have approved of my leadership and wish me to continue to be your unembarrassed spokesman in affairs at home and abroad."

Here are some other paragraphs in that most remarkable of all campaign appeals:

> "I am your servant and will accept your judgment without cavil. But my power to administer the great trust assigned me by the Constitution would be seriously impaired should your judgment be adverse. . . .
>
> "I have no thought of suggesting that any political party is paramount in matters of patriotism. I feel too deeply the sacrifices which have been made in this war by all our citizens, irrespective of party affiliation, to harbor such an idea. I mean only that the

THE PARADE TO PARIS—WILSON, HOUSE, LANSING, WHITE, BLISS, BARUCH, HOOVER AND CREEL

differences and delicacies of our present task are of a sort that makes it imperatively necessary that the nation should give its undivided support to the government under a unified leadership and that a Republican Congress would divide that leadership.

"The return of a Republican majority to either House of Congress would, moreover, be interpretative on the other side of the water as a repudiation of my leadership. . . . I submit my difficulties and my hopes to you."

The response from the people was the election of a Congress Republican in both branches—and Wilson promptly refused to accept their judgment "without cavil" or to assume that "his leadership had been repudiated."

It was still his duty to think, speak and act for America and he remained convinced that he could do all three with certain benefit to the world—that other minds would only confuse, perhaps thwart, the consummation of a purpose almost inspired.

WANTED NO ONE BY HIS SIDE

If he had only realized it, Wilson's long sought opportunity for achievement was now open wide to him—here was the time for him, by frank exchange of views with others, to make himself the accepted spokesman for all. But it was not in his nature to do so. When he expressed that desire in his campaign letter it would seem that he really meant spokesman *to* not spokesman *for* the whole nation. Never had he held himself apart more than in those days when his decisions were to be of such consequence to the world; even an autocrat would then have sought counsel.

The armistice had scarcely been signed before he was urged to bring men of all parties into conference, and seek to learn what the people had in mind regarding the peace to be made. As President he could draft into such service the experience, the wisdom and the patriotism of the nation. Everywhere it was hoped that he would. With such cooperation, his peace plans would have been invincible. He gave no heed to such suggestion. One man who urged it too strongly was met with angry flash from the eye, and those tightly gripped lips that indicated that the speaker was restraining unpleasant words.

We must remember that Wilson, despite his idealism, was an intense partisan. His reply that he did not propose to bring Republicans to the front in the peace negotiations was a true reflection of his partisanship, but it was only a small part of the truth—the part he could admit. The whole truth was that he did not propose to bring anyone to the front.

NOT WHAT YOU THINK, ONLY WHAT YOU KNOW

For peace commissioners he did not seek counsellors. He selected men who, with the single exception of House, would do no thinking on their own account, who would understand that Wilson was to do it all. One of the commissioners, anxious to be of real help in Paris, asked after six days of uncertainty on the George Washington, how he should go about it. "Never offer the President advice, never plead a cause with him," came the reply. "He is interested only in what you know, not in what you think. He will listen to your information but not to your opinion."

WILSON'S LIKING FOR "13"

With that deadened spirit among those who accompanied him, and in the mood himself that I have described, Wilson sailed for France on the George Washington. I think it was George Harvey who said that the ship speeded across the Atlantic at 18 "May-I-Nots?" an hour. The George Washington could have made Brest a day or so earlier than Dec. 13, but Wilson had it slowed down so as to arrive on that date. He had a liking for that unpopular number. Frequently in the White House he spoke of the 13 letters in Woodrow Wilson and of the fact that 13 States were the "originals"

AT 13 "MAY-I-NOTS?" AN HOUR

From Harper's Weekly.

in the Union. He grew to believe that there was something more than coincidence in the two thirteens. He thought it would be a good omen if, Columbus-like, he should set foot on French soil on the 13th and the George Washington's May-I-Nots were regulated accordingly.

"HOW FAR IS IT FROM PARIS TO VERSAILLES?" ASKED MARTIN

That voyage across the Atlantic was watched with deep anxiety by Democratic leaders back in Washington. They did not like the idea. Senator Martin, of Virginia, Democratic leader of the Senate, was especially disturbed. One day, during a dull session, he strolled over to Senator Lodge, and leaning far over Lodge's desk, asked in a low voice:

"Lodge, how far is it from Paris to Versailles?"

"Oh, about nine or ten miles," replied the Massachusetts Senator. "Why do you ask, Martin?"

"It seems to be too damned far for President Poincaré to go out there to meddle with Premier Clemenceau's conduct of the peace negotiations, but 3,000 miles does not seem to deter our President."

Whenever Democrats talked that winter as frankly as Martin talked with Lodge the same doubt of the wisdom of Wilson's course was heard. If there were any members of his party who believed the President was right, they did not make their opinion known.

CHAPTER LXII

THE "WILSON OF PARIS"

Amidst The Premiers Of The World He Was Acquiescent And Treated Them As Equals—"If We Could Only Bring This Wilson Back Home With Us!"—But Wilson Of Paris Could Not Cross The Atlantic—His Silent Break With House—Was House A Sage? A Myth? A Svengali?—One Or All?—Men Too Keen To Be Wrong Sought House As The Real Power.

WILSON pleaded constantly for a world of brotherhood and of heart; he lived in a world of loneliness and of what he himself called a single-track mind.

It is unfortunate that the track had neither sidings nor terminals, for if the *good* that was in Wilson could have been fused with the average purposes of men, a record of great achievement would have been made.

"Oh if we could only bring this Wilson back home with us!" a loyal Southern Democrat exclaimed in Paris. As a visitor at Versailles he had watched Wilson through many sessions presiding over the commission formulating the covenant. "What a hit he would make! He would have the Senate eating out of his hands!"

The Wilson of Paris, seated at the head of that table, saw as his associates those whom he felt he could accept as his equals. They were the premiers of the nations of the world, the flower of the world's statesmanship. He treated them accordingly.

The man whom I have quoted could contrast the Wilson of Paris with the Wilson of Washington, for in Washington he had seen and deplored Wilson's attitude of icy separation, even from his associates in the government; his not wholly

504

concealed contempt for the Senate. In Paris the considerate, acquiescent Wilson whom he saw day after day so enthused him that he had dreams of a changed Wilson returning to America; a Wilson who had come to realize the wisdom of conference and of considerate treatment.

But the Wilson of Paris could not cross the Atlantic. The nearer his ship approached his native land the taller in his own eyes he grew; and in those same eyes the smaller grew those at home who by election, or by appointment, were entitled to share with him the responsibilities of government. Instead of the changed Wilson he had with partisan pride hoped to see, this Southern Democrat on his return found in Washington a Wilson made more austere by his contacts abroad—more convinced than ever that, as he had said several years before to another supporter, it would be utterly futile and a waste of time for him to listen to others.

WILSON'S EARLY DOUBTS

In Paris Wilson at first doubted the wisdom of making a supreme issue of the League of Nations, as an integral part of the Versailles Treaty. Twenty-nine nations were seated at the peace table. He knew how far apart their views were. Each nation, regardless of size, believed it had been essential to victory, each felt its voice should be heeded. Indeed, the smaller nations were more certain than the larger ones that they had won the war.

To Wilson the prospect of unity seemed dim; he questioned whether he should thrust another brand into the fire. Some of his peace commissioners favored making the effort—Colonel House in particular. They believed that a treaty without the League in it would simply be one of the numberless and forgotten treaties of past centuries. A treaty with the League in it would be the most forward step ever taken for permanent peace; it would stand out by itself in all history. Wilson liked that prospect, and the League of Nations as a separate settlement was abandoned.

First, though, he had to settle the wisdom of sitting personally, as a member of the peace conference. It is the traditional policy of rulers of nations to have ambassadors represent them in such negotiations. No monarch had ever participated in an international tribunal, and, of course, that seemed to establish a precedent for the President of the United States.

Besides, no head of any other nation was then in Paris; Wilson outranked all who were officially there. Should he ignore that fact in an atmosphere where rank counts for so much—and hold himself in reserve, as a Court of Appeals? Lloyd George, Clemenceau and others thought so.

Wilson took a few days to consider the point; then decided to go in. Clemenceau, who presided, seated him at his right —the place of highest rank. He promptly made him responsible for the covenant. As chairman of the commission to formulate the covenant he became the "Wilson of Paris," a presiding officer more tolerant in his attitude toward all who desire to speak to their own time; so, also he became a member of the "Big Four"—Lloyd George, Clemenceau, Orlando and Wilson.

NO TRADING NEEDED TO SAVE THE LEAGUE

He bowed to their will as he had never bowed in Washington to any will. The "Big Four" got all they really desired—even the obligations of the secret treaties about which not a word had been said to Wilson during the war or until they were brought forward to be incorporated in the peace treaty. It is asserted in explanation of Wilson's surrender to the Allies' most important demands that he was fighting to save the League of Nations and that he sacrificed in order to do so, but not one scintilla of evidence has been produced that the League was ever in danger—that Wilson was any more eager for it than were his colleagues excepting Clemenceau. In America Wilson was accepted as the champion and spokesman for the League; in Paris he was only one of many.

It is not fair to the others around the peace table to picture Wilson as constantly engaged with them in a desperate battle over the League. A world in grief, in distress and in chaos crowded about them; peace was the prayer and purpose in every mind. Clemenceau alone regarded the old balance-of-power theory as the best assurance of peace; the other principals in treaty-making were as firm as Wilson for the League. They, or their successors, now constitute the League. Wilson's battle in Paris was over other features of the treaty, and into the struggle he threw himself with high purpose and a passionate energy that made its deep impress apparent on mind and body before the treaty was signed.

THE SILENT BREAK WITH HOUSE

It was at this time that the historic "break" with Colonel House occurred. Who knows the facts of that sundering of the most intimate ties that ever existed between the Executive of a great nation and a man in civil life? The relation began in silence, it continued in silence, it ended in silence. Was it a myth—that unity of purpose and of mind? Or was it real? Mystery of mysteries! Politics never saw its like!

Strange in its beginning, stranger still in its development through seven years of momentous problems, strangest of all in the mystery that still surrounds it, impenetrable, with the darkness of the grave on one side, and on the other side the only written evidence held back in deference to request.

Was House a sage? A sphinx? A Svengali?—one or all? In his day of power such queries were whispered among gossipers as softly as a spider spins his web. Since the "break" loud assertion has taken their place. Thus the glory of this changing world passes; surely we have here new evidence that its triumphs are of the moment—a frown, and they are gone!

As I Knew Them

I have studied with great interest the varied pictures of the Wilson-House intimacy as drawn by those who assume that they can fathom its depth and measure its extent, and I have reached the conclusion that until the entire correspondence—the letters *from* Wilson as well as those *to* Wilson—have been published, no man can judge the relations that existed, for no man knows.

What was Wilson's motive? What was House's? Here was a President who habitually shut the world out of his confidence—except this one man. Here was a President, new to public office and public policies, who yielded his judgment to no person except this one man. Here was a President unfamiliar with the problems growing out of a foreign war, who looked for guidance not to his Ambassadors in the Capitals of Europe, not to the leaders of his party, or of the nation, but to this one man.

Not once but several times this one man visited nation after nation at the suggestion of the President with the *written* authority of a supreme representative, and heard the potent voices of the world's leading men.

"As usual I listened" would come back to Wilson as, one by one, House conferred with the responsible men of Europe's great empires. Even in the Kaiser's presence he listened, as Germany's war lord laughed at the thought of committing Germany to a year of deliberation before engaging in war. The Kaiser's government was the only large nation that refused to sign the treaty prepared by Bryan. It failed in its main purpose because of the Kaiser's refusal. "With the German army and navy trained to the moment!" said the Kaiser, "why should I give another nation a year to prepare?"

ALL TURNED TO HOUSE

Perhaps you do not like this picture of the House relation; perhaps you are inclined to reject it; there are no official documents on file to attest it, no title gives it authority except the title of friendship, which, of course, has no place in government archives. Incredible it truly seems to be; incredible that another White House should be functioning in New York city, in addition to the official one in Washington. Yet European statesmen addressed their most confidential cables to New York because they believed it; our own leading men sought the House apartment in New York because they knew its power.

Were they right? And if they were right was such a condition right? I shall not attempt here to answer. My purpose is to show that men too keen to make a mistake in such matters acted upon that belief until after President Wilson's return to Paris in March 1919. There can be only one opinion about the relations of the two men up to that time; there is room for more than one opinion from that time, until Col. House in Madison Square Garden, New York city, listened to the radio report of his dead friend's funeral services instead of sitting, as he sought permission to sit, in the church in Washington, where the last words were being said.

THE STAGE IN PARIS AND ITS FIGURES

Now, let us look at another picture of House. We need not go into those seven years during which the President was his "grateful friend." Let us start with the assembling of the peace commissioners in Paris. There was the stage of tremendous events; the men to play a part upon it were destined to be historic figures. All eager, properly enough, to be in the limelight; all seeking to be identified conspicuously with any phase, every phase, of that difficult struggle to assess the penalties for a great tragedy and adjust the world to a better day.

Into that scene came Wilson, at once the central figure. Foreign statesmen did not know him; they had heard stories of his austere ways. Is it strange that at first they thought it best to continue using the channel he had indicated as an open and direct one to him? Even habit would have led them to do so. Evidently they did not realize that the House proxy from Wilson ceased when the giver of the proxy was present. The House apartments in the Crillon Hotel were the centre of many conferences that should have gone on where a President resided who wanted to do all and see all—even though the task must shatter him, as it did.

It is said that after an unsatisfactory talk one afternoon with Wilson, Lloyd George had hurried to the Crillon to talk it out with House. While the two men were thus engaged, Wilson entered. He excused himself for interrupting and said he would call again when House was at leisure. That later call was never made. At another time Lord Balfour, discussing with friends the differences still unadjusted, said:

"If we could only deal with House we would have nothing to worry about."

EAGER TO CARRY THE NEWS

On seven league boots that statement was rushed to Wilson; there were many persons eager to carry it and its like—so many that when Wilson left Paris on his first trip home in February, his mind had begun to close against House, though he was still on friendly terms with him. Back in Paris three weeks later the biggest budget of gossip awaiting Wilson was about House. He was told that during his absence House had cut the ground from under him, by agreeing to so many Allied demands that there was nothing left for trading purposes on other features of the treaty. Wilson's mind was so firmly fixed on doing everything himself that it yielded readily to suspicion that someone was intruding. He began an increasing avoidance of House.

"In Paris Wilson did not want tea party talks," said one of Wilson's Paris intimates to me, "he needed practical suggestions. House was good at tea parties where he agreed to everything and undertook to carry it through with Wilson.

As I Knew Them

The President needed a man who would take orders from him and not make compromises with others. House simply couldn't fill that bill. They had captured him as they had captured Page, and Wilson turned from both."

One can get the indictment drawn against House in Paris only bit by bit, from different individuals, he must then put the pieces together. President Wilson never uttered a word to House to indicate his separation from him. He just forgot, more and more each day, that such a man existed. No charges, no dissensions, no explanations. House saw him off for home, exchanged cables with him after he reached the White House, but there was another tone to their relation and shortly it died away entirely. I have never heard of a person to whom Wilson afterward ever mentioned the name of House.

The differences in April, with the "Big Four," that led Wilson, in temper, to order the George Washington made ready to carry him home, were laid by many persons at House's door. The President flatly refused to acquiesce in any of the understandings entered into by House during his absence. He let it be rumored to the other treaty conferees that House no longer knew his mind, or could interpret it. In the resulting tangle, he lost his balance in Paris, and came close to sailing home in pique. Finally with slight modifications he agreed to all that had been tentatively mapped out. The incident brought Wilson to the front as his own adviser; it also ended House.

After Paris, they never met again on the old terms. Finally sickness came to Wilson and meetings and letters ceased.

What did this man without title contribute to Wilson, that led him to make him his confidant, his spokesman, and, apparently, his guide? Colonel House's "Intimate Papers" give the clear impression that he was all three; the only authentic challenge to that picture of their relations lies in the unpublished letters from Wilson to House.

CHAPTER LXIII

THE EFFORT FOR "A SOLEMN REFERENDUM"

Wilson Was Determined To Make The Senate Yield Or Force An Issue In The 1920 Elections With Himself As The Candidate—Kellogg's Offer To Ratify Goes Unheeded—The Twelvemonth That Marked The Highest And Lowest Levels Of Wilson's Fortunes— Colby, Burleson and Daniels Worked for Wilson's Nomination—Colby's "Mingled Feelings" Returning to Washington—Wilson Said: "We Would Have Gotten That League Through Had My Health Been Spared—It Is God's Way and He Knows Best."

THE Wilson who on July 10, 1919, presented the Versailles Treaty to the Senate in person rather than by the usual messenger was neither the Wilson of Washington nor the Wilson of Paris, but a Wilson who had burst all narrower confines and now rated himself as a world figure without rival. You can get his own appraisement in his statement to Editor James Kerney four years later, as revealed in his enlightening book, "The Political Education of Woodrow Wilson"—"I realize that I am everywhere regarded as the foremost leader of the liberal thought of the world."

Happening to be in Washington at the time of his address on the treaty, I went up to the Capitol to hear it. I wanted to study the reaction of the Senators to what he had to say as he handed the document over for ratification. I was anxious, also, to contrast the Wilson I had heard deliver his war message with the Wilson now delivering his peace message.

Had I not known of his emotional breakdowns under the strain of Paris, I would have been shocked by the pallor of his face, the worn look that told a story no effort could wholly conceal. Zeal had plainly taken heavy toll. No thought of the tragedy then shaping itself crossed my mind. I realized, however, that I was looking upon a man who had returned to his native land with the hurrahs of Europe still ringing in his ears as a world call to leadership, who now regarded himself as the crusader for an inspired conception of the world's needs, the Messiah of his day, guarding his distinction with the avarice of a miser counting and recounting his gold to make certain that no one had robbed him of any of it.

There was a sureness about Wilson as he stood before the Senate that was almost defiance, the manner of one confident of the reality of his dream of a world Utopia with himself as its immortal figure.

WILSON'S FAITH IN A DEMAND TO RUN AGAIN

And on that July 10 began the period in Wilson's career yet to be fully revealed by those who know the facts, with all its intolerance of opposing views, its firm determination, if the Senate did not yield, to take the issue to the country; the tragic collapse on his western tour, the pathetic clinging to power while stricken and, finally, the abiding faith that his party and the people would re-elect him President and instruct the Senate to ratify his treaty.

Wilson's belief in such an outcome was so supreme that even those who knew his physical inability and the political unwisdom of his candidacy had not the heart to undeceive him. From his sick-room in the White House he waited expectantly day by day, hour by hour, for word from San Francisco that the national Democratic convention had put aside all lesser candidates and lesser issues and had chosen him to lead in what he had called "a solemn referendum." That word never came, but instead there came to him with crushing force the realization that the sceptre of power had passed to other hands, and with it the issue on which he had staked all.

Exactly one year from the day at Versailles when with glowing countenance he attached his signature to the peace treaty the Democratic convention met in San Francisco. Those two days, twelve months apart, marked the highest and the lowest levels of Wilson's quest for fame. On June 28, 1919, in Versailles, the signed document seemed a crowning triumph; on June 28, 1920, in San Francisco, his own party registered its preference for another as its candidate, and forced Wilson to a place with figures of the past.

KELLOGG'S OFFER TO RATIFY GOES UNHEEDED

It is not my province to rehearse the incidents of that year. I would like to say, however, that Wilson could have insured the ratification of the treaty within two weeks after his return to America had he chosen to do so on the basis of reservations suggested by Senators friendly to the League of Nations. I understand that the fact has not been published—certainly not widely published—that Senator Frank B. Kellogg, of Minnesota, now Secretary of State under Coolidge, called on Wilson at the White House about July 15 as the spokesman for a group numbering from 32 to 34 Republicans. The group did not include Senator Lodge. He explained to the President the reservations desired. Wilson listened attentively, but told Kellogg that their proposals were already covered in the covenant or by our Constitution. They were, therefore, not material to the treaty. "If that is so," urged Kellogg, "why not accept them? They can do no harm. We can furnish from 32 to 34 votes on this basis and with the Democratic votes you control you will have a safe margin for ratification."

"Thank you for the offer," replied Wilson courteously. "I appreciate your purpose. I'll think it over and if I can agree with your view I will let you know."

One week, then two weeks, passed without a word from the White House. Kellogg, Norris, and others in the group concluded that they would never hear from Wilson—and they never did. Nor did any other Senator ever get the slightest indication that any reservation, however mild, could break down the barrier in Wilson's mind.

As I Knew Them

In that battle with the Senate you have a Wilson striving solely for personal mastery—not a Wilson striving to achieve a great purpose in cooperation with those who by position had equal right with him to a voice in the decisions. His, and his alone, must be the treaty ratified. In November, 1919, in a letter to Senator Hitchcock he warned all Democrats against voting for it with the Lodge amendments; in January 1920, he revealed his mind more frankly when he wrote the Jackson Day banqueters in Washington:

> Personally I do not accept the action of the Senate of the United States as the decision of the nation. . . .
>
> If there is any doubt as to what the people of the country think on this vital matter the clear and simple way is to submit it for determination at the next election to the voters of the nation, to give the next election the form of *a great and solemn referendum*— a referendum as to the part the United States is to play in completing the settlements of the war and the prevention in the future of such outrages as Germany attempted to perpetrate.

No one who was not himself a candidate would have penned such a letter, for no national convention could have adopted such a platform without calling upon the man who embodied it to lead in the campaign. "We would have gotten that League through had I been spared my health," said Wilson a year or so later.

HE ALONE WAS THE ISSUE

In the weeks from the date of that letter until the Democrats met in San Francisco, the effort for recovery was buoyed and strengthened by his determination to be physically ready for the campaign battle he anticipated. That is why he had no regrets when in March 1920 the treaty failed of ratification

a second time. Perhaps it furnishes a reason for his continued refusal to save it. Seven or eight Democratic votes
would have given it the necessary two-thirds and men whose
loyalty he could not challenge urged him to permit that to
be done. The White House atmosphere, however, had then
become surcharged with thought of the coming campaign with
Wilson as the candidate. The President looked upon counsel
to save the treaty as the counsel of surrender; he was in the
mood of martyrdom and he had no other thought than that
the people would rise en masse behind his banner once it was
raised. He was looking out upon the world through the win-
dows of a sick-room, and with a mind long burdened with a
single purpose. There was no other leader to carry on the
battle—not even to Crown Prince McAdoo could the succession safely pass. In that mood, with body wracked by disease,
this pitiful figure in the world's greatest tragedy met with
stoic calmness a disappointment that shattered a dream such
as few rulers ever dared to dream.

COLBY PRIMED TO NOMINATE HIS CHIEF

The men upon whose strategy at San Francisco hope chiefly
rested were Postmaster General Burleson and Secretary of the
Navy Daniels. Burleson went so far in his prophecies of success that he never recovered his place in the President's confidence. Not for months afterward did he have conversation
with him. But I am told that the man who hurried 3,000 miles
across continent with polished epigram and brilliant peroration to rouse the convention to a noble duty was Bainbridge
Colby.

Colby says no, and Colby ought to know.

But Colby was Wilson's Secretary of State; he had many
world problems in his great office demanding his serious consideration; diplomats from thither and yon were paying their
calls of courtesy and urging and pressing for audience,—and
Colby breaks all precedents of his dignified office as to political
activities, grabs a suitcase, takes the fastest train to San Fran-

cisco. It would be a fair guess that Colby under similar circumstances today would take an aeroplane.

He paused only for a call at the White House.

Why the sudden resolve? Why the parting call? Indeed, why should a Secretary of State—the high-hatted member of every Administration—attend a nominating convention at all unless the interests of his chief were involved in a most important way? And what was at stake?

Certainly not the party platform. So far as the Wilson Administration was concerned the delegates were of one opinion. The President had no candidate to urge—even McAdoo had been disavowed; scores of loyal Wilson leaders were on the ground ready to defend their chief if need be. It was not defense that was needed but offense.

Colby like Sheridan was miles away—three thousand instead of twenty. Someone was needed to rally and enthuse a confused convention; someone was needed to reform the line of battle, to point the way to victory, and Colby was the man ordained by fate to be the Sheridan of his day:—San Francisco needed him.

And why?

Not to nominate "Jimmy" Cox; Colby didn't buy a ticket to Trail's End.

Nor was he seeking to bring to a close the Administration of which he was then the guiding and conspicuous member.

No, Colby had other motives in the Golden Gate city, and Wilson back in the White House awaited their consummation. The radio was on, preparations were made for newspaper photographers to gather and click their cameras at the thrice-named candidate when the news was flashed that Colby had begun to speak, that the delegates were in rapturous approval and that the new battle of the ballots was to be led by the man who had made the one real issue.

It was not to be. Somehow the cards didn't fall the right way; and a Democratic convention missed an opportunity to hear Bryan's cross of gold speech made to look like tinsel, for Colby would have done it.

What could the dependable Secretary of State telephone the eagerly-waiting White House of the developing conditions? Certainly not a blunt statement of the true situation. That shock was for the convention, not for him, to administer. He could telephone, however, that while prospects were not over-bright, he still had hopes, and that he was prepared to take the platform at the right moment. So Colby's "right moment" drifted from roll call to roll call but never came.

What a scene there would have been in that convention had it come! Far back in 1912 when Colby and I were engaged in that puritanic effort to return Roosevelt to the White House, he was a daring leader for the right, a spokesman who could face a thousand foe. And he would have been equal to that great occasion in San Francisco had there been a "right moment." There was not.

Think of Colby's poignant feelings as he saw the Cox vote climb to the needed two-thirds; think of his planning how to tell his chief the whys and wherefores of the failure—the "mingled feelings" with which he contemplated the disappointing result of the convention. There was so much to tell that it was nearly a month before Colby wrote the President he would like an opportunity to do so,—and neither Burleson nor Daniels ever found the courage even to go that far.

"THE WORLD NOT READY FOR IT"

And thus it was that Wilson resigned himself to defeat. He refused to be saddened. No one ever heard him complain. He let others do the talking. He lived to see two men follow him into the Presidency both sharing the opposition of their party to the League of Nations. "It is all right," he would say. "Perhaps we shall be all the better for the delay; the world was led to it by its sufferings; it might not have worked just yet; to be a sure success a League of Nations must not come from suffering but from the hearts and spirit of men. We are still in darkness but I am sure it is the darkness that eventually lightens. I realize now that I am only an empty tenement, a tool that has served its purpose in God's hand. I was stricken because it was His way of doing things. It was His will to set me aside; He knows what is best. I am content with the record as it stands."

CHAPTER LXIV

DAWES—POLITICIAN AND BANKER

TO MANY persons Charles Gates Dawes is an after-the-war development in national affairs. This presumption merely means that following his activities in the 1900 Republican national convention, as detailed in the McKinley chapter, Dawes undertook to build one of the big banks of Chicago, and, true to his character, put himself wholly into that effort until he had accomplished it.

The political public heard little from him for twenty years or more but Dawes was all the time looking over the fence into the old political pasture. When fortune came to him and gave him freedom of time and action, he found the World War a way back into the fold of public activities. "Over There" he acquired a pipe and a few mild swear words, but such things are only the outward evidence of a vigorous, hurry-up-and-get-there spirit,—intense, kindly and vigorous.

Dawes likes public service; he is really an old-timer at it—if the McKinley days are far enough past to be so classed. He was the first convention strategist—certainly the first to my knowledge—to card-index the delegates to a presidential nominating convention. Frank Hitchcock gained that reputation in the 1908 campaign to nominate Taft, but Dawes really began the practice in national politics back in the winter of 1896.

"A YOUNG MAN NAMED DAWES"

He had then moved from Lincoln, Nebraska, to Chicago, where he was establishing himself. As an ardent McKinley supporter, he was Mark Hanna's personal representative in the Illinois struggle to secure McKinley delegates. Illinois Republicans were then as ever since in a faction war; fighting was fierce and plenty. I was then to learn the situation, and found it baffling.

Someone in Chicago told me that if I really wanted the facts I would have to get hold of a young man named Dawes. So I hunted for Dawes. He had a little office up two or three flights of rickety wooden stairs in an old building on La Salle Street. I climbed the stairs, and found a room equipped with a roll-top desk, a wooden centre table, and two or three chairs. No pipe was in evidence.

I recall that whenever I asked Dawes about this or that county, he would rise from his chair, pull a little drawer from a case on top of his desk and look over half a dozen cards. Those cards had written on them the record of the day-to-day changes in each county. He would never answer a question until he had consulted his cards. He was so careful that I promptly made up my mind to accept his figures as the most dependable estimate to be had. When the State convention met, two months later, at Springfield, the Dawes prophecies of the number of McKinley delegates proved to be approximately correct.

A year later, Dawes became Comptroller of the Currency in the new Administration. He was known in Washington as McKinley's "white-headed boy." Next to Mark Hanna he was deepest in the President's confidence. McKinley's regard for him became deep enough to be called affection.

But banking on his own account was more attractive to the ambitious Dawes than office-holding, so he resigned as Comptroller and returned to Chicago to create the bank of which he was the head and principal owner when named in 1924 for Vice President.

ALMOST IN HARDING CABINET

How near Dawes came to be Secretary of the Treasury

under Harding is not well known; but for a week or so it was about settled that he was to be the man. Harding had called him to Marion, and had asked him if he could arrange his affairs so as to accept the Treasury portfolio if offered later on. Dawes replied that he could. Harding then said he had made up his mind not to make promises—he wanted to feel free as to appointments until the last moment for action; also he wanted others to feel equally free to decline.

"I expect and hope to offer you the place," said Harding, "but I shall not do so until I have my Cabinet complete and ask all members at the same time. I have no commitments. With this understanding let us both feel absolutely free to change our minds."

"That suits me perfectly," replied Dawes.

DAWES BUDGETS FOR AMERICA AND FOR THE WORLD

A week or so later, Senator Knox, of Pennsylvania, urged Andrew Mellon. Harding jumped at the opportunity; Mellon was willing. Dawes, when informed that Mellon would serve, heartily indorsed the Pittsburgh banker. Later, Harding sought a budget-maker, he asked Dawes to undertake that thankless task. Dawes agreed to do so for one year and with the definite understanding that he would be the direct representative of the President backed by his authority. He insisted that no budget could be made without supreme power over every Cabinet officer or bureau chief. Harding stood by him on that basis and the budget system of today, which has meant so much to the country, is the result.

Again, when a man was needed to budgetize German reparations, Dawes was brought into service—with the same fine results.

Back of Dawes' success, I have often thought, is that little case I saw on his roll-top desk in Chicago, thirty years ago, in which his card-index typified the thoroughness with which even in his young days he undertook everything.

As I Knew Them

Now he sits in the Vice President's chair—uneasily. He likes action, results, making each day count for something done and ended. The Senators like to talk, and while they indulge themselves in debate they expect the Vice President silently to listen. That is Dawes' job and he sticks to it, but with the Senate in recess the Senators hear from their vigorous presiding officer often enough to realize that he has some views of his own regarding the procedure of that "most deliberative body in the world." Moreover, having started on the road to political fame, there are many who believe Dawes has not yet finished his journey.

CHAPTER LXV

BORAH—INDIVIDUALIST

IF YOU are looking for an individualist among our national leaders, allow me to present the purest type in public service—William Edgar Borah, of Idaho, now serving his fourth term in the Senate, and, as chairman of the Foreign Relations Committee, the most potent voice on the subject next to the President and the Secretary of State. Europe, I suppose, wonders why we go almost to the Pacific for the man to conduct our foreign affairs insofar as the legislative branch of government is concerned. There must be a feeling of surprise over there, as there is here, that a Senator from Idaho should be so deeply interested in our attitude toward distant lands as to seek assignment on the Foreign Relations Committee when he could select committees whose work is closer to his constituents and seemingly more vital to them.

Borah picked the judiciary and foreign relations committees back in 1907 when he entered the Senate. Advancing by seniority in both committees he finally had to make a choice of chairmanships when Senator Lodge died, in 1924, and he chose foreign relations. So Idaho, the State of mountains, minerals, forests and distances, furnishes the parliamentary eyes, ears and mind for our country in matters across seas.

It is only a new demonstration that the east must face the fact more and more as time goes on that the Star of Empire westward takes its way. Next to Borah on that committee is Hiram Johnson, of California. Seven other members of the committee—making nine in all, or a majority—come from States west of the Mississippi River. When we keep in mind that Secretary of State Kellogg is a citizen of Minnesota, it is clear that our attitude toward other countries, for the present at least, except as the President voices it, has a distinct western point of view. It is not my province to say here whether that is a correct point of view or not, but it is certainly a more detached point of view, more of the isolationist pattern, than would be held if the majority of the committee were from the Atlantic States.

Borah in particular is an isolationist. He was more extreme as an "irreconcilable" during the League of Nations debate than was Senator Lodge; he was more responsible than any other Senator for hobbling our World court participation with so many reservations that Europe refused to agree to them; and he would be delighted if a way could now be found to recall our unaccepted acceptance rather than run even the slim risk that Europe may yet take us on our own terms.

You cannot get it out of Borah's head that Europe, still militaristic, only awaits opportunity to build larger armies and navies. He believes it is bred in the bone of her rulers and statesmen, and that the Versailles Treaty instead of serving the cause of peace is just so much dynamite to be exploded in a war more fearful than the war just ended. That is, largely, the ground on which he opposes cancelling the debt due us. Freed of that obligation, he believes that Europe would use the released credit to increase its military forces, and we would thus be uniting with her in a blow at peace.

If Europe would agree to cut down her present military expenditures, and relieve her people from that heavy tax burden, I am certain that Borah would be the first in America to urge that we do our share toward a world wide reduction of armies and navies by writing off the whole debt. Lacking such assurance he wants every dollar due us. He wants America to stand alone among the nations of the world,—in kindly but absolutely independent attitude—an individualist like himself. He believes that territorially we are big enough between the Atlantic and the Pacific and that our future is more secure if we remain in every sense between the two oceans.

Perhaps, I state it too strongly, but it seems to me that Borah favors letting the world take care of itself, believing that it will get along better without our intervention, and that we will have the same experience. That is why he urges recognition of the Soviet Government of Russia and independence for the Filipinos.

BORAH TRAVELS HIS OWN PATH

As a Senator for twenty years, Borah has gone his own way. He doesn't know how to follow. He so seldom travels a path another has trod that, if he were hunting bears in his Idaho mountains I doubt whether he would follow the tracks of Brother Bruin, as most hunters strive to do, lest he should feel that he was travelling a beaten path. He would get the bear, but in his own way!

If you were to study the Senate roll-call you would find that Borah votes more independently of party, of friends and of opponents than any other Senator. Nevertheless, he has more friends among his colleagues than have most Senators, and his attitude on legislation sways more votes. Why? Because of confidence in his integrity and ability, and because he makes no personal issues. He accords others the privilege he exercises of having his own opinion. There is nothing vitriolic about Borah; he never assails those who disagree with him; he fights their views but not them.

You will not find Borah in his Senate seat unless something important is before that body. Most of his time is spent digging for facts in the quiet of his office. There he determines whether he will support or oppose pending measures. He enters into no deals; he gives no votes as a bargain and seeks none. In all the gossip to be heard on Capitol Hill in Washington, I have never heard anyone claim that he had persuaded Borah not to speak his mind.

THE SENATE'S CONSTITUTIONALIST

Years ago William M. Evarts, of New York, and George F. Edmunds of Vermont were in turn known as the leading expounders of the constitution in the Senate; then John C. Spooner, of Wisconsin, then Elihu Root, of New York, Joseph W. Bailey of Texas and Philander Knox, of Pennsylvania. Today Borah is the accepted successor to that distinction. Borah studies the constitution, however, not to narrow it but to broaden it, and thereby keep it strengthened in the confidence of the people. He insists that its principles were intended to give effect to the fine purposes of the founders of our nation, and not to thwart them by technical interpretation.

Could a regular party convention be persuaded to nominate such a man for President? Who knows?

In 1924, he got out of bed in Washington after midnight to hear by telephone that the Republican national convention in Cleveland wanted him for Vice President; he promptly replied that he would not accept it and went back to bed. Borah would be the unhappiest man in Washington if he were fated to sit, silently, while the Senate was in debate. He delights in a conflict on the floor. Though he is "Bill" to most of his colleagues and they are "Jim" or "Frank" or "George" to him, those personal relations do not influence his attitude on legislation.

Borah's term as Senator expires in 1931—he will then have served twenty-four years. He has given the best years of his life to public service, and except for occasional newspaper writing he has limited his income rigidly to his salary. That means the sacrifice of many comforts. His reputation is his only asset as he moves into his later years; it assays of the finest quality but it is not convertible into those comforts that every man has a right to look forward to, and that every government should insure if it demands the kind of service that Borah gives it. He has now achieved the distinction of leadership of the Senate; that body holds no greater reward for him. The Presidency is the only promotion, but if Coolidge is to be reelected in 1928 the earliest date for Borah would be 1932— a long time to wait with many intervening uncertainties. Borah would then be sixty-seven years old. William Henry Harrison is the only man to enter the White House at a greater age. He was 68 when inaugurated.

The Presidency has yet to go west of the Mississippi—other places of power are going in that direction, and, of course, it is only a question of time when the presidency will go too. If Coolidge should refuse to run again, perhaps there will be a call for the able, earnest individualist Senator from Idaho,— the kindliest figure in the Senate personally, the most "uncertain, coy and hard to please" in legislation.

CHAPTER LXVI

CALVIN COOLIDGE

"THERE is no right to strike against the public safety by anybody, anywhere, any time," rang through the country in September, 1919, from the Governor of Massachusetts, like the clear, sharp peal of a Liberty bell.

It was a new voice. With thousands of others I listened, aroused.

"This is the people's cause," came a few days later in a proclamation from the same Governor of Massachusetts, declaring that he proposed "to support all who are supporting their own government," and that "the authority of the Commonwealth cannot be intimidated, coerced or compromised."

Again, with more thousands, I listened, aroused.

Here was a voice calm but firm, decisive but not defiant, capable of stating the substance of a great issue in a few understanding words.

Though Calvin Coolidge was the Bay State's Chief Executive, the Boston police did not know their man. They were now to know him better, so was the nation. Everywhere people applauded; everywhere newspapers gave columns to the struggle to maintain the supremacy of government. They were not slow to rally back of a Governor with the courage to challenge Samuel Gompers' contention that public servants had a right to strike even though such action imperilled public safety.

THE PEOPLE WANTED TO KNOW MORE OF COOLIDGE

The battle was quickly won, and the "news" was out of the incident. Like other nine-day wonders it soon faded away through the back pages of the newspapers. But Coolidge remained in the minds of the people as the defender and exponent of orderly government. Never did any man in public life win the interest and confidence of a nation so completely. Speeches delivered long ago—even his valedictory at Amherst—were dug out of a neglected past and widely discussed. A series of addresses were finally gathered into a book entitled "Have Faith in Massachusetts"; even that was seized by the newspapers for serial publication.

The Calvin Coolidge who had never sought to push his way to the front now found himself in the front line of national figures, well liked for his modesty, well liked for his philosophy of life, well liked for the courage with which he held to his beliefs.

Nor was this liking a political liking. The talk of Coolidge was not at first heard among politicians; it soon got to them, however, for a presidential contest was not distant and a candidate was needed. Since the days of Blaine and of Reed, the country had not looked seriously to New England for a President. In 1916, John W. Weeks, then Senator from Massachusetts, had sought nomination, but the support he received was largely a compliment to a man highly esteemed. The trend of political availability had long been steadily away from New England; Coolidge turned it back.

HE STUCK TO HIS DAY'S WORK

But not by seeking newspaper notoriety or indulging in stump speaking. He spread no propaganda about himself. Newspapers discovered that the people were interested in him, and gave him space on their own account to satisfy that reader interest. I was among those editors attracted by the Coolidge speeches and even more strongly impressed by his "approach," to use a golfing term, to the presidential nomination. He stuck to his day's work. All the progress he had made in life had been made by doing each day's work within the day and not crowding it with plans for ambitious tomorrows.

The possibility of the Presidency did not lure him away from that wise habit. He refused campaigning tours, refused alluring offers to write for magazines and newspaper syndicates, refused interviewers and photographers. If the people were to judge him he preferred to be judged on his record and not on any representations he might make to them as a candidate.

Take the Coolidge of today and recall the Coolidge who first came to your attention and you will find him following the same quiet habit of doing thoroughly his day's work and letting results tell his story.

LODGE COULD NOT SEE COOLIDGE

In the 1920 convention, my thoughts ran to Coolidge as more likely than others to interest the country. He had no antagonisms, he had made a good impression, and he had proven his courage in public service.

I said so frequently in my newspaper. Though new to the people in a national sense, I believed that he had secured a substantial following among them. I was prepared to see the Wood-Lowden forces end their deadlock by turning to the Vermont-born Governor of Massachusetts.

I have already referred to that convention as a convention of "ifs" so I may be permitted to add one more. *If* Senator Henry Cabot Lodge, head of the Massachusetts delegation and chairman of the convention, had not insisted that only a candidate acceptable to Boston's Back Bay aristocracy could possibly be the real choice of Massachusetts for national honors, a compromise on Coolidge might have been secured. But Lodge could not see a President in the occupant of a modest home in Northampton and he held a majority of the Massachusetts delegates in opposition.

"Nominate a man who lives in a two-family house?" he

exclaimed to me while at dinner in the Chicago Club. "Never! Massachusetts is not for him!"

That was not the comment heard among the delegates, however. They liked Coolidge. They believed that brains and purpose were more desirable assets in a President than wealth. Their liking was not reflected in actual votes on the nominating roll-calls for President because nearly all State delegations were committed to candidates with more "organization" backing; but a clear demonstration of Coolidge strength came in the quick responses to that unexpected call from far-off Oregon for Coolidge for Vice President.

The men sitting as chairmen of their delegations manipulating the convention did not have Coolidge in mind for a place on the ticket; in those closing hours, however, the bulk of the delegates got out of hand, and Oregon's demand had to go through. It voiced the uncontrolled desire of the.convention, —too emphatically to be denied. In the chapter on the 1920 nominations I have described that scene.

THE PEOPLE'S FAITH IN COOLIDGE

The people see in Coolidge the fine simplicities, the sturdy patriotism, the firm unpretentious character, the spirit of New England; they have faith in him beyond any they have shown in any other President of my time. I say this without lessening in the slightest my admiration for Roosevelt. Roosevelt commanded an intense, emotional enthusiasm never equalled by any other man.

There is a different meaning to the faith the people have in Coolidge. His period is a period of world-healing, of restoration—of an effort toward what Harding called normalcy. Vision clear, judgment cool, course always marked straight ahead toward a fixed purpose, he inspires a deep, nation-wide confidence that all will go well with the country while he is in the White House.

We will live within our means and meet all our obligations;

CALVIN COOLIDGE BEING SWORN INTO OFFICE AS PRESIDENT IN THE HOMESTEAD AT PLYMOUTH, VT., 2 A.M., AUGUST 3, 1923. HIS FATHER, JOHN COOLIDGE, AS JUSTICE OF THE PEACE, ADMINISTERED THE OATH. THE ABOVE IS A REPRODUCTION OF THE PAINTING BY ARTHUR I. KELLER, WHICH APPEARED IN THE LADIES HOME JOURNAL AND IS NOW IN POSSESSION OF MRS. COOLIDGE

we will travel a sure road, taking no quick turns to prosperity nor quicker turns to adversity; we will respect the rights of others and see to it that others respect ours; every hope for permanent world peace will be strengthened by our example; every department of government will be well financed for its real necessities but not for extravagance; our house will always be found ready for any emergency, equal to any test.

A BIG TASK WELL DONE

It has been the good fortune of our people that in times of crises they have had at the head of their government the man suited to the task beyond any other man then known to them. Calvin Coolidge is in that class of Presidents. Harding's term was too brief for him to do more than realize the appalling extent of the chaos following war, and to undertake tentative plans; he did well all that was possible for him to do in two short years; the real task of making good on his plans and of making new ones came after Harding had passed on. Coolidge took over that task. I do not minimize its importance or the splendid results obtained when I rank another need as of equal importance. One hundred million people dazed by immense wealth, newly aroused to ambitious endeavor, thrilled by the consciousness of world-wide opportunities, needed the restraining example of a President whose own experience had shown him the wisdom of prudent living and of calm reasoning before acting.

AN EXAMPLE THAT THE NATION FOLLOWED

No example from the White House would be impressive if made for the occasion only; it had to have the backing of lifelong habit. Coolidge gave it that backing. He did not suddenly acquire those traits; they are his by intuition. Neither great power nor the pressure to seek quick solutions of pending problems has ever led him from them.

As I Knew Them

The people knew this of Coolidge—big people, little people, all people. It has influenced them to follow the same course. We have not had the "frenzied finance" of the McKinley days or the sensational industrial expansion which Hanna declared had been voted in 1900. Our prosperity is sound. Business men have kept their heads and wage-earners have put their savings into banks, into home-ownership or securities to an amazing amount. To no one person so much as to Calvin Coolidge is this due; by example not by preaching he has persuaded a whole nation to this habit. And the influence of his course is not lessening.

With him as President there will always be progress, steady and sure; greater progress, when the final accounting comes, than if it were too eagerly sought. Coolidge believes that back of every advance there must be effort and purpose if the advance is to count, and he knows that effort and purpose require time. He is willing to wait results, but waiting does not mean idly hoping; he is working to accomplish all the time.

COMPARISONS WITH LINCOLN

I am tempted to say that in this respect Coolidge suggests Lincoln, who was our most patient President, and who often waited long and anxiously for the thing he had in mind; but thought of a Lincoln comparison recalls to me a remark made by Roosevelt at a time when many extravagant comparisons of him with Lincoln were being made.

It was not long after my newspaper had published Homer Davenport's popular cartoon, "He's Good Enough for Me," showing Uncle Sam standing back of Roosevelt with his hand on Roosevelt's shoulder. We had followed that cartoon with another drawn by Davenport showing Lincoln in similar attitude. The second cartoon led Roosevelt to mention the subject to me. He said:

"I've got to let this talk about Lincoln and myself run its

534

course, but you must know that I am not fooled even a little
bit by it. I am not in Lincoln's class. He had his work to do
and I have mine; the two are far apart. He did his work
mighty well, and I am doing mine the best I know how. I
think I have a fair estimate of my possibilities. I understand
myself, and I'm making no comparisons with Lincoln."

So, too, Coolidge is not to be compared with any of his
predecessors, for, like the period during which he has been
at the head of our government, he stands apart. His record
when completed will be that of a President who knew at all
times the exact direction and purpose of his undertakings,
and who gauged with accuracy how far the people were prepared to go with him. Of all the men in the White House the
past half century Coolidge senses most surely the desire of
the average person; he has the keenest mind for knowing just
how that person would react to each separate situation. He
has referred to it as just plain common sense, and perhaps he
is correct; if so then common sense is the one quality that
hereafter should determine our choice of President.

A book of reminiscences is not the place in which to deal
with an administration not much more than half-way through,
or to estimate the work of a President with much still to
accomplish. I shall not attempt it with Coolidge further than
to repeat that, in my opinion, judged by the record as it stands
to date, he has made good as the man best fitted to our
nation's needs, the man who more than any other is regarded
by the people as an accurate interpreter of their desires.

He has made no prophetic boasts, has fixed no ambitious
outposts of achievement, and has sought no glory but the
satisfaction of performance of the tasks at hand. The record
as stated in figures of debt reduction and of tax reduction and
in legislature is available from many other sources than here.

When Coolidge said in an Associated Press interview in the
autumn of 1926 that he liked to do things for himself, that
on his father's Vermont farm that was the habit and pleasure
of his day's work, he gave the country a picture of its Presi-

dent that took him out of the austerity of distinguished office and into closer relationship with his fellows. The man who "likes to do things for himself"—he is the man in whom the people have an abiding faith.

COOLIDGE FURNISHES A SENSATION

Wednesday, August 2, 1927.—This book written and finally given over to the tender mercies of the Publishers. A perfect summer afternoon, the country calm, serene and prosperous.

"I do not choose to run for President in 1928!"

This time, it was not a new voice, but, as in 1919, I listened, amazed.

"I do not choose to run for President in 1928!"

Out of Dakota's Black Hills the voice came like a rifle shot—sharp, clear, direct at the target.

Amazed, not a nation but a whole world now listened. Those twelve words meant the turning aside from power and place greater than any man ever held, and the free choice of the life of a plain citizen of the republic. No fanfare of trumpets heralded this unexpected renunciation of the finest title in the world,—just the calling of the correspondents into the class-room of a modest Dakota schoolhouse and handing to them, one by one, a folded slip of paper, with the historic words typewritten.

Where is there such dramatic force as in the simplicities of life? And of all the men in the Presidency who more than Coolidge has illustrated in his manner of life, and in the things he has sought and prized, that splendid, outstanding quality of American birthright that values contentment more than titles and one's own fireside more than the seats of the mighty?

As I pictured that scene with the newspaper men filing one by one past the President, I could not repress a feeling of keen regret that Time had eliminated me from participation in one of the most historic events in American history. The thrill of playing a part in such a scene would last a lifetime.

As I Knew Them

This book is reminiscent, not prophetic, and I claim no power to foresee who is to be President after March 4, 1929, but I do know that when Calvin Coolidge goes back to Northampton or to the farm in Vermont—to the place called Home —he will be on the way to his heart's desire.

"YOU DON'T LIVE IN THE WHITE HOUSE," SAID ROOSEVELT

If the reader will turn to another chapter and read again the talk I had with Roosevelt on the subject of life in the White House he will learn the truth about it. "You don't live there," said Roosevelt. "You are only Exhibit A to the country."

Many illustrations could be given by anyone familiar with Washington life. Let me give one.

When it was announced that President Coolidge had selected the Dakota Black Hills for his summer vacation, the cry went up throughout the country that he was going out there on a hunt for delegates—that he was to make an effort to repair the damage done to his political fortunes by his veto of the McNary-Haugen farm bill. Now, what was the truth? Within a week after his return from his Adirondack vacation in 1926, the President told me, while discussing vacation places, that he had made up his mind next year to try the Far West. He said that he had enjoyed the Adirondacks, but he wanted to get into unfamiliar territory—into entirely new surroundings. Of course he had neither farm legislation nor Presidential delegates then on his mind—just a desire to get to some place on vacation where life would be freer, simpler, less formal and official than had been possible at Swampscott or in the Adirondacks.

Yet months later, when it became public that he was going west, the wise men of politics instantly sought for a reason beyond the one simple reason that he really wanted to go there! The twelve-word message of August 2 is only another evidence that the hardest thing in the world to judge is the

537

motive of another man. Seldom is it correctly guessed—particularly when a President is that man. Perhaps the Coolidge incident will hasten the time when the head of our government, whoever he may be, will be credited with an earnest purpose to do what he believes to be his duty or his real desire instead of being met with the suspicion that every move he makes is dictated by self interest.

There are more men in Washington doing the right thing at cost to themselves than there are men there doing the wrong thing at cost to the nation.

CHAPTER LXVII

THE "INABILITY" OF OUR PRESIDENTS

Who Is To Determine That The Chief Executive Is Incapacitated?
—Only Eight Years Since Vice President Marshall Might Have
Taken Over The Presidency—Several Other Instances That Have
Led To Repeated But Unheeded Warnings—Wilson's Collapse Meant
A Bedside Government—The Timid Visit Of Senators To The White
House To See For Themselves.

IT IS only a matter of eight years since there were many people—some in high position—who honestly believed that Vice President Marshall should declare President Wilson physically unable to perform the duties of his office, and assume the Presidency himself. The President's collapse on his western tour, the paralysis that followed his return to the White House, created a mild panic among the Cabinet officers. There was a strong feeling that preparations should be made in anticipation of a complete breakdown if not worse. Precedents were sought, but none could be found.

Was the President incapacitated enough for the Vice President to succeed him? Who was to guide the Executive branch of government while the President was ill? Death speaks for itself and creates its own vacancies, but "inability" is an elastic term.

There was but one case at all comparable—that of Garfield, who was shot in July, 1881, but did not die until September. A period of unquestioned "inability" existed between the two events. Had the shooting occurred during winter, with Congress in session, instead of in summer, the serious question faced when Wilson broke down with Congress about to convene would have had to be faced in the Garfield case. Some authorities insisted that Vice President Arthur succeeded automatically when Garfield fell mortally wounded. Others thought the Vice President should decide when "inability" existed to an extent justifying action. The Garfield Cabinet and the whole country debated until death made further discussion unnecessary for that particular occasion—and then Congress calmly passed the question on undetermined.

THE WILSON BREAKDOWN

The same debating course was followed in the Wilson crisis. Fortunately Wilson in time regained sufficient strength to be outside the "inability" zone. Promptly he took the position that those who had considered the possibility of a successor to him were in a conspiracy "to oust" him from the Presidency, to use his own words. Secretary of State Lansing bore the brunt of his anger. But Lansing's activities settled nothing on the main question.

The one thing settled by the Lansing-Wilson correspondence is that for weeks the President knew nothing of the world outside of his sick room—not even that his Cabinet had met. Here is an extract from his letter to Lansing dated Feb. 7, 1920, showing how remote he was from the government, and yet how tenaciously he clung to Presidential rights.

"Is it true, as I have been told, that during my illness you have frequently called the heads of the executive departments of the Government into conference? If it is, I feel it my duty to call your attention to considerations which I do not care to dwell upon until I learn from you yourself that this is the fact.

Under our constitutional law and practice, as developed hitherto, no one but the President has the right to summon the heads of the executive departments into conference, and no one but the President and the Congress has the right to ask their view or the views of any one of them on any public question.

I take this matter up with you because in the development of every constitutional system, custom and precedent are of the most serious consequence, and I think we will all agree in desiring not to lead in any wrong direction. I have therefore taken the liberty of writing you to ask this question."

As I Knew Them

Private Secretary Tumulty states in his book that Lansing called at his office a day or so after the Wilson collapse, and urged him to make public announcement of the President's inability. He refused. Lansing then called the Cabinet in special meeting "to consider the situation." Actually they had no "situation" to consider because they could get no facts about it. Vice President Marshall was anxious for sick-room news lest he be called upon when unprepared, but even he got none. Naturally newspaper attention was attracted, and Washington was full of rumor as to the possibilities—even that Lansing and Marshall held the same views. An emphatic statement by the Vice President settled the matter, in the sensible way characteristic of him, but until he spoke there was public feeling that he was likely to take action.

Suppose there had been no Vice President? There was none during the three years after Coolidge succeeded Harding, after Roosevelt succeeded McKinley, and after the death of Vice President Hendricks in 1885, and of Vice President Hobart in 1899.

Suppose Secretary of State Lansing, next in line, in case of a vacancy, had felt called upon to declare himself President? He went so far as to formally notify Marshall; he called the Cabinet in meeting. The Cabinet responded, demonstrating by their acquiescence how promptly the man at the foot of the table senses who sits at the head.

The next step in the same direction would have seemed a short one. Ambition has often led men in other nations to attempt that next step and one not so well justified. No weak man ever makes the attempt. The peril lies in a strong man with a stronger "cause."

A BEDSIDE GOVERNMENT OF THE COUNTRY

No jury of doctors at the time would have pronounced President Wilson capable of performing any serious duties of his office. Their diagnosis might easily have been used by a Vice President or Secretary of State to declare the "inability" of the President, and assume the place himself.

Despite the refusal of everyone in authority to act, and despite the considerate report of a committee of Senators as to the President's condition, it is a fact beyond dispute that President Wilson was physically incapacitated. There was complete collapse of the executive branch of government. Whether, as dependable report had it, Mrs. Wilson and Secretary Tumulty together or Mrs. Wilson and Dr. Grayson together ran the Executive department, or one or the other of them ran it alone, I do not know. If they did not, nobody did. For months, it was a bedside government, and as time wore on, the figures around the bedside lessened to an irreducible minimum.

Secretary of the Treasury Houston throws some light on the subject while detailing in his interesting book, "Eight Years in Wilson's Cabinet," how he learned of his promotion to that place. One Sunday in January, 1920, he received a telephone message that Mrs. Wilson wished him to call at the White House at 4:30 that afternoon. She greeted him with this remark, "You are wondering why I sent for you this afternoon. Of course, I did not ask you to come merely to drink tea. The President asked me to tell you he is anxious for you to accept the Secretaryship of the Treasury."

That settled, Mrs. Wilson said the President would like to have a suggestion as to who should succeed Houston as Secretary of Agriculture.

That settled, Mrs. Wilson "asked whether I had anybody in mind for Secretary of the Interior, Mr. Lane having resigned—in the press."

Further conferences that Secretary Houston had with Mrs. Wilson from time to time are not revealed in his book, except as they may be inferred from this closing paragraph in his letter of official farewell to President Wilson March 3, 1921: "I feel that I cannot close this note without an expression of indebtedness to Mrs. Wilson and of admiration for the part she has played and the judgment she has shown in dealing with important matters."

Thus, we get a glimpse—eight years later—into the White House in the last eighteen months of Wilson.

THAT TIMID VISIT OF SENATORS

Everyone will recall that Senatorial visit in December, 1919, to learn the truth about the President's condition. There was something of the hippodrome to their call at the White House, attended by two score reporters and almost as many camera men. The Senate had not authorized it. That august body was doubtful of its right to cross the White House threshold for purposes of inquiry—even an inquiry as to whether the President was incapacitated. It made no attempt. Rarely has it shown such restraint when the rights of the "coordinate branch" were involved.

The Senate Foreign Relations Committee, with Senator Lodge as Chairman, appointed Senators Hitchcock and Fall a committee "to lay before the President some papers relative to Mexican affairs and to confer with him regarding their disposition." What a pitiful subterfuge! Everybody wanted to know the President's condition. Surely some people with responsibility had a right to know. Yet nobody was permitted to know, and nowhere in our laws could there be found authority to know. The only way was by asking a conference about Mexico!

The Lansing cabinet meetings, the Marshall rumors, the White House barred to everyone, the unrevealing doctors' bulletins—all created uncertainty. Most uncertain was whether either House or Congress, or both in joint action, possessed the right or duty, formally, to inquire and determine whether a coordinate branch of government was capable of functioning or not.

Remember the Senators' timid overtures to Tumulty as to

whether they could or would be received? Remember the conferences between Mrs. Wilson and Dr. Grayson as to whether the President could stand it? Of course he could, they stoutly declared—after some hours of doubt.

The Senators saw—and graciously blinded themselves. They said hardly a word about Mexico, or anything else.

As Senator Fall, of New Mexico, left the President's bedside, he said:

"I shall pray for you, Mr. President."

"Pray don't, Senator," came back the quick rejoinder.

Senator Fall told waiting reporters the President seemed to be in excellent mental trim.

WHO IS TO DETERMINE WHEN AND HOW?

At a time of great panic, or partisan disputes, or differences with other nations;—it might be the duty (or the ambition)—of a Vice President or a Secretary of State to declare himself President.

Who is to determine when, and how? If the silence of the Constitution is deliberate, then its framers probably meant the initiative to be taken by the official upon whom responsibility falls. What power could have prevented Vice President Marshall from declaring himself President had he chosen to do so? Wilson certainly would have resisted. Congress also might have refused to recognize him if in session at the time, but such action would have meant chaos. If Congress were not in session, the new executive would have full swing until it reassembled.

A most serious weakness in our national structure is revealed—an inability through existing law, definitely and beyond question to establish under every situation that can be anticipated, and at all times, who is entitled to be recognized as the executive head of our nation. There are likely to be occasions in future when we cannot stand the strain of a collapsed executive department for so long a time as that of President Wilson's illness.

As a people we are so sure of ourselves, so certain that with us right will always prevail, that we ignore the fate of other nations as powerful in their day; we take no precaution to make the "man on horseback" impossible among us at crisis times.   Our remissness gives point to a remark Roosevelt once made in private conversation; that our country may have to be "shot over" once more before it settles down to its ultimate destiny.   He added that even the thought of such a possibility horrifies; we reject and scorn it as too remote for consideration, but if in years to come control of our government is ever to be in conflict just such uncertainty as exists governing election and succession to the Presidency is likely to be responsible for it.

WHAT THE CONSTITUTION SAYS

The Constitution speaks only in broad terms.   It says:

> "In case of the removal of the President from office, or of his death, resignation or inability to discharge the powers and duties of said office, the same shall devolve on the Vice President; and the Congress may by law provide for the case of removal, death, resignation or inability both of the President and Vice President, declaring what officer shall then act as President, and such officer shall act accordingly until the disability be removed or a new President shall be elected."

Unfortunately, while Congress has enacted a "succession" law it has merely stated who after the Vice President shall succeed the President; it has deliberately failed to provide for the determination of "inability."   That vital question is still in the air—where the makers of the Constitution left it.

Probably no man was more disturbed by the Wilson crisis than Secretary of the Treasury Houston.   He was in the thick of its perplexities, and knew how closely we came to trouble then, how unwise it is not to clarify such situations before prejudice, passion and personal desires control them. I quote from his "Eight Years in Wilson's Cabinet" as follows:

> "The problem presented by the illness of the President is one for the handling of which machinery ought to be created. The Cabinet is in good position to pass upon the government's exigencies, perhaps in better position than any other body, but, for various reasons, it is not the body that should be charged with the final determination of the inability of a President to discharge his duties.
>
> "The Congress also is not the proper body. It might be of different political complexion from the President and there might be situations in which partisanship would enter.
>
> "It would seem that either a Commission should be set up composed possibly of Supreme Court justices, members of the Cabinet, and members of Congress, to sit as a jury and to determine the matter, or the determination might be left to the Supreme Court.
>
> "But whatever may be the best machinery, it is clear that some machinery should be set up."

A STUBBORN FACT YET TO BE FACED

Of the four causes of vacancy in the Presidency listed in the Constitution only two are definitely operative. Death, of course, is an obvious fact and the Vice President automatically succeeds; so would be removal by impeachment. But to whom would a President resign? Would he merely walk out of the White House, and notify the Vice President? Law provides for the resignation of every other officer except the President and Vice President. Of course, resignation is a remote contingency, but since it is mentioned, a way to resign ought to be definitely provided. I know that Vice President Fairbanks was anxious to leave Washington on account of his wife's health. He attributed her death to the exactions of her social duties; he would gladly have resigned if he had had any precedents.

Twice, in the past fifty years, the President's "inability" has been a stubborn fact; the Vice President in both cases

546

blinded himself, and the country "muddled through." It "muddled through" five electoral count disputes, simply because they did not affect the results. Then came the Hayes-Tilden controversy, and a serious situation developed,—so serious that neither party dared attempt settlement in Congress.

Garfield's case was so hopeless from the start that I doubt whether a declaration of "inability" by Vice President Arthur would have been contested, but Wilson's resentment of Lansing's activities is proof that Vice President Marshall would have had to lay siege to the White House, had he assumed the Presidency.

No wonder that John T. Morgan, of Alabama, who for years ranked as one of the leading men of the Senate, wrote of the "inability" and the electoral count under the heading "Some Dangerous Questions."

CHAPTER LXVIII

"FIGHTING BOB" LA FOLLETTE

*The Czar Of His State And Spokesman For More Than 4,000,000
Voters In The Nation—He Had Much To Give The Country, But
He Failed Because He Would Not Do Team Work—Hiram Johnson
In California Won And Holds His State As La Follette Held
Wisconsin.*

THE death of Robert Marion La Follette in 1924 closed
the career of the only man except Theodore Roosevelt
able to lead more than 4,000,000 voters from their party
affiliations into support of his candidacy for the Presidency.
Speaking in terms of proportion I suppose that the bolt of the
Democratic faction headed by Breckinridge in 1860 was
greater than that headed by either Roosevelt or La Follette.
It certainly proved to be of more significance to the nation,
for it insured Lincoln's election and that result led to a quick
decision by the South to seek separation.

Roosevelt's 4,125,000 votes represented a little more than
30 per cent of the total cast in 1912, while La Follette's 4,-
800,000 votes, because of the increase caused by woman suf-
frage, represented a little less than 15 per cent of the total
in 1924. La Follette secured the 13 electoral votes of his
own State of Wisconsin—against Roosevelt's 88 from seven
States.

That more than 4,000,000 voters would give their ballots
to any man despite their knowledge that they could not elect
him is a tribute no one may dispute; the recipient must be
accepted even by his severest critics as the spokesman for a
great many people.

And La Follette was such a spokesman. When he entered
the Senate in 1905, he was the acknowledged dictator of

As I Knew Them

Wisconsin politics. He had been five years Governor, had utterly demolished the old Republican organization machine, had freed the Badger State government of corporation control and had enacted legislation so distinctly in the public interest that no one has ever sought to repeal it. He took the Wisconsin State University at Madison out of the deep ruts of tradition and made it an institution commanding the respect of the nation.

HAD TO WIN OVER PREJUDICE

Philetus Sawyer, Isaac Stephenson and John C. Spooner had been the spokesmen in the Senate of the old Wisconsin régime, and the appearance there of a man known to the political world only as "Fighting Bob" was as comforting to the Aldrich-Gorman bi-partisan crowd as a bull in a china shop.

Like "Pitchfork" Tillman, of South Carolina, La Follette when he took his place in the Senate, found the bars up against men of his "extreme" views; also like Tillman his early speeches were made to crowded galleries but empty Senate seats. The two Senators had a common experience, however, in soon being accepted as men who had to be heeded. Even those who rarely voted with them paid them the compliment of attention. A Senator who never supported a La Follette proposition told me once that no Senator was so thoroughly prepared on the subjects he debated as the Wisconsin Senator.

I doubt that it ever deeply concerned La Follette whether his colleagues listened to him or not; the Senate was to him merely the platform on which he stood. His appeal was to those beyond the two-party machine that even now holds the Senate in its grip, though not so firmly as in years past. He thrived on defiance. On several occasions he held the floor of the Senate for several days while filibustering against legislation. Never in strong health, he was tempting fate in such trials of endurance, but he liked heroic rôles, full of dramatic intensity, and he did not fear the consequences.

549

As I Knew Them

NEVER A COMPROMISER

La Follette was "Fighting Bob" when at 26 he defied the party machine in Dane County, Wisconsin, and won nomination and election as District Attorney; he was "Fighting Bob" when in 1884 he had himself elected to Congress against the same machine influence; and he was still "Fighting Bob" in his final days when he held his own national convention at Cleveland, Ohio, and had himself nominated for President on his own platform. Throughout his career he had no mood for compromise. Unlike Bryan, he never abandoned an issue. Whatever else may be charged against him, he was not an opportunist. He believed strongly—never timidly or for the moment.

Moreover and again unlike Bryan, he loved good books and he did not care for wealth. He sought knowledge and power, not riches. Every thought, every act, was devoted to his advancement in politics; he wanted power—always power —and always power for himself; never power for himself and others. His beadlike, deep-seated eyes, small beardless face, high forehead and high pompadour hair accentuated in the minds of those who watched him from the Senate galleries the traits he was known to possess. He seemed an actor playing a part, but in truth he was always in earnest.

HAD MUCH TO GIVE PUBLIC SERVICE

Of all the members of the Senate during La Follette's three terms, I doubt whether there was one who in steadfastness and courage of conviction, in personal integrity and in comprehension of governmental needs had more to give to public service than he. And the pity of it is that aside from the Seaman's law that bears his name, he is credited with so little. Why? Simply because he lived in and for his own ambitions; unless he could be commander of the ship he preferred to scuttle it rather than share with others the glory of bringing it to port. There were potentialities in La Follette that would have meant a great deal in directing government toward helpful policies for the people, but his passion for control, for a leadership that meant in fact dictatorship, stood in the way of accomplishment.

La Follette was the most self-centred man I ever met in politics. His lieutenants feared him and he distrusted them. Teamwork was impossible for him. He tolerated no equals. Every man who joined with him in Wisconsin was conscious of a watchful and suspicious eye upon his every move. All lived politically in dread of him, for his power to ruin was absolute and he used it as ruthlessly as a pirate of old. Bryan was self-centred, too, but to no such extent as La Follette; and he did not use his power to make men fear him. Bryan had multitudes of friends—"they would die for me," was his proud boast often and often repeated; but there were none that even in his own mind La Follette believed "would die for him."

Yet the voters of Wisconsin stood by him solidly through the nearly 30 years that he reigned as czar of their politics—while Governor and while Senator. Irvine Lenroot managed to be elected Senator in the great Harding sweep of 1920 though La Follette opposed him, but with that exception Wisconsin knew but one master in politics, and La Follette was the man.

WISCONSIN BETTER FOR THE LA FOLLETTE REIGN

Judging it from afar, it has been a well-governed State—no scandals have reached the public, while a persistent, intelligent effort has been made to bring the benefits of government to all. Every now and then we hear critics sound the praises of autocratic government—a government in which one man directs all. Wisconsin has been used as an illustration. Primaries and elections there have been only a formality, for whatever La Follette decreed was accepted at the polls.

As I Knew Them

The State was a little empire in the political world with La Follette as its emperor.

We may not like to acknowledge it, but Wisconsin is better for having its La Follette than New York with its Tammany, Illinois with its Democratic and Republican machines and Pennsylvania with its Quays, Penroses and Vares.

California is another State that has benefitted by leadership away from old moorings. There Hiram Johnson has been Czar since 1908 when he routed the Southern Pacific crowd from control of the State government. .Conditions had become intolerable—a man of courage and independence was needed—and Johnson came to the front. The "interests" are more powerful in California than in Wisconsin, and Johnson has had a hard battle to hold the State. Nevertheless he has done so, electing himself Senator twice and always naming his own candidate for Governor. With all their mistakes, with all their self-centred ambitions, Johnson and La Follette, each in his own way, stand out as justified protests against influences that surely were in defiance of the public interest.

LA FOLLETTE'S ONE AMBITION

From the moment La Follette entered the Senate, he had but one purpose—to be President. He undertook to make a career at Washington that would be recognized by the country as entirely his own. His support of the Republican Presidents from Roosevelt to Coolidge was always perfunctory; he had no real interest in any of them. He was careful to allow nothing to go on record from him that would stand in the way of an attack upon their policies whenever he desired.

In all his speeches in the Senate you will seldom find a line indorsing any Administration policy. For twenty years he stood on the side-lines of politics awaiting his opportunity as hungrily as a fox watches a hen-coop. Like a flash he looked upon the overthrow of a Republican Congress in 1910 as a call to him to rally the Republican party to his standard and against

As I Knew Them

Taft in 1912. When he found that Progressives turned to Roosevelt as their leader, his vindictiveness led him to help Taft to secure control of the Chicago convention. Though nominally, later, in the campaign he supported Taft, he gave his State to Wilson on election day. I say "gave" because it was then literally in La Follette's power to give Wisconsin's vote to any candidate he really desired.

In another chapter I have written of La Follette's course at that time. So long as he could not persuade the Republican party to accept him as its leader, he was determined to have it remain under the control of the reactionaries. By contrast, he could thus build up an organization of his own. And after 1912 that was his one purpose and hope—a sick man engaged in a race with death to satisfy something more intense than ambition—a consuming passion to be President.

The last time I spoke with him was just before his convention met in Cleveland in 1924. Speaking of his campaign he said: "I don't care what the newspapers print in their editorials about me, if I can keep in their news columns. Give me a fair show on the news pages and they can damn me to their hearts' content in their editorials. Now that we have the radio and can reach people through it, I think newspaper influence in politics is steadily lessening."

INDEX

555

Index

Index

557

Index

Index

Index

Index

Harding, Warren G. (*cont'd*)
Cabinet, strong, 475
estimate of, 473 *et seq.*
experience, lack of, 476
frankness of, 471
friends, loyalty to, 474
ill-health of, 475
interview with, 470
labor, efforts for, 477
nomination of, 465
policies of, 476 *et seq.*
post-war problems, 475
President, unhappy as, 472
speeches, 477 *et seq.*
Harlan, John Marshall, 365, 366
Harmon, Judson, 281
Harper's Bazaar, 129
Harrison, Benjamin, 1, 11, 39, 81, 92,
93, 120, 149, 158, 159, 178, 197, 202,
251, 269, 312, 315, 370
advice, attitude toward, 56
administrative ability of, 36
ancestry, 181
bargain, refusal to, 170
campaign song, 164
character, 76
diplomacy, 218
election returns, awaiting, 172
epigrams by, 181
Hawaiian treaty, 217
home life, 175
negroes, on the, 184
nomination of, 217
personality, 165 *et seq.*
President, an able, 164 *et seq.*
Presidential campaign, 169 *et seq.*
second term, campaign for, 179
tariff bill signed, 236
Harrison, William Henry, 528
Hartranft, John Frederick, 98, 101
Harvey, George, 188, 501
"Have Faith in Massachusetts," Calvin Coolidge, 530
Hawaiian Islands, 10, 71, 73, 216 *et seq.*
American minister in, 218
annexation, plea for, 216
government recognized, 219
Liliuokalani, Queen, 218 *et seq.*
marines in, 219
recognition of, 220
Hawley, Joseph R., 69

Hayes, Rutherford B., 59, 71, 93, 232, 312
administration, 92
Arthur, dismissal of, 120
Cabinet, 84
candidacy of, 99
cartoon, 82
civil service reform, 106
memorials, 76
newspaper men, honored by, 25
nomination of, 82
personality, 81
policies of, 83
President, as, 76 *et seq.*
prophecy of, 91
services, public, 82
silver, veto on, 91
South, attitude toward, 87
vetoes of, 88, 91
Hayes, Webb C., 76
Hayes-Tilden controversy, 72, 82, 136, 547
Hays, Will, 471, 475
chairman, national, 462
political methods, 24 *et seq.*
Hearst, William Randolph, 441
Hendricks, T. A., 136, 150, 541
Heney, Francis J., 405
Hepburn, A. Barton, career of, 105
Hewitt, Abram S., 77
Hill, David B., 32, 40, 56, 158, 239
Hill, James J., 170
Hinman-Greene Direct Primary Bill, 380
Hiscock, Frank, 32, 172, 271
Hitchcock, Frank, 343, 386, 515, 520, 543
Hoar, George Frisbie, 32, 100, 108, 233, 234, 279
Hobart, Garret A., 248
Hoey, John, 68
Hooker, Joseph, 167
Hoover, Herbert, 466, 475, 476, 496
Hoover, Irwin Hood, 1
Hornaday, Dr. W. T., 302
Hot Springs, Virginia, 341, 347, 350
House, Colonel Edward M., 56, 71, 174, 245, 285, 484, 491
capitals, in foreign, 508
influence of, 509
Paris, in, 505 *et seq.,* 510
Wilson, break with, 507, 510
Wilson's spokesman, 492

Index

Houston, David F., 542, 545
Howell, Clark, 42
Howell, Evan, 42
Hudson, New York, 2
Hughes, Charles Evans, 81, 136, 280, 304, 319, 329, 380, 442, 475
  across-the-continent tour 451 *et seq.*
  campaign, Presidential, 449 *et seq.*
  candidacy of, 333
  career of, 438 *et seq.*
  cartoon, 458
  defeat, causes for, 448 *et seq.*
  foreign policy of, 458
  Governor, as, 441 *et seq.*
  insurance investigation, 441
  nomination of, 436
  Presidency, opinion of the, 447
  primaries, fight for, 443
  Roosevelt, conference with, 444
  Secretary of State, as, 458
  Supreme Court, on the, 446
Hurley, Edward N. 496
Hyde, James Hazen, 134

I

Illinois, political leaders, 32
Immigration, restriction of, 177
Imperialism, 10, 72, 256
Indiana, political leaders, 32
Industries, American, government control of, 365
  fruit, 214
  iron, 214, 477
  Standard Oil, 366
  steel, 214, 260, 477
  sugar, 217, 219, 260, 365
  tin plate, 215
  tobacco, 366
  wool, 214
Ingalls, John J., 33, 159, 188
  eloquence of, 194
  politics, on pure, 194
Ingersoll, Robert G., 87, 99, 160, 410
Inglis, William O., 65
Insurance Investigation, 441
"Interests, The," 217, 219
"In the Good Old Summer Time," 356
"Intimate Papers of Colonel House," 491, 511
Iowa, political leaders, 32, 33

J

Jackson, Andrew, 149, 282, 367
Jay, John, 174
Jefferson, Thomas, 9, 35, 282
Jewell, Marshall, 99
Johnson, Andrew, 123, 203, 210
Johnson, Hiram, 306, 394, 405, 410, 413, 467, 524, 552
  political power of, 451 *et seq.,* 552
  Presidency, loss of, 464
Johnson, Samuel, 89
Jones, B. F., 137
Journal, Kennebec, 97

K

Kansas, political leaders, 33, 405
Kearney, Patrolman, 114
Keesling, 454
Keller, Arthur I., 530
Kelley, W. D., 32
Kellogg, Frank B., 514, 524
Kentucky, political leaders, 32, 33
Kerens, Richard C., 126, 157, 180
Kerney, James, 512
Key, David M., 84, 85
Kilgore, Constantine Buckley, 176
Kitchener, Lord, 493
Knox, Frank, 390, 391
Knox, Philander C., 329, 522, 527
Koenig, Samuel S., 398
Ku Klux Klan, 273, 286

L

Ladies' Home Journal, 530
La Follette, Robert M., 33, 247, 274, 329, 330, 394, 401
  ambition, his one, 552
  candidacy, 1912, 416
  compromise, refusal to, 550
  independence of, 549
  political power of, 548 *et seq.*
  public service, 550
  reactionaries, leader of, 403
  slogan, campaign, 388
  state boss, 551
Lamar, Lucius Q. C., 32
Lamont, Daniel S., 141
Lane, Franklin K., 482, 542
Lawton, Henry Ware, 308
League of Nations, 11, 183, 423, 489, 505, 518, 525

Index

Index

Index

Index

Index

Index

Index

Index

Index